THE HOLOMOVEMENT
Embracing Our Collective
Purpose to Unite Humanity

Let's ignite the Holomovement together!

Emanuel & Joel

THE HOLOMOVEMENT
Embracing Our Collective
Purpose to Unite Humanity

EDITED BY EMANUEL KUNTZELMAN
AND JILL ROBINSON

Books may be purchased through booksellers or by contacting Sacred Stories Publishing.

The Holomovement: Embracing Our Collective Purpose to Unite Humanity
Edited by Emanuel Kuntzelman & Jill Robinson

Tradepaper ISBN: 978-1-958921-15-9
Electronic ISBN: 978-1-958921-16-6
Library of Congress Control Number: 2022952430

Published by Light on Light Press
An imprint of Sacred Stories Publishing, Fort Lauderdale, FL

Printed in the United States of America

TABLE OF CONTENTS

INTERVAL

PART II: Attributes of the Explicate Order—Experience, Practice and Action
Towards Wholeness

FOREWORD

by William Keepin, PhD

"What is needed today is a new surge that is similar to the energy generated during the Renaissance but even deeper and more extensive; ... The essential need is for a "loosening" of rigidly held intellectual content ... along with a "melting" of the "hardness" of the heart. ... The "melting" could perhaps be called the beginning of genuine love, while the "loosening" of thought is the beginning of awakening of creative intelligence. The two necessarily go together."
— David Bohm

Genuine love and creative intelligence are the twin forces that together weave the profound pathway for the future unveiled in this remarkable book. "Holomovement" is the elegant term—coined by the late physicist and spiritual practitioner/philosopher David Bohm—to denote the totality of the cosmos as an "unbroken wholeness in undivided flowing movement without borders." The 'holo' in holomovement refers both to the holistic inclusion of all dimensions of reality, and the fractal or holographic structure that enables every element to reveal "detailed information about every other element in the universe." The holomovement integrates scientific, spiritual, aesthetic, and artistic truths and sensibilities, including all forms visible and invisible.

This book provides inspiring applications and implications of the holomovement developed by Bohm, whose contributions span many different fields including science, spirituality, philosophy, literature and beyond. Bohm's primary field was physics, and before proceeding further with introducing this wonderful book, it feels essential to digress briefly in order to acknowledge a unique recent development that raises Bohm's scientific work to a new level of unprecedented importance and recognition.

The 2022 Nobel Prize in Physics was awarded to three physicists (Alain Aspect, PhD; John F. Clauser, PhD; Anton Zeilinger, PhD) for experiments based on pioneering work done by David Bohm 70 years earlier, plus subsequent follow-up work from physicist John Bell. Had either Bohm or Bell been alive, they might well have shared the prize.

The backstory goes back to 1927, when Albert Einstein and Niels Bohr began their infamous debate on quantum physics. Bohr maintained that a complete description of quantum reality is provided by probabilities from the Schrödinger wave function and that, when a measurement is taken, the wave function "collapses" into a specific physical outcome. This became the orthodox "Copenhagen interpretation." Einstein objected to this quantum indeterminacy and probabilistic formulation, and he famously quipped that "God does not play dice" with the universe.

Beyond this, Einstein harbored an even greater objection to quantum mechanics, which emerged clearly in 1935 when he and two colleagues, Boris Podolsky and Nathan Rosen, conceived "the EPR paradox," a thought experiment designed to demonstrate that quantum physics is incomplete. They showed that, for two quantum-entangled particles, any measurement on one particle must instantaneously influence the other, no matter how far apart they are located in space. For Einstein, this was absurd, because nothing could travel faster than the speed of light, and he famously dismissed quantum entanglement as utter nonsense, calling it "spooky action-at-a-distance."

Then in 1952, David Bohm published a radical reformulation of quantum mechanics that postulated non-locality and challenged quantum orthodoxy by proposing a deterministic "pilot-wave" theory of quantum mechanics based on "hidden variables." Bohm and Einstein had worked closely together for a few years at Princeton University, and both shared strong misgivings about the Copenhagen interpretation. The new theory—called "Bohmian mechanics" today—was based in part on a deep conviction that quantum physics was in need of radical revision.

Although widely rejected by the orthodox physics community, Bohm's work was a major epiphany for physicist John Bell, who also had been troubled by the quantum orthodoxy. Writes Bell, "But in 1952 I saw the impossible done. It was in papers by David Bohm."

Bohm developed a deterministic "pilot wave" theory of quantum mechanics, expanding upon ideas originally introduced by Louis de Broglie in 1927. In his theory, quantum particles such as electrons are "guided" by a pilot wave function that influences their behavior. The evolution of the pilot wave over time is given by the Schrödinger equation. The metaphor that Bohm used to elucidate this theory is an airliner that crosses vast oceans, guided throughout by radio navigation signals. The radio waves don't provide any energy to the airliner, which proceeds entirely under its own power, yet the airplane's trajectory is fully guided by those radio waves. In like manner, the quantum particle is guided by the pilot wave, and Bohm developed an ingenious mathematical quantum theory that yields the exact same predictions and results as quantum mechanics, while eliminating all the murky quantum strangeness.

Bohm's theory postulates that the universe is inherently "non-local," i.e., fundamentally interconnected beyond the limitations of space and time. John Bell was deeply inspired by Bohm's hidden variables theory, yet like Einstein, he concedes that, initially, "The non-locality which I first met in Bohm's 1952 theory is very odd and very hard to accept, so I resisted it." Bell continued wrestling with it for 12 years and tried his best to eliminate non-locality from Bohm's theory. However, he found it couldn't be done, and this eventually led him to develop his brilliant "Bell's theorem," published in 1964, which provided a criterion based on the contravention of certain mathematical inequalities that theoretically could decide the non-locality question: "As a result of resisting it, I came to the theorem that [non-locality] is inevitable." The importance of Bohm's breakthrough also was recognized by others, and Bohm was nominated for a Nobel Prize in 1958.

Bohm also had earlier reconfigured the EPR paradox to measure particle *spin* (rather than position and momentum as originally conceived). This set the stage for practical experimental tests based on measuring the spin of paired photons. The first prototype experiment was conducted by John Clauser in 1972, and many subsequent "Bell experiments" based on generalized versions of Bell's theorem were conducted to rule out potential loopholes, including key experiments carried out by Alain Aspect in 1982, and by Anton Zeilinger in 1998 and 2017. These and other refined experiments consistently validated non-locality in quantum mechanics.

When the 2022 Nobel Prize in Physics was awarded to Clauser, Aspect and Zeilinger, the Nobel Committee affirmed that their experiments "supported quantum mechanics by clearly violating a Bell inequality," thereby firmly establishing non-locality as a fundamental feature of the universe. However, as physicist Tim Maudlin points out, much of the history around this has been garbled, and even the Nobel Committee's press release was mistaken in saying, "This means that quantum mechanics cannot be replaced by a theory that uses hidden variables." Maudlin writes:

> "That statement is flatly false. On the contrary, it was a theory that uses hidden variables—Bohmian mechanics— that inspired Bell to find his inequalities, and Bohm's theory makes the correct prediction that the inequalities will be violated. The most well-known and highly developed

'hidden variables' theory is that of Bohm, and Bell not only did not refute it, he was one of its most vocal proponents."

Today, there is a long-overdue revival of Bohmian mechanics, with extensive experimental and theoretical research being done at several universities. This vindicates John Bell's impassioned plea from 40 years ago that Bohm's hidden variables or "pilot wave" theories should be widely taught:

"Why is the [Bohmian] pilot wave picture ignored in textbooks? Should it not be taught, not as the only way, but as an antidote to the prevailing complacency? To show that vagueness, subjectivity, and indeterminism [in the Copenhagen interpretation of quantum physics] are not forced on us by experimental facts, but by deliberate theoretical choice?"

The Bell experiments also showed that the quantum-mechanical states that permit violations of Bell's inequality are precisely the entangled states, which means that quantum entanglement can be cultivated in practice to create quantum network systems, applying innovations such as "entanglement swapping." This enables the practical application of quantum entanglement for quantum computing and information science, which has launched the "second quantum revolution."

As Albert Einstein once said, referring to the need for a radical new quantum theory, "If anyone can do it, then it will be Bohm." His declaration was prophetic. Bohm did precisely this, and a major consequence is that the "spooky action-at-a-distance" that Einstein found so implausibly absurd is not only *real*, but 70 years after Bohm made it the cornerstone of his reformulated quantum physics, it has now become the foundation of today's rapidly emerging technological breakthroughs that are driving the "second quantum revolution."

Sadly, the physics community shunned Bohm's theory, in large part because it challenged the prevailing orthodoxy of the "Copenhagen interpretation," which finally today has begun to lose much of its earlier dominance.

During Bohm's lifetime, his "hidden variable" theory and "ontological interpretation" of quantum mechanics were met with rejection and sheer silence from the scientific establishment. At one point, Robert Oppenheimer even enjoined the physics community, "If we cannot disprove Bohm, then we must agree to ignore him." This astonishingly unscientific response to Bohm caused him much pain. Nor were his later theories of the implicate order and the holomovement taken seriously by most scientists. Bohm was hurt by this rejection, which along with the plight of the world, contributed to his occasional crippling bouts of depression.

Bohm's pioneering work has been groundbreaking on multiple levels. Yet, as Tim Maudlin laments:

> "To this day, [mainstream physicists] commonly claim that Bell's result proves Bohm's theory to be impossible and indeterminism to be inevitable, while Bell himself was the staunchest advocate of Bohm's deterministic theory. Even now, the average physicist has no understanding of what Einstein argued in the EPR paper and what Bell proved. ... What the work of [the new Nobel laureates] John Clauser, Alain Aspect and Anton Zeilinger has shown, building on John Bell's ideas, is not that quantum mechanics cannot be replaced by a deterministic, hidden variables theory. What it has shown is that quantum mechanics, as well as all of physics, is non-local."

The 2022 Nobel Prize in Physics honors the experimental proof of non-locality and quantum entanglement. In effect, this constitutes unprecedented scientific proof of "undivided wholeness" in nature, an intrinsic oneness that Thich Nhat Hanh describes as 'interbeing.' David Bohm was the first to develop a brilliant theory of quantum physics built upon nonlocality. It was disregarded by Einstein (because he rejected nonlocality), and it was ignored or misunderstood by most physicists, with few notable exceptions such as John Bell. May Bohm's work, and Bohmian mechanics, now finally begin to garner the attention that has so long been denied, yet so richly deserved.

Remarkable as this scientific story is, it covers only a portion of David Bohm's profound contributions. Bohm was not only a pioneer at the pinnacle of quantum physics, but he also carried his burning quest for truth far *beyond* science. As F. David Peat put it, "He had the courage to pursue truth no matter where it took him, yet he was guided by a strong moral sense." Bohm entered into deep dialogues with leading spiritual masters including Krishnamurti, the Dalai Lama and others. What Bohm and Krishnamurti pioneered together—as physicist and mystic—now needs to be replicated on a much larger scale between entire disciplines of science and spirituality. Fortunately, this is happening increasingly today through various organizations.

The far-reaching implications and potential applications of the holomovement, and the subtle dimensions to which quantum entanglement is now leading, could one day enable not only routine teleportation of information in quantum networks, but could also potentially help unravel unknown secrets of currently unexplained phenomena. Bohm stressed that "a hidden order may be present in what appears to be random," pointing to vast potential undiscovered connections between matter and consciousness. Quantum entanglement may help unravel some of these, such as "synchronicity," the "a-causal" connection between matter and consciousness that Carl Jung and physicist Wolfgang Pauli explored collaboratively. Or, it might explain the interpenetration of spiritual and physical realms as reported by advanced mystics, ancient and contemporary, such as in the hidden lands (or *beyul*) of Tibet. Or perhaps, it will explain the 80 rigorous scientific studies that demonstrate highly significant correlations between astronomical configurations of planets and terrestrial phenomena of human events, consistent with traditional astrology. As Erwin Schrödinger wrote in 1935, "I would not call entanglement one but rather *the* characteristic trait of quantum mechanics."

The "holographic principle" in physics is a contemporary theory that could potentially unify quantum physics and relativity theory. It shares a close parallel with the spiritual and mystical traditions of the world: the physical universe is a holographic projection, from a "higher" plane of reality. Hence, the physical universe is not *ultimately* real. Time and space are not ultimately real; they have relative existence only. Thus, the universe is a manifestation of a "higher" spiritual reality, represented by a two-dimensional hyperplane in physics. What is ultimately *real* therefore cannot be seen through the telescopes and instruments of science, which are themselves manifestations within the physical cosmos and can only perceive phenomena within that domain. So, neither the scientific instruments nor what they perceive or measure are *ultimately* real. It may well be that, in order for quantum mechanics and general relativity to *both* be correct, the universe must be structured along these lines of the holographic principle, and this may also one day help to explain the inner structures of the holomovement.

Bohm's holomovement provides a radically different and far more inspiring view of the living cosmos—and humanity's integral place in it— than the contemporary mainstream astrophysics view, as expressed for example by physicist Stephen Hawking:

> "The human race is just a chemical scum on a moderate-sized planet, orbiting around a very average star in the outer suburb of one among a hundred billion galaxies. We are so insignificant ..."

Religion offers a profoundly different perspective: "We are made in the image of God." Perhaps, borrowing on Bohm's holomovement, we might put science and religion together in one sentence, as follows: "We are made in the *holographic* image of the Cosmos."

For as Stanislav Grof has observed, "After five decades of consciousness research, my deepest conviction is that each of us is everything." We each have inner access to the entirety of cosmic awareness and consciousness, deep within our being. This is the core discovery of mystics across the ages and traditions, and it is possible ontologically precisely *because* of the holomovement, by whatever name it was called in previous millennia. As the poet Rumi expressed it:

> You are not just a drop from the infinite ocean.
> You *are* the infinite ocean, contained in a single drop.

The full "infinity of divinity" is contained in the human heart. This is an experiential fact, affirmed by mystics across the ages and traditions. It is also the basis of the fractal or holographic structure of consciousness. Bohm showed that science itself is bringing this revelation forward, through quantum physics and the holomovement.

Why have these truths not been widely recognized in science? Bohm summarizes the problem succinctly: "Thought creates structures, and then pretends they exist independently of thought." This is the central blind spot of science, and it also applies to most human thought structures.

It is this unwarranted certitude, born of unrecognized *pretense*—that this book strives to go beyond. To get at the truth, the reader is invited here to approach this book with a truly open mind and heart, and strive to suspend cherished beliefs and perspectives, even if only temporarily, in order to open to new ideas and perspectives.

Science today is asking this humility of us. Physics tells us that 94 percent of the cosmos is dark matter and dark energy—we don't know what's going on there. Similarly in biology: over 75% of the human body is considered to be "Junk DNA" —biologists don't know its purpose. Our most advanced sciences have only mapped out a portion of the physical universe, to say nothing of the spiritual universe. All this should give us a huge hint: tremendous ignorance remains in science.

Given this background, a core message of this Foreword is to invite the reader to approach this remarkable book in a spirit of humility, curiosity, openness and sincerity. The richness and depth of the essays here deserve nothing less.

If David Bohm were with us today, he would applaud this book, *not* because he would want us to engage in either 'verifying' or 'discrediting' his holomovement theory—dear though it was to his heart. Bohm would implore us to keep the spirit of genuine inquiry alive as we delve into these ideas. He would ask us to hold all theoretical views and positions "lightly"— meaning not only to remain open and unattached, but also to actually hold them up to the shared *light* of collective awareness and insight, examining them together as a community, and from there, to explore our various points of view, including lines of agreement and disagreement, with a gracious view toward pursuing Truth.

In this way, disagreements are not occasions to pick sides or to engage in mutual criticism—or to stop talking when we disagree (as Einstein and Bohr did, which prompted Bohm to develop Bohmian dialogue). Indeed, these seeming 'rifts' and contradictory fault lines may provide the source of the deepest revelations and fruits of our inquiry. This is what Bohm intended in developing Bohmian dialogue.

A welcome and perhaps unexpected surprise from this book is the beautiful spirit in which it is written. Behind the wonderful ideas and inspirations in these essays is a palpable sense of tremendous care and concern for the human family, and our collective destiny—perhaps itself an expression of undivided wholeness. Far from having the feel of a dry philosophical tome, this book radiates a gracious warmth and supernal light that nurtures the soul, as the ideas inspire the mind. This was an unexpected pleasure, unusual for a book of this type.

For those of us who were privileged to meet and interact personally with David Bohm, two qualities stood out strongly: his genuine humility, and his deeply earnest temperament. Bohm most wanted to engage with others on a shared quest for truth, wherever it might lead. May we all adopt this same spirit of deep humility and earnest inquiry, as we embrace the wonderful spectrum of ideas in this book.

As David Bohm suggested, it's time now to open your mind, soften your heart, and enter into these expansive, magnificent essays …

PREFACE

Integrating the Parts of the Whole
by Robert Atkinson, PhD

The greatest challenge of the Holomovement in our time may be getting all the various parts to work together as one. There was a time when that happened organically. Lao Tzu called the wholeness of existence the "nameless," which is all there was at "the beginning of heaven and earth."

Everything was created whole. Unity was the organizing principle. The whole had a quality that went beyond the parts. The meaning of the whole was in the parts and in the harmony of all their relationships. This is the way it was from the beginning, the way it was intended and the way it is still. The first Indigenous peoples seeking wisdom to live by incorporated this understanding into their unitive narratives.

However, eating the forbidden fruit in the Garden of Eden and opening Pandora's box separated humanity from this original wholeness. The "nameless" was fragmented into the "named," into "ten thousand things," as Lao Tzu noted.

Adding to unitive narratives, this fall from wholeness created divisive narratives. After millennia of stories focusing on duality and maintaining separation, what the world needs now is unitive narratives that will lead us through a process of returning to our original wholeness, as we'll see developed further in Chapter 2 of this book.

Among the earliest unitive narratives expressing a holistic worldview is the Hermetic principle of "As above, so below; all things accomplishing the miracles of the One thing." Plato, as well, imagined a pattern that tied all things in the universe together:

> Perhaps there is a pattern set up in the heavens
> for one who desires to see it,
> and having seen it, to find one in himself.

This pattern, perhaps set up in the heavens and found in ourselves, would be an expression of the organizing principle of wholeness, one that integrates all levels of reality from the macrocosm (the universe as a whole) to the microcosm (i.e., the human being, a miniature universe). It bridges the divide between duality and nonduality and shows that the individual and the collective mirror one another in their essential nature and processes.

This image of an original wholeness across all existence is what David Bohm discerned as well from his studies in quantum physics. He recognized a primary unifying agency in the universe that he called the holomovement, or wholeness-in-motion. Within this coherent and harmonious whole, everything flows in orderly patterns of action, undivided and borderless.

Our challenge though, as this wholeness became hidden, even divided, after the One thing split into "ten thousand things," is to reclaim the perennial mystical wisdom that has long maintained a vision of the inherent wholeness of a living universe. Completing our long cycle of knowing, there is now scientific evidence that also reveals this wholeness to be an ever-evolving unified field.

The significance of this deep understanding of the whole (from the Greek *holos*) is that by definition and make up, the whole always consists of parts that are inherently diverse. Each part is essential for carrying out a different function to maintain harmony and balance within the whole. Over many millennia, especially on the social level, this diversity spotlighted oppositions that created tensions essential to bringing about and completing a process of transformation that is needed periodically to evolve our consciousness to higher and higher levels of understanding existence, and what is inherently possible.

Though there is a built-in tension to all oppositions in the whole, there is also a built-in balance to all oppositions. We see this in all opposites—yin and yang, feminine and masculine, light and dark, etc. They are all parts of one whole, co-existing as interdependent systems within the whole, designed to maintain the wholeness of the Whole.

An example of a whole sub-system within the greater Whole that functions with this inherent balance is the human body. Consisting of multiple systems, an organization of organs, all connected one to another, they function as a whole. Cooperation is its governing principle. There may be no greater diversity of parts in a whole system than in the human body, yet the harmony of all the diverse parts maintains a fully functioning whole being.

While the human body may be Bohm's holomovement in microcosm, its macrocosm is everything in the universe moving together in an interconnected process, as an undivided, flowing wholeness.

Consciousness is its own holomovement as well. The evolution of consciousness can be seen as a continuum or a keyboard within which all levels or states of consciousness co-exist in the same whole. Our evolving consciousness is wholeness-in-motion, taking us from one state of consciousness to another, from a consciousness of separation to a consciousness of wholeness. Looking at consciousness as a continuum allows us to see a borderless movement, or flow, from one state of consciousness to another within the whole.

Our challenge is to understand, accept and integrate all the diverse parts of the whole. There is a pattern designed to do just that for us. The pattern of wholeness that Plato imagined as "set up in the heavens" and found within us also defines and assists the orderly movement of our evolving consciousness within the whole.

This pattern, with transformation at its core, is understood by many ways of knowing as a means of merging opposites into a new unbroken, unified whole. Mythology, mysticism, ritual and psychology all share a three-part process leading to transformation and a restoration of wholeness.

These ways of knowing, expressing variations on the same pattern, as explained in my book, *A New Story of Wholeness: An Experiential Guide for Connecting the Human Family*, all derive from the familiar narrative pattern of beginning—middle—end. The deeper level of this pattern is most succinctly represented as *beginning—muddle—resolution*. The muddle is the crisis, or challenge, appearing as an opportunity, to prepare us for completing our personal journey to wholeness.

All this illustrates that the greater purpose of this universal pattern of transformation is to bring the diverse parts of the whole, even opposing forces within the whole, into balance, harmony and unity to re-establish their undivided wholeness, ensuring the highest level of functioning of the whole. The Holomovement, in our time, must be able to resolve differences within the whole so it can function as one, while maintaining its inherent diversity.

Wholeness-in-motion on the social level includes a transformative process connecting personal transformation to collective transformation. Individual transformation carries within it a collective function of contributing to the betterment of the world—what Kabbalists call Tikkun Olam, the work of repairing the world or restoring the world to wholeness. This comes naturally to those who have consciously experienced this pattern.

For the Holomovement to be effective, people need to acknowledge and accept all the diverse—even opposing—parts within the whole, so the whole can function in its entirety. Diversity is not an inherent problem for organic wholeness. In fact, it is needed. David Bohm was very clear on how to deal with this inevitable diversity of the parts in the whole on an interpersonal or social level, as well:

> "People have to make a cooperative effort to have a dialogue in which we not merely exchange opinions, but actually listen deeply to the views of others, without resistance. We cannot do this if we hold to our own opinion and resist the other. We have to be able to look at all the opinions as suspended in front of us without suppressing them."

This is a very appropriate description of the scientific method itself, as well as of the art of consultation, which is designed to arrive at the spark of truth from a variety of viewpoints. It is the nature of the whole to organize the parts into a unity, an undivided wholeness in which all parts make a cooperative effort without resisting or suppressing the flow of the other parts.

This is the nature of reality. The One, though split into what appear to be separate parts, is always One. This book on the Holomovement is designed in the same way. Many diverse and even far-ranging views make up an understanding of the whole. Despite their differences and diversity, the views in this book serve the function of spotlighting various aspects of the whole while emphasizing how its parts all fit together. In the holomovement, everything in the richness of its diversity moves together in an interconnected process expressing and forming a coherent and borderless wholeness.

This book is mapping the holomovement in such a way to illustrate a totality, a singular system that contains nested sub-systems. While there is a diversity of wholes in all the sub-systems, there is only one over-riding wholeness that connects all these sub-systems together through a universal consciousness from which orderly action flows throughout the whole.

With the Holomovement understood as this universal consciousness, or unitive consciousness, which we are continually evolving toward, as expanded upon in Chapter 15, we see this as a movement toward, yet within, wholeness. This book, in all its diverse variations of expressions, is a primary tool for assisting us all toward an understanding of wholeness as well as for living into a consciousness of wholeness.

INTRODUCTION

The Flow of the Holomovement
by Emanuel Kuntzelman

"Y ou know, it's tantalizing," said David Bohm to his wife Saral on the phone as he left Birkbeck College, University of London (as it was formally called) on October 27, 1992, "I feel I'm on the edge of something." An hour later, as he arrived at his home in a taxi, Bohm was stricken by a heart attack and died.[1]

The world lost one of its grandest visionaries before he was able to finalize his alternative quantum theory to his highest expectations. Today, however, we see that his work not only lives on, but it also has become the centerpiece of quantum physics and, in its application, a sociological model for guiding humanity to its proper flow on the path of the Holomovement.

As we contemplate the state of our world today, we surely can say the same: it is, indeed, tantalizing that we are on the edge of something. Whether that edge is the danger of civilization falling off a cliff or the cutting-edge breakthrough into a transformative new era of holistic understanding, these times are certainly keeping us all on the edge of our seats. It is our hope that this book is a call to action in finding our purpose, to help resolve our differences and bring us together in a spirit of Oneness.

As William Keepin, co-founder of the Gender Equity and Reconciliation International project and mathematical physicist, so brilliantly described in the Foreword, Bohm's theory of quantum mechanics, proposed back in 1952, has now been vindicated by the Nobel Prize in Physics 2022. The award establishes non-locality, which Bohmian mechanics requires, as a scientific reality.

For most of us, this theory is nearly impossible to comprehend intellectually, yet we inherently sense that everything is interconnected. However far our imaginations may stretch into the infinity of existence, whether as consciousness or physical reality, it is all One. No matter how many computations of multiple metaverses our vision can hold, both in unbounded physical space and timelessness, it is still but One.

As hard as it was for Einstein to imagine a universe that can instantaneously interconnect beyond the parameters of space and time, and this "spooky-action-at-a-distance" was hard for him to accept, what Einstein did appreciate about Bohm's theory was that it postulated that the quantum world is at least somewhat deterministic. Bohm proposed that an ontological pilot wave gives rise to the universe, and this alleviated Einstein's concern as to whether "God plays dice with the universe." In Bohm's theory, not everything is left to random chance. In the beginning, there were not simply elementary particles bumping around like billiard balls, but rather a vibration producing a process—the flow of the Holomovement.

The flow between the core of consciousness and the material manifestations of its information represents the interwoven components of the holomovement: the implicate order as the Source and explicate order as physical reality. Pure consciousness vibrates and then flows out in waves from the center of timelessness as the holomovement and unfolds into the density of the material universe. Humanity's existence is a result of this vibrational expression, our evolution leading us to seek an understanding of this oneness. We are beginning to recognize the call to serve in healing humanity and facilitate its transformation into a higher level of consciousness. In doing so, we enfold our consciousness back into the flow of the holomovement, bringing all of the explicate order's diversity into wholeness.

Along with acting as the cosmic flow of the quantum field of existence, the term "holomovement" also represents the sociological phenomenon that heralds the convergence of individuals, organizations and movements around the globe into a worldwide movement. This sociological Holomovement will gain strength and unity as it grows as a solution to the immense challenges that face our society. It is a call to unity, but not uniformity. We may not be separate, but we are certainly different. The Holomovement recognizes this diversity and asks for all to heed the call—back to the cooperative, loving and altruistic nature of the human spirit.

In his Preface, Robert Atkinson writes how Plato proposed there was a universal pattern behind our existence. Atkinson states that "the greater purpose of this universal pattern of transformation is to bring the diverse parts of the whole, even opposing forces ... into balance, harmony and unity to re-establish their undivided wholeness, ensuring the highest level of functioning of the whole." These opposing forces, although uncomfortable at first, also drive cultural evolution when a contrasting thesis and its antithesis find a synthesis that gains acceptance to move our development forward.

Our universe, described by physicist Sir James Jeans as being more akin to a grand thought than a great machine, began with a primordial vibration that was not necessarily a big bang. In this anthology, it is also referred to as the Big Breath by cosmologist Jude Currivan in Chapter 2. From that initial and profound gasp, a wave arose that has carried us through both physical and cultural evolution in its undulating flow.

The holomovement has unfolded from the implicate order, evolved into the physical universe, then enfolded into life, leading to human consciousness. Now this consciousness has unfolded yet again into our human civilization and has brought us to our present-day situation. Here is what it looks like within the context of a wave:

The Evolutionary Pilot Wave

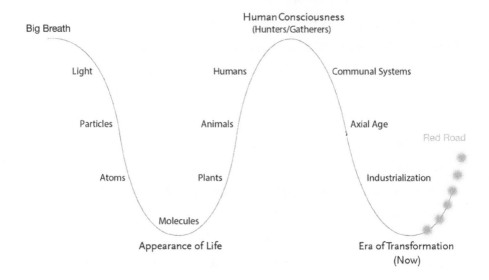

Big Breath

Human Consciousness
(Hunters/Gatherers)

Light

Humans

Communal Systems

Particles

Animals

Axial Age

Red Road

Atoms

Plants

Industrialization

Molecules

Appearance of Life

Era of Transformation
(Now)

The Evolutionary Wave is an octave, flowing through seven stages of process in the same way that the western musical C-scale would go DO-RE-ME-FA-SO-LA-TI-DO. Evolution follows the wave from DO to DO, returning to the same note, but having doubled the frequency in the process.

Some Indigenous cultures have stated that there have been three great miracles in our journey through existence: the beginning of the universe, the appearance of life and the dawn of self-reflective, human consciousness. We can see the three miracles on the Evolutionary Wave at two crests and one trough as the emergence of the Big Breath, Life and Human Consciousness. The fourth great miracle now awaits, as we struggle to pass through our current trough—the cliff's edge we are hanging on.

In the flow of the holomovement, the Big Breath of the implicate order *unfolds* into materialism. The explicate order reaches the limits of its manifestation at the bottom of the wave trough, where molecules finally figure out how to become reproducing life forms. The wave makes its miraculous turn into Life and *enfolds* upwards in the ascending wave back towards the implicate order of Source Consciousness. Upon reaching the crest of Consciousness, *Homo sapiens* appears to utilize its emerging sense of self-reflective awareness to develop the social organization that will become (for better or worse) our civilization. The process of creating this human civilization follows the same *unfolding* process that produced the physical nature of the universe. It can be a rather messy and random unfolding. Just as the universe erupted into supernova explosions and convulsed into black holes in the process of creating our universe, the unfolding of human civilization mirrors this bumpy and dramatic ride into the explicate order of now: the Era of Transformation.

As we can also see from the previous wave diagram, just as with the creation of the universe, the making of civilization involves the development of materialism as it unfolds and descends from the implicate order. This descent, which is part of the natural flow, brings some unruly side effects with it. In the process of "civilizing" ourselves, we also have subjected our fellow humans to piracy, terrorism, torture and all kinds of abuses. The temptations of materialism are many, and it is this downward flow of the wave that has given rise to our various cultural efforts to explain it in our creation stories, from the fall from grace in the Garden of Eden to a dismembered Osiris floating down the river in Egyptian mythology.

This notion of the fall has haunted humanity throughout history as we inherently sense that something is wrong in our world. Christianity explains it by saying that we are born with original sin. A more compassionate explanation would be that the development of human consciousness coincides with a descent into materialism, which fosters a negative feedback loop as we lose sight of our divine Source and become gradually more absorbed in the accumulation of material possessions. It seems the more we have, the more we want at the sacrifice of our spiritual nature.

The downward flow of unfolding into the explicate order seems to have its own gravitational pull and tends to accelerate into a free fall if we are not able to control the descent with our innate, moral value system. It is the flow of the descending wave that makes us think we have "fallen from grace."

Allowing our spiritual nature to be overcome by materialism is a fault we need to rectify if we're to make the turn in our evolutionary process.

Once we have hit rock bottom in the depths of the trough, it is not easy or natural to reverse the momentum. Greek-Armenian philosopher George Gurdjieff, who proposed the law of octaves upon which this evolutionary wave is based, also described the difficulties of passing through intervals. In the acceleration of frequency in going from musical notes DO to DO, there are two points in the process where the increase slows down, as we approach the troughs and crests of each wave. This is especially true when it is a great turning, when the large-scale process needs to reverse direction. That is the case now. We have bottomed out as a civilization, and it will take the equivalent of the fourth great miracle of all time to pull us out of our tailspin.

Whether or not we can do so is uncertain. Gurdjieff believed it required some kind of shock to make the wave reverse its direction. At the time in history when molecules were bogged down before the emergence of life, they simply kept building longer and more complicated chains of hydrocarbons, but no life appeared. It was a similar situation to our current day dilemma in which we keep trying to find solutions with the same materialistic mindset that gave rise to the problem. With molecules, it is likely that a shock from outside ignited the emergence of life, such as a lightning bolt, that triggered the chemical reaction to produce single-cell organisms that suddenly knew how to reproduce themselves.

In our current times, we are receiving plenty of self-imposed shocks—climate change, overpopulation, the threat of nuclear annihilation—but we remain stubbornly slow in waking up to the need to shift the wave into an ascending flow, in an enfolding of the holomovement toward the implicate order. It's not easy to build life out of nothing or reverse the course of society, but we need to find a new way, based on unifying principles, to make this historic turn and ascend to higher consciousness.

In attempting to take on this singular challenge, however, we should explore what we can really do to make a difference. If Bohm's ontological pilot wave is deterministic, we need to ask if that means there is no free will and that our existence is all a result of a pre-determined plan. In Bohm's later life, he became more open to the notion that this determinism arose as a purposeful intention and led to what he called quantum potential, as described in the posthumous book entitled *The Undivided Universe: An Ontological Interpretation of Quantum Theory*, co-authored by Bohm and Basil Hiley.

We can surmise from his description that the universe begins as deterministic but also allows for free will, a concept known as *compatibilism*, allowing the two seemingly opposed concepts to intertwine. Thus, we venture to say that the implicate order coded the universe with a general plan—in this case the Evolutionary Pilot Wave—but left it open to the cosmos and consciousness to see how it all played out. Thus, evolution is not a result of random chance, but it does tend sometimes to meander as much as it progresses, and occasionally, it swerves off course or even reverses itself when materialism overpowers the free will of human consciousness.

Even so, we could say that God (in our case, the Implicate Order) still doesn't play dice with the universe by leaving it all up to chance, going back to Einstein's concern; however, maybe the best analogy is to say that the Implicate Order plays with loaded dice, meaning the dice game has a preference for rolling out in waves of sevens creating octaves, but it is left up to us to make sure we create our own "good luck" and keep rolling those sevens. We need to stay on course and make this tricky turn, like a good surfer catching the power of the wave, and not get distracted by the material temptations along the way.

To maintain our balance and hopefully ride this wave home, we do need some pilot wave orientation of our own; therefore, we have developed eight core principles that arise from our scientific understanding of the Holomovement. Alongside these foundational tenets, we also call upon the wisdom traditions to guide us in their long-held understanding of wholeness in our interconnected web of life. By embodying these principles, we can begin to explore the nature of this Holomovement as it draws us toward unity and accelerates the evolution of both our individual and collective consciousness. The eight core principles of the Holomovement are as follows:

1. *Interconnected Wholeness.* Although dazzlingly complex and multidimensional, the cosmos is a single, living process, profoundly interconnected and sacred in its Oneness. All knowledge systems, including science and spirituality, exist to discover and express the reality of this interconnected wholeness and arise from our innate curiosity to explain the implicate order and are, at their essence, potentially in harmony with each other.

2. *A Conscious Living Universe.* Dynamic and alive, the universe arises from a source of consciousness, offering meaning to every component of our interconnected wholeness. The "difference" between spirit and matter is a question of frequency, density and the degree of bonding, but they come from the same Source.

3. *Purposeful Evolution.* Oneness is evolutionary in its conscious awareness of existence, engaging in a purposeful evolution of its own nature. Over time, the Cosmos, the Earth and all living things develop increasing levels of complexity, interconnectedness, consciousness and cooperation.

4. *Wholesomeness as Our Natural State of Being.* All of reality, including individual beings and social and cultural systems, tend to be attracted to health, wholeness and the mutual flourishing of life and consciousness. Seemingly "evil" motives and behaviors are not fundamental to human nature, but rather arise from an unbalanced state when materialism and a sense of separation dominate human consciousness.

5. *A Self-Healing Cosmos.* Our existential civilizational Meta-Crisis (of climate, culture, society, economics and more) is naturally coinciding with a widespread awakening of virtuous social projects, analogous to an immune response. These contrasting forces, or levels of consciousness, although challenging, offer the necessary impulse to propel our ongoing evolution.

6. *Embodying the Holomovement.* Bohm's term holomovement describes how undivided wholeness is expressed in every seemingly separate entity, event and action. "The Holomovement" is an apt name representing the diverse sociocultural movement toward a just, fulfilling and sustainable human presence on Earth in accordance with the cosmological parameters of the physical universe.

7. *Unity in Action.* The Holomovement is an inherent expression of the endemic nature of reality and amplifies the pull of collaborative coherence that simultaneously awakens individual purpose to discovering how it can also best serve the good of the whole. Especially needed now in all interpersonal relationships at all levels of society are social justice principles that support the collective well-being, such as equality between men and women, balance between wealth and poverty, freedom from all forms of prejudice and justice that is unitive, not punitive.

8. *Self-sustaining Development of Unity Consciousness.* The Holomovement, like the universe itself, emanates from a spiritual Source that defines the action of the undivided cosmos working to reassert health and wholeness in the face of what appears to be fragmentation. As individual human beings become increasingly conscious of their connection to Source and discover a deeper sense of their own purpose in connection to it, they are naturally motivated

to improve their psychological outlook and build communities with like-minded people drawn to the shared values of truth, beauty and goodness of the holotropic attractor. Thus, a positive feedback loop naturally arises in the development of individual consciousness as it gains an intuitive understanding of a self-reinforced unity consciousness, where individual purpose flourishes as it discovers ever better ways to contribute to the collective well-being of humanity.

These principles, elaborated through years of discussion, are explored further within the context of values in Joni Carley's and Phil Clothier's Chapter 6 contribution to this book. Perhaps the growing use of these principles will allow us to provide our own shock to the process—our collective wake-up call—and make the great turn of the evolutionary wave. The proposal from the Holomovement perspective would be to take self-reflective consciousness to a new level and find our deepest meaning in collective purpose.

Radical Collaboration in Action

It's time for a spiritual revolution from the inside out, one that is ignited by peace and love and manifests in purposeful social action. Despite the illusion that we are all separate, the implicate order is wholeness, and there is an attraction to bring us back to wholeness, or as Ervin Laszlo suggests in Chapter 3, our driving evolutionary force operates as a "holotropic attractor." Laszlo breaks down the term into parts, "holo" meaning *the whole*, and "tropic" meaning *the orientation or the tendency*. "Holotropic" is defined as a fundamental, orienting drive toward wholeness. An "attractor" is something that lures us onward: purpose, love and ideals. It is what creates order when chaos is involved, as mentioned in Chapter 15; thus, the holotropic attractor of the Holomovement could, with a little help from its friends, provide the impetus to lead civilization out of chaos and back to our natural state of harmony.

As Laszlo also states, "The holotropic is the effect of the wholeness-oriented information coded in the implicate order, on the explicate order." This is the determinism in Bohm's model, but it is up to us to exercise our free will to turn things around. Bohm tells us that "active information" arises from the implicate order to guide us towards our quantum potential, and Jude Currivan describes this information transfer in more detail in Chapter 2. In the chaotic situation we find ourselves, we would be wise to follow the call of that holotropic attractor in our ascent toward a higher state of consciousness in the implicate order.

Cosmologically, psycho-spiritually and sociologically, the Holomovement is quite literally a movement of the whole towards truth, beauty and goodness. Our earliest ancestors, with their close connection to the natural and spiritual world, understood the essence of unitive consciousness as we are now exploring it, based upon a purposeful universe. Now is the time to merge the understandings of our elders with our knowledge of quantum reality, such as proposed by David Bohm, and fuse it all into a grand, worldwide movement for social renewal.

In the same way Bohm described the implicate and explicate order moving in an unbroken whole, each of us are entwined as co-creators within our evolutionary flow. We must move beyond the transactional nature of relationships and embody the transformative power of deep spiritual connection. The good news is that the Holomovement is endemic to everything we do. It is consciousness flowing in the universe, through us and the manifestations of our souls. Thankfully, we don't have to "find it" but rather slow down and drop into a mindful place of deep knowing and feel the force of love that weaves our humanity together.

We can no longer afford to fall back into habits of complacency, ignorance and denial. So profound is our entangled connection with people and planet that there is decreasing distinction between who is suffering and who is not. Ultimately, we all suffer from the malaise of society.

It is imperative that we form and nurture relationships across all divides and belief systems if we are to rediscover our collective sense of purpose and spiritual worth. Love and compassion are not finite resources within the flow of the Holomovement. In fact, the more we connect with others through goodwill, compassion, joy and curiosity, the more abundant these qualities become. This can no longer be the work of a few.

Imagine the beauty and wonder and feeling of flow that we could experience if eight billion people, acting with compassion and purpose, moved together in phase for the good of the whole. Each of us has a soul-based purpose to contribute within this diverse sociocultural movement to restore the dignity and integrity of humanity as a functioning whole.

The Holomovement is the call to action in following our individual purpose toward the enfolding of collective purpose. This doesn't mean sacrificing our individual well-being or our personal resources to an extent that may slow our evolutionary service, but it does mean that we vow to find our deepest purpose in life so we can visualize how we can best serve the whole in what is also the right livelihood for ourselves.

Thus, we will ignite the Holomovement, bolstering relationships, building communities and establishing the eco-systems of social support to co-create the great turning of the wave. Now is the time to rediscover our inherent unity in the Source of the implicate order. In doing our part to ignite the spark of the Holomovement, we shall not be consumed, but rather mutually catalyze a transformational shift of consciousness that will empower and guide us into a whole new future.

Enfolding the collective purpose of the ascending holomovement means exactly that: enfolding it. It does not unfold, because it is aways present—the inherent unity and nondual reality of the entire cosmos. We simply need to embrace it anew, with a huge hug of gratitude as it helps us find our path to unity. It is our choice, and it is also our birthright and our destiny.

To help readers follow the flow of this anthology, Part I offers a first octave wave of eight chapters that explores the understanding of reality in its wholeness, which comprises our admittedly limited human attempts to describe the nature of the implicate order. As Chapter 1 confesses, it is a daring task to use our human thought and language to describe it, but it is also our duty to try.

After the first octave wave, we find ourselves in an interval at the turning point between waves. We are in a time of deep reflection when it behooves us to consider all possible perspectives if we truly want to succeed in firmly establishing a worldwide movement of consciousness called the Holomovement. Thus, the Interval gives us a summary of what we have learned so far and introduces the key components of integral theory. A contribution from philosopher Ken Wilber provides a detailed description of the integral playground and how we need to keep all quadrants of perspectives in mind while simultaneously "Waking Up, Growing Up, Opening Up, Cleaning Up and Showing Up." Wilber ends his essay by questioning whether our perspective is "fully-baked."

Part II comprises the book's proposed answers to Wilber's challenge as to whether we are indeed waking up (Chapter 9), growing up (Chapter 10), opening up (Chapter 11), cleaning up (Chapter 12) and showing up (Chapter 13). The final two chapters address additional questions as to how we are "linking up" and "lifting up." We end the full octave by exploring a re-awakening of the purpose of the human soul in service to the whole.

PART I

Attributes of the Implicate Order—
Understanding Reality in Its Wholeness

CHAPTER 1
NAMING THE NAMELESS

by Ben Bowler
including interviews with Patricia Anne Davis,
John Cobb, PhD & Ramesh Bijlani, MD

"The Tao that can be told is not the eternal Tao; The name that can be named is not the eternal name. The nameless is the beginning of heaven and earth."

— Lao Tzu

"That which we call a rose / By any other name would smell as sweet."

— Juliet (Shakespeare)

Language is a wondrous thing. We take it so much for granted—the rules, grammar, familiar word symbols we see and the sounds we make and hear every day. We talk, think, process, imagine and even dream in our primary language. How deeply we are grounded in the prism of our mother tongue is extraordinary. It isn't until we learn a second or third language that we may realize how arbitrary in many ways our own language is in describing reality. That's when we realize that "that which we call a rose" has a great many "other names" all equally valid and suitable.

Growing up in Australia, like in many anglophone parts of the world, English is so dominant that there is little need to speak any other language. For me, it was not until an immersive three-month experience in China in

1985, as a 12-year-old learning basic Mandarin, that this realization hit with full force. I was overwhelmed by the language, the culture, the worldview and the food! The boy from the sheltered Canberra suburbs would never be the same again.

How then can we approach the naming of ideas and concepts so profound, that no symbols could hope to truly encapsulate them? This is the dilemma that sixth century B.C.E. Chinese philosopher Lao Tzu lays out for us in his epic poem the *Tao Te Ching* in the line: "The name that can be named is not the eternal name." How can we talk about things eternal, infinite, cosmic, spiritual and universal when reduced to basic word-symbols and sounds humans make with their tongue and lips?!

It is a profound challenge and one that must be met with compassion and curiosity. The power of a common language, a shared terminology, however imperfect, is essential in driving forward the movement toward wholeness, greater unity, sympathetic understanding and intercultural harmony on this planet.

The concept of this anthology is to utilize American physicist David Bohm's term *holomovement* and apply it to the unfolding reality of a grand movement for holistic transformation on Earth and beyond. The authors in the following chapters collectively show that Bohm's cosmological understanding of an unfolding dance between the implicate and explicate order can unify this global social—spiritual—cultural phenomenon that is hitherto, without a name.

Bohm did not create the holomovement; he discovered it. He *named* it. For Bohm, the holomovement brings together the principle of "Undivided Wholeness" with the understanding that everything is in a state of flow, of "evolutionary becoming" that Bohm referred to as "universal flux." Holistic physicist and author F. David Peat further articulates this foundational concept:

"The implicate order is not so much a set of objects but a process. It's a process of constant movement of constant unfolding and enfolding. So, what we see as our explicate world is really the result of a process of unfolding and enfolding. The explicit order comes out of the implicate."[2]

These beautiful ideas of wholeness-in-perpetual-motion, the universe as a grand interconnected *process*, did not originate with David Bohm. Such insights have been accessed by seers, mystics and prophets of many traditions throughout the ages. That the deep awareness Bohm arrived at through his scientific discoveries matches and meets what far older wisdom traditions already "knew" is perhaps the most remarkable feature of this whole synergizing story.

In this chapter, we will explore a variety of spiritual philosophies and how they resonate with Bohm's views. We will take a journey into Indigenous wisdom, Western philosophic tradition and Eastern philosophic tradition and find out what they may say about Bohm's own insights into "undivided wholeness," implicate order, explicate order and the Holomovement. In laying this foundation, we can better understand why it is important to define this extraordinary sociological movement and identify the manifold attractors bringing humanity together.

Indigenous Wisdom and Teachings

Mutthi Mutthi man Jason Kelly says, "We aboriginal people are universal; our dreaming doesn't separate heaven from earth, as we are connected to the universe from the ground—our Mother, to the trees, to the animals, to the sky, to the stars, to the sun and the moon."

A deep notion of how we are connected to the cosmos through the holomovement has been with us for millennia. Let us explore the deep wisdom Indigenous peoples have gleaned from their experiential understanding of our sacred connection and communication with nature.

In my interview with Patricia Anne Davis, of the Diné People (also referred to as "Navajo"), she shares her thoughts on the teachings of Hózhó:

Words from Patricia Anne Davis

"There is no other reality other than Hózhó. We are existing in our sacred self in our sacred place in the universe, our eternal self in the eternal now. My lifelong work is simplifying and conveying to the general public the ceremonial terminology which is coming from a different thinking system than English.

Euro-centric, dualistic thinking often means "either-or," "for-or-against," "right-or-wrong." This thinking system of the Western world, the root cause of mind-body dichotomy, arises from what we can call Cartesian philosophy after René Descartes and all of the reductionist philosophers who focused on the physical aspect of what we think we see, and not the interconnections. This leads to a belief in a deficient self-image which entraps us in this sense of separation from who we really are. As Einstein eloquently said, "We cannot solve the problems with the same thinking that caused them." So, I am speaking from an affirmative thinking system where we are eternally existing within time and space and within the spiritual realm, simultaneously—this is Hózhó.

David Bohm used words that attempted to conceptualize this wholeness—I use Wholeness with *H* (Holeness) and Holiness with *W* (Wholiness). In my academic work, I had to be careful not to use religious terms but to use terms like holographic and holistic to describe Hózhó. There is dualism, and there is semi dualism and non-dualism. Then there's pure non-dualism. Pure non-dualism is Hózhó.

Pure non-dualism is often incomprehensible to Western Thinkers who are entrenched in the Cartesian model of thought. Indigenous language speaking within the context of Hózhó is from the *whole to the specific*— that's "process"—whereas Western culture is speaking from the *specific to the whole*. It's like the difference between inductive and deductive thinking.

Western culture is speaking of specifics which are not meaningfully related but when we're awake to Hózhó, the holiness and wholeness that we are existing in, we are using our "whole brain thinking." I call this conscience, which is holy thinking. Conscience—moral reasoning—is the appropriate function of our whole-brain thinking. From the whole to the specific, that is collective conscience.

Carl Jung talked about synchronicity as a spiritual concept of interconnectedness and interrelatedness, but there is no form of mathematics or form of statistics that can prove it because the causality of left-brain thinking understands only that "a causes b," which is dualistic. However, in reality, ABCD causes E, the culmination of meaningful co-occurrences—*that* is synchronicity.

Reductionist scientists do not have a form of math sophisticated enough to prove synchronicity; all the while, they are existing and living within the synchronicity of the universe in which temporal and eternal time are the same. In our Diné language, when we say "now" it means the ongoing, eternal now. It is this idea of "process" that eliminates the concept of compartmentalized and binary thinking.

In the West, dualistic left-brain thinking is built into us and built within us. At a personal and a societal level, we have been systemically conditioned. When I use the "art of making distinction," I do it to assess and facilitate our conversations and discussion into unifying principles. For example, schooling is not education. Schooling is focused largely on left-brain activity whereas education is a lifelong process.

What I know of process theology is its belief in unfolding Holiness and Wholeness. For us that are Hózhó, we understand life as an all-encompassing concept that we exist in, and no one can exist outside of, or separate from it. We are our eternal self in the eternal now, and whether we are in or out of the body, we exist accordingly in our sacred self in our sacred place in the universe.

Diné Bizaad is *not* the Navajo language; it is ceremonial pronunciation sounds and vibrations that are interconnected and interrelated within the natural order. Our body is but the earth element, and we are 72% water, fire is our temperature and the air is "in breath, out breath" which is not our own breath; it is the perfect peace and love of Creator. Whether we exist in the body or out of the body, we are existing in the perfect peace and love of Creator *and* within creation simultaneously! That's the closest way in English that I can describe to you Hózhó.

We're not an Abrahamic tradition, and we're not pagan either in the classical sense. Hózhó is not a theory and not philosophy; it's not new age, not alternative medicine and certainly not superstition. It is not a belief system; you don't have to *believe* in seasons or the four directions or gravity or moon phases or the equinox—these are all existing within this natural order, as are we, together in alignment.

I make a distinction between the criminal mind and the sacred-self intellect. The criminal mind is using *our thinking for what it is not for*—such as "I win;" "You lose;" and "Winner takes all." Such thinking leads to the destructive and death-producing outcomes we are experiencing at a global crisis level right now. The appropriate function of our whole-brain thinking is conscience, moral reasoning. I make these words in English synonymous— whole-brain thinking, conscience, moral reasoning, intuition, creative imagination. Our creative imagination is the gift we are given that allows us to design co-creative solutions.

Holo means the micro and the macro are reflecting. We're a hologram, and we're *in* the hologram! We look like we're separate, and everything looks like it's separate, but it is not so. "Holo" is Bohm's terminology for understanding this oneness, so the individual, family, community, society, nation all reflect the same patterns. It's the same. It's exactly the same for any race, any religion, any age, any language, any land—it's the same. That's the "Holo" he is speaking of. We are the holistic in the holographic.

In the Navajo ceremonial language of Hózhó, there are the four directions clockwise—East, South, West and North—and then the ordinal directions, which makes eight. These cardinal points are like the particles, and the movement among them is the wave, so it is quantum physics. The Holo is quantum physics meaning there's process, there's movement, what Bohm calls holomovement. The sequencing is very important—earth, water, fire and air. We have: sunrise, noon, evening, midnight; spring, summer, fall, winter; and child, youth, adult, elder. There is sequencing. We don't rearrange the clock or the time of the seasons. There is a sequencing that, in the natural order, one follows the other as a process and practice that we are experiencing and living within. It is not something outside of ourselves; we're *in* this place of sacred self—the power *within* to use power *with* others.

When I use the term Hózhó I am only interested in the unifying principle. I am informing and clarifying. I am teaching; I am describing, illustrating and defining the unifying principles that are built within us. Let us be cognizant and awake and begin using this awareness instead of denying that we are already in alignment. It's not like we have to overcome something or "We're gonna get there someday." In our language, "Holy People" does not exclude anyone. We are all equally "holy earth surface people."

In the Euro-centric, dualistic, inverse, thinking system, consciousness produces perception. Reality is relative to perception, and there's no spiritual morality because there's only conversion and competition for who has the one right way and who has the one right truth. So, people polarize into perpetual adversity and conflict and warfare. This repeats itself so that, eventually, people don't even know that they are trapped and entrenched.

To reframe our thinking, I'm not going to describe consciousness and perception or reality's relation to perception, but rather will describe conscience, collective conscience, whole brain thinking and moral reasoning. Reality is exact in the natural order; there's no "maybe." Does the fire work? Does the sun work? Does the Earth gravity work? Does the air work? Do you have to have faith and belief in it? Reality is exact, so there's spiritual morality within it. That's where group consensus or decision making for "I win—you win" is natural, because we're each a spark of divinity with inherent sovereignty. We are born with this sovereignty; it is not politically granted, and we are governed equally by the laws that govern us. We each have our genius gifts; yours and mine and each person's is for our collective survival. Decisions are made for our collective survival, for the greatest good for the greatest number of people—that's justice. Justice is love; the whole universe is the essence of the substance of love—that's Hózhó!

Complete holiness and wholeness exist within me and around me. That is the total truth, and truth is the only real power, and it's our protection. So, conscience, reality, is the natural order, and there is morality in our decision making and designing of the co-creative solutions for our collective survival. That is another description of Hózhó.

We don't have to think about how to experience the beauty of this wholeness; *we don't have to do anything other than give up our denial of it.* And that we can do in a split second—it's not tomorrow, next week, next year or next millennium. The words in the vibration are *right now.* We're already in alignment; we don't have to do anything other than to speak truth and then have a witness, and then we're all doing this work together. We are not sacrificing anybody or ourselves. We're not believing that pain and suffering is the only spiritual path. The path is the true spiritual joy of true spirituality, not the mood changes of avoiding pain or seeking pleasure, which is a substitute for having gratitude for our spiritual identity. This means to be in our original state of sacred self. Using Navajo language and teaching: "Making distinctions" helps people get to the "aha! moment" where there is the reframe to not be trapped in dualism and compartmentalization. Simplicity is where to find interconnection and interrelatedness.

Within Hózhó, throughout one's life, there is joy and happiness and good health. It's complete, and we're going to travel accordingly on this epic way-path together, because we're all born within this existing complete unity. We don't have to make it; we're not the one making the unity—it IS. And because "it is," then we think, act, speak, and make our decisions accordingly. That's where the group consensus comes in and then we save time; we're not confronting and debating, and we're not bantering on and on. We can do the work."

⁂

Dr. Leroy Little Bear, a friend and associate of David Bohm, says in the film *Infinite Potential: The Life & Ideas of David Bohm*:

> "David Bohm was interested in Blackfoot metaphysics because the English language has to become a lot more process-oriented [as opposed to noun-oriented] in trying to explain some of the things that happens in the subatomic level. And that process-oriented approach to English he was referring to as the 'real mode.' And that's what he was working on. And when I understood that, I said to him, 'Hey, Blackfoot,' which I grew up in, 'is a whole lot more process-oriented and so on,' and I jokingly told him, 'Hey, quit the real mode. Hey, just learn Blackfoot.' You know? In the Blackfoot mind, nothing is static, everything is always on the move, and you can never predict what is going to happen. So that the only thing you can really say is happening is The Now."[3]

Process Theology and Judeo-Christian Thought

Considering Bohm's interest in process-oriented language and the challenge of expressing something akin to the Holomovement with a single noun, I was fortunate enough to interview Dr. John B. Cobb, Jr., a founding co-director of the Center for Process Studies and the author and editor of over 40 books, including *Sustaining the Common Good: A Christian Perspective on the Global Economy.*

As one of the foremost experts on Process Theology and Thinking, his insights on the attempt "to call a rose by any other name" were enlightening. Here is a transcript of what he shared with me:

Words from John Cobb, PhD

"On one occasion, David Bohm and I spent two weeks in Claremont, California, and we talked almost every afternoon. We discovered that, in terms of our cosmological thinking, we were extremely close. The language you speak largely determines how you think, and it is very hard to think against your language. This is something Bohm talked about a lot.

Our Indo-European linguistic frameworks require us to use a stable entity as the subject of all of our thinking. That stable entity is thought of as being self-identical through time when all the attributes are changing. That's the idea of a "substance." The idea of a substance is a given object that has no fixed relationships, so it is an independent entity. Relations are obscured by substance language.

Bohm said the only hope for science to understand the quantum world is to stop using nouns and pronouns as the subjects of our sentences and instead use gerunds (verbs acting as nouns, ending in "ing"). Grammatically that's possible but a very minor part of our normal conversation. In substance thinking, the world is made up of things; in process language, the world is made up of "events," and the gerunds that Bohm was talking about are much more suggestive of events. Substance thinking forces a kind of separateness of each entity, whereas process says everything is interrelated, interconnected. In this way, process thinkers feel we have *not* moved far away from the original wisdom of Indigenous and other spiritual cultures.

The Indo-European languages all grow out of the world of vision—seeing. The Bible, written in Hebrew, which is not an Indo-European language, is much more about hearing. "The *word* of God"—God *speaks* the world into existence. The Hebrews did not develop a philosophy; their explanations of what is and what is not, what is valuable and what is not, are mostly in story form. They don't identify some unchanging thing; they tell a story about events. There is nothing about Yahweh being unchanging or all-powerful; all that language comes later from the substance language throughout Western thought.

There are people in the West who, in spite of their language, try very hard to think of relations as fundamental. It is a well-accepted philosophical notion that no two substances can occupy the same space at the same time. And that's true if there was such a thing as substances. The idea that God is in everything, and everything is in God, is the exact opposite of that and is much closer to biblical thinking.

We don't think we are radical in the sense of distancing ourselves from what Christians have thought, but since most Christian theology has become completely substance-oriented, we are seen as quite heretical. So, what is common to "process thought" is a fundamentally different understanding, which we think is closer to the biblical understanding. We feel like we are recovering truths rather than just going off on our own and creating something new.

If you forget about substances and tell stories, you can certainly talk about how God is with us and in us and we are in God. That is fundamental to Christian thought and is not given up by the people who use substance language—it is just in unresolved tension with how they think.

Alfred North Whitehead (the father of Process Philosophy) thinks that the one, actual entity that we can be surest of is our immediate experience. That is different to Descartes who says, "I think therefore I am," where the I is a substance. For process thinking, the "I" entity is the coming-together of a whole-past constantly enfolding into a new entity. It is creativity, it is an *activity*, and the world is made up of units of activity. It is not only human beings who have experiences; everything that IS is an experience.

We are also quite critical of the way science formulates things, as was David Bohm. Scientists announced that they can explain everything as clockwork. In Aristotelian science, there were four causes, and one of them was "final cause," which deals with ultimate values and purpose. In the rise of Western science, they did away with "final cause." It was a brilliant move for science and allowed it to make much more progress focusing on "efficient cause" than when it was inclusive of "final cause." It was a mistake, but it was a brilliant mistake for advancing materialistic science! Now they have become so dogmatic on this point that purpose, meaning and value play greatly diminished roles in today's world. If there are no purposes, if things are determined solely by efficient causes, this leads to determinism and materialism. I think scientists must pay attention to evidence, otherwise it ceases to be science. The evidence is overwhelming that the world is not made up of substances.

Philosophically, if you believe that there is real novelty in the world, then there are potentials that have not yet been actualized but remain potentials. Both Heidegger and I use the word "calling"—*Der Ruf, the call forward*—we experience a sense that there are possibilities that are better than what we are and have been. I think this idea of the "call forward" is possibly the most pervasive and significant experience of God. Once again, it's very biblical— calling is very common in the Bible. Every event includes God as one of many things each event includes. Whitehead says the primordial nature of God consists of all potentials, and many of them have not yet been actualized. God provides the potentiality that is essential for life to have meaning and purpose.

Bohm's idea of the explicate order is the order of the world that we see and the patterns that we find there. Science thus far has focused its attention on the order that is continuous with our visual experience. I think you get much closer to causality if you talk about *smelling* than if you talk about *seeing*. The implicate order is the order of the experience itself, and it is in that order that everything is interconnected, that everything is process.

The world is not made up of substances; it is made up of events. To be an event is to be an experiential synthesis of everything that has been. That means that the things that have been in the past are in some sense flowing into the present—flowing in incarnation. So, we incarnate a great deal of our own past every moment of experience. Everything is constituted by a creative synthesis of relations. The way I use "creative synthesis" is pretty much the same as holomovement for Bohm."

Eastern Philosophy and Thought

In the latter part of his life, David Bohm developed several extraordinary relationships with "giants" of Eastern spiritual traditions. His friendship with Krishnamurti is celebrated and well documented through the many dialogues they engaged in together. Similarly, his friendship with the 14th Dalai Lama became a profound relationship, resulting in the Dalai Lama calling Bohm his "science guru."

Bohm's friendships are in part a result of the wonderful synergy his discoveries in quantum physics had with these ancient, mystical traditions. Connected to the Dalai Lama's own Vajrayana Buddhist tradition is Dzogchen, also called The Great Perfection. This "secret" tantric teaching encompasses three interrelated stages or states—the Ground, Path and Fruition. There is a deep resonance with the "Ground" of Dzogchen and Bohm's implicate order, as there is with "Fruition" and the explicate order. The "Path" that unites them is the holomovement itself.

Dzogchen has a connection to Tantric schools and so a relation to Advaita Vedanta, the grandmother of non-dualism, which held such deep resonance with Bohm's own discoveries of reality as "undivided-Wholeness." Sri Aurobindo was one of the sages who connected the non-dualism of the East with 20th century process theory. I had the opportunity to discuss this connection with Ramesh Bijlani, an Indian medical scientist, inspirational speaker and author.

Below is his insight on Sri Aurobindo and the resonance between Eastern philosophy and Bohm's work:

Words from Ramesh Bijlani, MD

"Sri Aurobindo's philosophy of Supermind represents the unmanifest divine, totality, holistic vision (implicate order). The Overmind and lower gradations represent the imperfect manifest world (explicate order). Sri Aurobindo's approach was as a seer and a mystic, whereas David Bohm started as a scientist and discovered, just as many other physicists have, that physics at the highest level is consistent with the spiritual world view.

There are two things at least which are striking in their similarities. First, is how Bohm looks at the universe in a holistic manner. This corresponds more or less to what Sri Aurobindo calls the Overmind. It has been looked upon as two hemispheres, the upper hemisphere is the unmanifest divine, the total truth in itself without manifesting, and the other half, the Supermind, is the highest that is conceived in manifestation.

The second point of agreement is that the world is moving in a direction toward higher grades of consciousness. This futuristic vision, as well as these higher grades of consciousness in which we have this sense of oneness and unity, are quite consistent with what David Bohm has said. They might have approached the same truth from different angles, one through the doorway of science and the other through the doorway of yoga, but ultimately, they are talking of very similar things.

The evolutionary thrust is so strong that it is inevitable, the world will move in that direction, and this is one of those events that is taking the world in that direction. The Holomovement and its 8 Core Principles—all these are essentially taking the world in the direction that Sri Aurobindo had foreseen about 100 years ago. So once the time for an idea for a certain stage of evolution has come, it is inevitable, it will happen.

Sri Aurobindo's philosophy is essentially rooted in Vedanta (non-dualism). The world is a manifestation of the divine, and therefore, you cannot reject one form of the divine and accept the other form; to accept the unmanifest and reject the manifest is something you cannot do. Since the manifest is imperfect, what we have to try and do as human beings, who have both the urge and capacity, is to reduce this imperfection and make human life and the world more worthy of what is manifest. That is the life-affirming, life-embracing view of Vedanta. It is qualified non-dualism, ultimate truth is one, ultimate reality is one—everything else is different ways of looking at the same one reality. That is the basis in Vedanta Sri Aurobindo also subscribes.

One thing about Sri Aurobindo which stands out, even compared to this qualified non-dualism, is this stress on evolution and his futuristic vision. In that sense, he is perhaps the first to emphasize it to such a great extent and gives the certitude that this is something inevitable. It will happen."

It Is What It Is, By Whatever Name It Goes

There are, of course, countless other examples from wisdom traditions that point to the similarities between the history of spiritual understanding and the meaning of the Holomovement. In doing so, there are also numerous references to the difficulty—indeed, even the audacious impossibility—of trying to put a name on the ineffable essence of a movement of movements. The Sufi Master Bawa Muhaiyaddeen stated in *The Resonance of Allah: Resplendent Explanations Arising from the Nur, Allah's Wisdom of Grace*:

> "Oh Man! You think you can know all things solely by your investigation. There is, however, a Truth that governs such knowing. That Truth is this: The State of Silence will be invaluable to you. Let the form of Divine Luminous Wisdom grow from this inner Silence. See yourself as

the consciousness within the form of Divine Luminous Wisdom. It will appear as One. That form is That. And That is you. That State is One. It is That which is the All-pervading Radiant Effulgence."

Just as Lao Tzu warned us about the folly of attempting to name the nameless, so does Bawa Muhaiyaddeen alert us here to the epistemological dangers of any truth-claim rooted in "language." So, let us say this: It is not the name—the word—that is of significance. It is the message. And the message is, from time immemorial in all of our wisdom traditions, "May They Be One." Let us honor this divine calling to come together in a social/spiritual meta-movement to unite humanity and move forward in positive ways! Call it by whatever name you will; a rose is a rose, and it still smells as sweet as it is, by whatever name it goes. Let's look to all our five senses and beyond to identify with this movement that is calling us ever forward, that exhorts us all to keep moving, keep growing, keep becoming.

Through this chapter, we have explored various and distinct wisdom traditions representing Indigenous, Western and Eastern spiritual perspectives that each have deep, profound resonance with David Bohm, his discoveries in quantum physics, his notion of "undivided wholeness" and the Holomovement itself. What an extraordinary time to be alive, when the discoveries of modern science are validating diverse mystical teachings of thousands of years ago! Or perhaps, is it the other way around? Either way, the idea that we inhabit simultaneously a perfect unity beyond time and space as well as an evolutionary process in the manifest world that is always on the move and is becoming more perfect, is an idea with deep roots in the collective soil of humanity's rich cultural, philosophical and spiritual heritage.

May we now take these insights, these revelations affirmed by both spirituality and science, and use them together for the advantage of all life on Earth. Working in partnership with the unfolding, evolving cosmos, what great achievement could ever be beyond us! In the flow of the Holomovement, the cosmic wind is truly at our back. Let us hoist high our sails and harness those prevailing winds of truth, beauty and goodness to bring us to the fairer shores of justice, love, healing, peace, unity, wholeness and ever onwards into the Great Mystery that lies beyond all.

References:

Renard, Gary. *The Disappearance of the Universe: Straight Talk about Illusions, Past Lives, Religion, Sex, Politics, and the Miracles of Forgiveness*. Hay House Inc.: 2004.

CHAPTER 2
A UNITIVE NARRATIVE: COSMOLOGY UNDERPINNING THE HOLOMOVEMENT

by Jude Currivan, PhD

The emergence of a Holomovement, as a wholistically interrelated movement of movements, is essentially inspired by American physicist and idealist David Bohm's perception of the fundamental wholeness of the nature of reality. Yet, until now, our collective world-view would have been unable to stand with Bohm to underpin and frame a Holomovement initiative.

Our challenge is a collective perspective of the world based in materialist science and a mindset of separation. Whilst the technologies of this prevailing paradigm have enabled us to achieve much, including communicating as a global species, its cosmology describes a Universe devoid of meaning and bereft of purpose. The narrative of our times considers evolution as driven by random occurrences and mutations and treats immaterial mind and consciousness as somehow arising from material brains.

However, a new story is unfolding. Evidence of scientific breakthroughs, at all scales of existence and across numerous and wide-ranging fields of research, is now revealing a radically expanded realization. This emergent wholeworld-view and its new paradigm is converging with universal wisdom teachings and spiritually-based traditions to create an integral and unitive awareness. It seems Bohm was ahead of his time as his insights have been significantly extended and founded on and framed by a further three decades of scientific investigations and discoveries.

Instead of a Universe based on materialist separation, (r)evolutionary insights are showing that the appearance of energy-matter and space-time, do indeed, emerge from deeper levels of causation, as maintained by Bohm and time-honored traditions. And they are describing a Universe that not only exists and evolves as a non-locally unified entity, but, vitally, that it exists TO evolve; from simplicity to complexity and ever greater levels of individuated and collective self-awareness, interdependence and perceived interbeing.

Above all, leading-edge science is discovering that, fundamentally, mind and consciousness aren't things we *have*, they are what we and the whole world *are*, which, alongside Bohm, also has been the understanding of scientific pioneers such as Sir James Jeans, Max Planck, Albert Einstein and John Archibald Wheeler.

An emergent cosmology of evolutionary consciousness, based on increasingly compelling evidence, is finding that everything in our Universe is in dynamic and collaborative relationships with everything else. It shows how cosmic mind, articulated in a universal "language" based on digitized and vitally meaningful in-formation and pixelated at the most minute scale of existence, literally and actively in-forms the entire appearance of our Universe. Empirical evidence from atomic to cosmological scales also demonstrates that it does so holographically.

Essentially, our entire Universe is a (W)holomovement, whose unified existence and evolutionary purpose is expressed in the holarchic diversity of its nested holonic complexity. And now, the conscious evolution of humanity may also be seen as having an intrinsic role in its ongoing emergence. For as we link up and lift up together as a Holomovement, we too are reflecting and embodying what our Universe does in its entirety, from its unified wholeness to the holons of its constituent parts.

The evolutionary story of our Universe, our planetary home, Gaia, and our human family, began 13.8 billion years ago, not in the implied chaos of a big bang, but in a minute, exquisitely fine-tuned and incredibly ordered state. It was, as the ancient wisdom teachings of Vedic India maintained, the first moment of an ongoing Big Breath.

Its universal and non-locally unified nature, the meticulous order and simplicity of its birth and the invariant nature of its space-time appearance had the inevitable consequence of a one-way flow of time. This, alongside a holographic expansion of space, which will continue throughout its finite life-cycle, has enabled ever-more and vitally meaningful in-formation to be embodied within space-time.

As a finite thought of an infinite and eternal Cosmos, the extreme fine-tuning of its in-formationally relational laws of physics also instills it with an innate evolutionary impulse and essential purpose—to evolve from its original simplicity to ever-greater complexity and individuated and relational levels of self-awareness.

After some eight billion years, its evolutionary arc had formed in the mid and outer reaches of galaxies, creating vast interstellar nurseries of elemental abundance. Here, in the deep cold of space, ordered by magnetic fields and bathed in ultra-violet light, assembled the prebiotic building blocks of organic lifeforms for planets still to form.

Around five and a half billion years ago, one such nursery, nested in a spiral arm of our Milky Way galaxy and around two-thirds of the way out from the galactic center, was buffeted by the shock waves from a nearby exploding star, or supernova, and began to gravitationally collapse in on itself. As it did so, it started to spin, and its material formed a rotating disk around a central hub of its protostar. Gradually, the disk separated out into planets, and its central star ignited to become our Sun. Located in the so-named "Goldilocks zone," not too hot and not too cold, a small rocky planet formed at just the right distance away, and our planetary home, Gaia, came into being.

Gaia's elemental makeup is extraordinarily abundant. Literally embodying all the natural elements of our Universe and blessed with abundant water, our planetary home took the next step within the universal (w)holomovement four billion years ago. Gaia was ready to embody the subsequent and vital stage of the Universe's and her evolutionary impulse and holarchic complexity.

A number of fundamental aspects of Gaia's onward emergence have particular significance and offer guidance and opportunities as to how we may optimize our emergent human Holomovement. These relate to the inherently co-evolutionary processes of the entirety of Gaia's planetary 'gaiasphere' with the evolution of the biosphere, comprising all her organic children, in dynamic relationships with the rocks and minerals of her geosphere, the waters of her hydrosphere and the air of her atmosphere. And indeed, embedded within her wider relationships with our Sun, Moon and entire Universe.

With regard to biological evolution, recent and unfolding discoveries are radically reappraising the role of genes and the genetic code, or genome, superseding the supposition of random mutations as driving evolutionary emergence. These findings are reframing our understanding of how simplicity evolves to complexity and holarchic organization, with a deepening appreciation of multilevel collaboration and cooperation.

While the DNA genome codes for the inherited attributes of an organism, it isn't an unchangeable instruction manual. Responsivity to ongoing environmental and potentially evolutionary in-formational flows and processes allows genes to be expressed in different ways. Along with numerous roles served by DNA's complementary partner RNA, the genetic code is an organism's servant in co-existing and co-evolutionary holonic and holarchic relationships. Taking place dynamically within organisms themselves and other organisms and with the conditions of their immediate and wider environment, in-formational processes are underpinned by so-named holotropic attractors of in-formational causation. Our building blocks of existence within our biosphere and entire gaiasphere act as an innately interdependent and holarchic whole.

In addition, the foundational presumption of random mutations to the genome as the primary driver of biological evolution is being shown to be fundamentally flawed. Instead, from the initial emergence of prebiotic molecules, the precursors of organic lifeforms are now being shown to originate in pre-planetary interstellar clouds of gas and dust; to their further evolution nurtured by Gaia, resonant and collaborative relationships have been embodied. From the inception of the genome in the earliest of Gaia's organic children and progressively in the onward emergence of complexity, contingencies, redundancies, checks, balances and corrections in the genetic replication processes, extraordinary lengths are taken to dramatically reduce coding errors and so minimize the possibilities of random mutations. Such enormously complex processes, for example, reduce an estimated error rate in human protein synthesis of one in 10,000 copies in transcribing the initial DNA instructions to a minuscule level of only one in more than a billion copies.

So, if random mutations were in any way significantly helpful for evolution, such extensive and complex efforts would not be worthwhile in terms of the energy and effort to prevent them from occurring. While the tiny number of error mutations that do evade the editing process almost always result in disadvantage and dis-ease, they're still affected by the inexorable logic of natural selection with their surroundings. Such random mutations, though, rather than persisting, generally result in an evolutionary dead end.

Instead, an organism's highest priority is to sustain its integrity and coherence while being able to proactively and beneficially adapt to environmental and evolutionary threats and opportunities.

The hitherto evolutionary model based on random mutations and the allied presumption they are only passively embodied through natural selection, also requires very long timeframes for other than minor evolutionary change. There is now significant evidence that shows otherwise. It is revealing, rather, that meaningful and intelligent in-formational processes, arising from underlying causative attractors, guide the progress of evolutionary complexity and can initiate such changes over much shorter timescales.

Scientists are finding it is via 'horizontal' gene transfers (HGT) and a myriad of genetic processes, rather than the so-named 'vertical' inheritance through the DNA lineage, that evolutionary opportunities can be quickly accessed. As Gaia's story is now revealing, these can include radical transformations with the emergence of not only new and more complex species, but also entirely new groups of organisms and multiple holarchies. By incorporating a widespread, mutually beneficial and multi-level biological collaboration and in-formational dialogue, opportunities to survive and thrive are further enhanced, enabling major changes to be brought about and often with remarkable speed.

It is becoming apparent our understanding of such an emergence cannot occur by attempting to separate a biological entity from its environment. Entire ecosystems are being revealed to be in intimate co-evolutionary and dynamic partnerships, not only inclusive of their biological organisms but with the entirety of Gaia's planetary gaiasphere and in even wider relationships with our Sun and Moon.

Competition for environmental niches and resources does have its role and does, indeed, encourage the 'survival of the fittest' in the sense that an organism that most effectively fits its environmental niche is likeliest to survive. However, it is cooperation and holarchic organization that fundamentally drive evolutionary complexity. Collaborative relationships that are win-win, whether through competitive tensions or cooperative mutuality, supported the earliest emergence of biological evolution and have continued to do so ever since.

Over some four billion years, the ongoing emergence of Gaia's biosphere has been embodied in a series of evolutionary ebbs and flows trending over time to greater holarchic complexity, all the while maintaining a dynamic balance between the elasticity and resilience of simplicity and the greater evolutionary potential, and the fragility and rigidness that comes with progressive individuation, diversity and self-awareness.

The waves of her evolutionary impulse are literally pulsed through such epochs of relative quietude and times of radical transformation. In periods of environmental stability, which until now has included our own Holocene epoch for some 12,000 years, only minor biological progress has occurred and generally within species. Longer, medium term cycles caused primarily by the variations in Gaia's orbit and axial tilt, however, engender greater levels of biological responses. The progressive die-off of preexisting species generally corresponds, though, with the emergence of new, environmentally-adjusted variants, often closely linked to their forebears. With ecosystems increasingly understood as existing close to what are known as critical states, on the co-creative edges of order and disorder, such apparent instability actually confers a level of flexibility. It enables the optimization of such responses with minimal levels of genome reconfiguration, so offering maximum evolutionary benefit with least effort.

However, when environmental change is rapid, extensive, drastic or involves catastrophic extinction, such disruption drives (r)evolutionary innovation and emergence throughout the entirety of Gaia's inherently interconnected gaiasphere. These evolutionary waves require dynamic and radical co-evolutionary collaboration, each evolutionary pulse embodying increased complexity, diversity and sentience.

As more complex species evolve, their bodily templates, however, become progressively inflexible to their ability to incorporate further and significant change. A series of transformational extinction events in Gaia's past five hundred million years have shown that, whilst numerous extant species die-off, these are generally the most complex of their time and often at the end of their evolutionary arc. Instead, Gaia's ongoing evolutionary impulse continues through innovative surges in organisms with greater emergent potential and ability to adapt themselves to enormous changes to carry the next wave of evolutionary progress forward.

The ongoing story of Gaia, and her innate evolutionary impulse and processes, have essentially embodied an increasingly complex and planetary-wide holomovement throughout her four billion years in the making. As I share in much greater detail in my book, *The Story of Gaia: The Big Breath and the Evolutionary Journey of Our Conscious Planet,* as a planetary mother, Gaia and the ebbs and flows of her evolutionary journey are replete with innate wisdom and profound guidance for us and our own emergent Holomovement.

Throughout the long arc of her story, Gaia has and continues to exist, evolve and thrive within the wholistic limits and emergent opportunities of her planetary gaiasphere. In doing so, she embodies innate simplicity to achieve her evolutionary purpose. Her unity is expressed in diversity, optimizing, rather than maximizing, flexibility, resilience and collective genius. Skills and best practices are in-formed and shared locally and globally. She appreciates "healthy" competition and encourages multi-level cooperation to guide emergence of complexity. Minimum effort is used for maximum impact. Forms are fitted to functions, again with optimum efficiency. And everything is recycled, often repurposed, and nothing is wasted.

Applying such wisdom to the emergence and holarchic complexity of a human Holomovement finds us in and aligns us with Gaia and her marvelous web of sentience. As the youngest of her organic children, we embody her legacy and that of her and our entire Universe's evolutionary impulse. An emergent Holomovement offers us a vital opportunity to re-member, experience and embody a realization of our profound relationship with her and an evolutionary recognition that we are all Gaians. For us to do so successfully, we also need to ground ourselves in a new and unitive narrative of wholeness and innate belonging.

During the Winter of 2021, into the Spring of 2022, as the impulse to initiate the Holomovement was emerging, members of the SDG (Sustainable Development Goals) Thought Leaders synergy circle of the Evolutionary Leaders were convening to articulate this unitive narrative. Aligned in serendipity and synchronicity with the Holomovement, members of the SDG based their work on the emergent and wide-ranging scientific evidence of a conscious and evolutionary Universe. This unitive narrative underpins and frames a wholistic and transformational approach to the implementation of the United Nations Sustainable Development Goals.

Converging with universal wisdom and spiritually-based teachings, the unitive narrative aims to "provide an emergent cosmological, planetary, interspiritual and societal foundation to serve and support the conscious evolution of humanity and heal our collective worldview from separation to a perspective of unity in diversity." The text contextualizes its urgent calling by paraphrasing the great narrator of human experience, mythologist Joseph Campbell:

"The only narrative that will be worth thinking about in the immediate future will be the one talking about the planet and all beings on it. This new narrative will need to be grounded in widespread, unitive consciousness, which includes a felt sense of unity with all life, unity with source of being and unity with evolutionary flow."

This unitive narrative and its wholism "invites us to inwardly hear the wisdom of our hearts and respect the complementarity of feminine and masculine attributes. And thus, its unity expressed in diversity guides us to a wholeness of both the inner being and outer doing in our lives. It supports us in integrating our innate health and wholeness, both individually and communally and as a planetary species."

In realizing the unified nature of reality, this unifying message "calls for a collective celebration of our inner lives as a doorway that opens us to an evolutionary shift of consciousness and the emergence of an inclusive interspirituality which provides essential practices for awakening to this unitive consciousness. Vitally, it recognizes our fundamental interbeing; our interconnectedness, interdependence and belonging with the whole community of our planetary home, Gaia, and with the entire Universe."

Perhaps, and above all, what this unitive new narrative does is "empowers us to envision and gives us hope to co-create a love-based rather than separation-based future where regenerative and sustainable development is a natural outcome of a world that works for all people and our planetary home."

The synergy circle members and authors of this message have worked with the United Nations, global governments and organizations and civil society for many years. Collectively, they recognized that this unitive narrative, founded on the latest scientific evidence across all scales of existence and numerous fields of research, is essential to underpin and frame a unitive worldview and mindset to inspire and empower transformational change in the world.

The innate interspirituality and inherent multidimensionality of the emergent cosmology of a conscious and evolving Universe not only integrate the inner being and outer doing of our lives, as a unitive narrative invites and encourages, but they also naturally encompass nonlocal sentience. Intuitive insights, coherent group consciousness and the occurrences of synchronicities, such as the co-emergence of a convergent Holomovement and unitive narrative as Bohm perceived, invite us into deeper and experiential relationships with the whole of reality.

At this moment of our collective choice, this is indeed the time for a Holomovement to come into being. Propelled by a unitive worldview and narrative, and inviting a shared (r)evolutionary purpose as an overarching and coherent perspective, we are enabled to facilitate multi-level distributed intelligence and holarchic actions from the bottom up as a movement of movements. Its allied universal principles based on loving truth and embodying inclusion, equity and justice, can additionally empower and ethically guide us. Thus, its overall coherence is attuned to and aligned with the emergent and evolutionary flow.

By reflecting the coherently dynamic design principles, patterns and processes that are embodied by Gaia's entire and emergent gaiasphere, a Holomovement can co-create holarchies, rather than hierarchies, of interdependent and nested complexity and synergistic empowerment and co-creativity. The inclusion of Bohm's multidimensional perspective, now shared and extended by the latest scientific evidence, offers the evolutionary potential for humanity's collective consciousness to be coherently embodied in such generative transformation.

Bohm's friend and colleague F. David Peat shared the significance of this emergent opportunity when he said: "It is this collective consciousness that is truly one and indivisible, and it is the responsibility of each human person to contribute towards the building of this consciousness of mankind." And Bohm himself states: "There's nothing else to do. There is no other way out. That is absolutely what has to be done and nothing else can work."

﹡————————﹡————————﹡

As I've previously mentioned, evidence is increasingly showing that varied and rapid progressions of horizontal gene transfers (HGT) have assembled to in-formationally guide biological innovation, especially following periods of dramatic ecological breakdown. Now, and instead of such biological emergence, it may be that the corresponding ideas, behaviors and cultural symbolism of our collective consciousness may be called into evolutionary play, in processes of "horizontal meme transfers" to guide us to the next level of evolutionary awareness as a species.

Such memes arising from new stories based on a unitive narrative and allied with the activation and behavioral developments of a Holomovement, can inspire and empower our conscious evolution and enable us to step forward to become co-evolutionary partners with our planetary home.

As referred to in the founding text of the unitive new narrative, and to paraphrase philosopher Teilhard de Chardin: Someday, we shall harness the energies of love, and then, for a second time in the history of the world, humanity will have discovered fire.

That someday is here and now. As we wake up to the radical reality of a unitive narrative and our emergent opportunity as a Holomovement, we also will discover as a species, perhaps for the first time, who we really and truly are and who we can evolve to become.

References and Resources:

Cosmological:
Wilber, Ken. https://integrallife.com.

Atkinson, Robert. *The Story of Our Time: From Duality to Interconnectedness to Oneness*. Delray Beach, FL: Sacred Stories Publishing, 2017.

Berry, Thomas. https://thomasberry.org.

Currivan, Jude. *The Cosmic Hologram: In-formation at the Center of Creation*. Rochester, VT/Toronto, Canada: Inner Traditions, 2017.

Currivan, Jude. *The Story of GAIA: The Big Breath and the Evolutionary Journey of Our Conscious Plane*. Rochester, VT: Inner Traditions, 2022. https://wholeworld-view.org.

Swimme, Brian. *Journey of the Universe*. New Haven & London: Yale University Press, 2014.

Walach, Harald. *Galileo Commission Report: Beyond a Materialist Worldview Towards an Expanded Science*. Scientific and Medical Network, 2019. https://galileocommission.org/report.

Planetary:
Earth Charter. https://earthcharter.org.

Brown, Peter. https://www.humansandnature.org/peter-g.-brown.

Nadeau, Robert. https://www.humansandnature.org/robert-nadeau.

Interspiritual:
Teasdale, Wayne. *The Mystic Heart: Discovering a Universal Spirituality in the World's Religions*. Novato, CA: New World Library, 1999.

Social:
Laszlo, Ervin. https://thelaszloinstitute.com.

Smitsman, Anneloes. https://earthwisecentre.org.

Transformational Change:
Evolutionary Leaders Circle, https://evolutionaryleaders.net.

Atkinson, Robert, Johnson, Kurt, et al. *Our Moment of Choice: Evolutionary Visions and Hope for the Future.* New York: Atria Books, 2020.

Evolutionary Leaders SDG Thought Leaders Synergy Circle. https://sdgthoughtleaderscircle.org.

Universal Principles and Action Steps:
Johnson, Kurt, Ulfik, Rick, and Winters, Shannon. "Universal Principles and Action Steps." *The Convergence Magazine.* New York, NY: Light on Light Publications, 2021. https://issuu.com/lightonlight/docs/universal_principles_and_action_steps.

Unitive Narrative:
https://www.evolutionaryleaders.net/unitivenarrative.

https://sdgthoughtleaderscircle.org/unitive-new-narrative/.

https://www.unitivenarrative.org/.

CHAPTER 3
THE HOLOTROPIC ATTRACTOR

by Ervin Laszlo, PhD

A Conceptual Clarification

Let me begin by suggesting my interpretation of the concept of the holomovement postulated by American physicist David Bohm, and then show its relation to the concept of the holotropic attractor.

The holomovement is the transfer of information from the implicate order to the explicate order. It is the implicate order "in-forming" the explicate order. In the course of evolution in the explicate order, increasingly coherent ensembles of elements create complex and coherent systems. The holotropic attractor is how this in-formation is transferred: it is how the "in-formation" of the explicate order by the implicate order appears to observers in the explicate order.

The holotropic attractor is the effect of the wholeness-oriented information coded in the implicate order, on the explicate order. This effect is subtle but effective, and in the cosmic context, it is decisive. It is the "bias" created in interactions within the explicate order toward wholeness and coherence. Interactions in the explicate order are constant and universal in space and time, but not random. Their non-randomness produces a cumulative effect. It is the bias that makes for a universe of whole-systems from quanta to galaxies, evolving on multiple levels of structure and organization.

The transfer of wholeness and coherence-generating "in-formation" is the meaning of the term "holomovement." In the absence of the holomovement, the universe would still be a random swirl of inert plasma without structure and order. That the universe has a coherent aspect—due to the presence of nonrandom interactions—is due to the effect of the holotropic attractor.

In the systems sciences, the term "attractor" denotes the factor that impels dynamic systems toward particular states of order with a particular form of evolution—order in the "phase-space" of the systems. The states of the natural systems that appear in the universe change over time. If the change does not follow a discernible sequence, the system is considered chaotic and is not representable by attractors. But if an element of order can be discovered in the phase-space of the systems, the evolution of the systems can be represented by one or a combination of attractors.

There is compelling evidence for the presence of an attractor in the universe, even if the evidence is indirect. Not enough time has elapsed since the Big Bang for random interactions to have created the complex and coherent systems we observe. The 13.7-billion-year dimension of that interval does not offer a reasonable probability that random processes would have created the DNA of a fruit fly, much less the complex architectures of living organisms. The conclusion is inescapable: there was, and is, something other than mere chance underlying interactions in the universe.

The story of the universe is not the story recounted by classical physics—it is not based on random interactions producing the phenomena we observe. There is guidance in the way the universe evolves, even if it is intrinsic and not extrinsic to the universe. It took 13.7 billion years for the systems that emerged in space and time to achieve the complexity and coherence that now meets our eye, and this evolution was far more rapid than random interactions could have produced. It began following the release of the energies by the singularity known as the Big Bang. These energies produced increasingly ordered and stable systems—units of in-phase vibration that could maintain themselves in the chaos of the early universe. They were *leptons* (electrons, muons, tau particles and neutrinos), *mesons* (pions) and *hadrons* (baryons including protons and neutrons). In the course of time, they clustered into atoms, and the atoms clustered into molecules and molecular assemblies. On the astronomical level, stars and stellar systems and entire galaxies came about.

That evolution would be a universal process is now recognized, but it is not clear what is responsible for it. French philosopher Henri Bergson speculated that it is an *elan vital* that counters the trend toward energy-degradation in natural systems, and biologist Hans Driesch suggested that it is a counter-entropic drive he termed *entelechy*. Philosophers Teilhard de Chardin and Erich Jantsch postulated a dynamic tendency called *syntony*, and others spoke of the structuring factor as *syntropy*. Eastern thinkers call the energy that drives the evolutionary process *prana*, a Sanskrit term, and in the West, psychoanalyst Carl Reich suggested the term *orgone*. Rudolf Steiner called it *etheric force*.

Newton himself recognized the presence of a dynamic, creative factor in the universe and sought to accommodate it in his theory. Mechanistic laws, he admitted, are not full descriptions of reality; they need to be completed with the recognition of what he called an "enlivening and ensouling spirit in all things"—"animating" or "enlivening" spirit of "vegetation." Today, we can recognize this force or factor as a universal attractor that shapes the processes that unfold in space and time.

There is indeed a "grand movement taking place around the world, based on the emerging principles of what has been called the new paradigm." That movement is "a movement guided by a unifying worldview and outlined by defining principles giving us hope, meaning and evolutionary direction." It has meaningfully denoted the Upshift Movement: a movement of awakened people seeking alignment with the cosmic attractor, which is the manifest effect of the Holomovement in the observable universe: the explicate order.

More on the Deep Dimension

The idea that a deep dimension underlies the world we observe and inhabit goes back to the Hindu seers of India. Their concept was embraced and elaborated by the philosophers of the metaphysical branch of Hellenic thought: the Idealists, and the Eleatic school of thinkers, including Pythagoras, Plato, Parmenides and Plotinus.

The Hindu seers and the Hellenic philosophers were united in their belief in the existence of a dimension of reality beyond the domain of observed or observable things. For Pythagoras, this dimension was the *Kosmos*, a trans-physical, unbroken wholeness, the ground on which matter and mind arose. For Plato, this was the realm of Ideas and Forms; Plotinus referred to it simply as "the One." The *Lankavatara Sutra* in Indian philosophy called it the "causal dimension" and maintained that it gave rise to the "gross" phenomena we observe with our senses. Hermes Trismegistos described two levels, or two worlds, present in what he called The All—the cosmos. The level we observe is the "sensible" (that is, sense-perceivable) world of material things. Below that world is the "intelligible world"—a world that is not "substantial" and cannot be observed. The sensible world of change and motion derives its existence from the unchanging reality of the intelligible world.

The classical, metaphysical thinkers affirmed that the phenomenal world, the world we observe, is secondary: its existence stems from a deeper level. The deep dimension is eternal, and it is eternally unchanging. It is that which gives rise to the changing and shifting kaleidoscope we regard as the real world.

The Hindu seers used the Sanskrit word "Akasha" to name the deep dimension. The Akasha is the fundamental dimension of the cosmos, prior to the dimensions of *vata* (air), *agni* (fire), *ap* (water) and *prithivi* (earth). The universe is a cyclic phenomenon, emerging from, and again falling back into, the Akasha. In his classic *Raja Yoga*, Indian spiritual master Swami Vivekananda anticipated this concept of contemporary cosmology:

> "Akasha is the omnipresent, all-penetrating existence. Everything that has form, everything that is the result of combination, is evolved out of this Akasha. It is the Akasha that becomes the air, that becomes the liquids, that becomes the solids; it is the Akasha that becomes the sun, the earth, the moon, the stars, the comets; it is the Akasha that becomes the human body, the animal body, the plants, every form that we see, everything that can be sensed, everything that exists ... At the beginning of creation there is only this Akasha. At the end of the cycle the solid, the liquids and the gases all melt into the Akasha again, and the next creation similarly proceeds out of this Akasha."

At the dawn of the modern age, Giordano Bruno brought the idea of a dimension that subtends the observed world into the ambit of science. The infinite universe, he said, is filled with an unseen substance called *aether* or *spiritus*. The heavenly bodies are not fixed points on the crystal spheres of Aristotelian and Ptolemaic cosmology, but move without resistance in this deep dimension under their own impetus.

In the nineteenth century, French physicist Jacques Fresnel revived the idea of a space-filling medium beyond the observed world. He called it "ether." Fresnel sought experimental proof for his theory. The ether, he said, is a quasi-material substance in which the movement of heavenly bodies produces friction. This creates an observable effect: the "ether drag."

Physicists Albert Michelson and Edward Morley tested Fresnel's hypothesis. They reasoned that, if the Earth moves through the ether, the arrival of light beams from the Sun would display a drag. In the direction of the Earth's rotation toward the Sun, the beams should arrive faster than in the opposite direction. But the experiments failed to detect such a drag. Michelson noted that this does not disprove the existence of the ether, only of a particular mechanistic friction-producing conception of it. But the science community assumed that the negative outcome of the experiment meant that there is no ether. Einstein accepted this view. There is no concept of a space-filling, physically friction-producing substance in his special theory of relativity, no fixed background underlying the space and time. All movement in the four-dimensional spacetime continuum is relative only to its own reference frame.

In the second half of the twentieth century, physicists revived the idea of an unobservable plane or dimension grounding the observed universe. In the Standard Model of particle physics, the entities of physics are not independent material things even when endowed with mass; they are part of the unified matrix. The entities of the matrix are the smallest identifiable units of the universe: the quantum particles. The matrix, described as a unified or grand-unified field (and sometimes as "nu-ether") harbors all the fields, forces and constants of the universe. It is more fundamental than the quanta that appear in it. The latter are critical points—crystallizations or condensations—of the underlying matrix.

The deep dimension of the universe found its influential current definition at the end of the twentieth century in the work of David Bohm. As already noted, Bohm called the deep dimension underlying the manifest universe the implicate order. It is from here that the observable/measurable phenomena of the explicate order emerge. The phenomena of the explicate order are not separate realities, but projections of the implicate order. Each moment of time is a projection of the enfolded "pre-space" from which the observed order has arisen.

The theorems of quantum physics deal primarily with the structure of the implicate order. The laws of nature are in that dimension, and they act on the manifest dimension. Thus, inasmuch as quantum physics deals with the reality of the world, it deals primarily with deep dimension. The real world is not an ensemble of quantum particles moving in space and time. It is the deep dimension that governs movement and development in space and time.

These hypotheses are cogent, but scientists are not generally inclined to appeal to quasi-spiritual factors to complete their theories. Bowing to this preference in the contemporary sciences, we shall eschew theological and metaphysical explanations in favor of a simpler concept. We suggest that what scientists and other thinkers have been meaning by higher intelligence, *elan vital*, *prana*, or etheric force, is a universal "attractor."

The presence of an attractor in a system defines the state or condition toward which the sequence of states and behaviors in the system tends or drives. If the sequence exhibits elements of repetition over time, the attractor is said to be "periodic." If it exhibits a tendency toward a single state or behavior, the system can be represented by a point attractor. The evolution of a system can also be complex, including unpredictable elements and incomprehensible sequences, and in that case, the attractor is said to be "strange" or "chaotic." A complex system can exhibit diverse attractors at the same time, operating simultaneously or in temporal sequence.

The presence of an attractor is the simplest explanation of the nonrandom directionality manifested in the evolution of the clusters of in-phase vibrations that are the observable entities of the universe. These entities are coherent, and they are staggeringly so in their ensemble: they could not be the product of mere chance, even when we extend the timeframe of evolution to cosmological dimensions. Serendipity does not explain the existence of the atoms of the elements, much less the DNA of the simplest organism: the known age of the universe would not have been sufficient even for the atoms that fill the periodic table of the elements to have come about by a random mixing of their components. There must be "something" that biases random interactions in the universe and creates the observed evolution of systems toward structure, form and coherence. That "something" may well be a supernatural or at least super-cosmic intent, will or design, but for our purposes, it is sufficient to consider it as an attractor.

The cosmic attractor need not be a separate, *sui generis* law or principle: it is enough to consider it as the formative effect of the laws of nature. Even in this "modest" concept, we get a complex quasi-metaphysical hypothesis. The attractor needs to be considered as originating "beyond" the manifest universe, in the same way as the laws of chess, for example (or of any law- or rule-based system), are "beyond" the processes (or games) that take place in accordance with those laws. The relation of the cosmic attractor to the manifest universe is analogous. The attractor is the impetus Bohm calls "in-formation" and is not part of the processes that take place in the manifest universe.

We define the attractor in reference to the way it governs processes in the universe. The term we chose is "holotropic" (from *holos* meaning whole, and *tropic*, exhibiting a tendency or orientation toward a point or a condition). Thus, we say that the attractor that forms and in-forms processes in the universe is "holotropic." Processes in the universe are governed by a holotropic attractor, and consequently display an orientation toward wholeness.

The holotropic attractor, being the formative effect of the ensemble of the laws of nature, determines that the processes in the universe tend toward the creation of systems with holistic properties. A case in point is the formation of atomic structures. The energy configuration under which a proton is in resonance with a neutron, and accepts electrons in permissible energy shells around the nucleus, and excludes them from others (the "exclusion principle" associated with the name of Wolfgang Pauli), is a holistic (i.e., whole-system creating) process: it leads to the formation of coherent and, in time, increasingly complex atomic structures.

The exclusion principle, and hence the feature of the attractor to which we ascribe it, is the foundation of the evolution of coherent systems in the universe. Through gravitation and particle inclusion and exclusion, the attractor impels particles and ensembles of particles to create ordered structure, counteracting in particular spacetime domains the physical trend toward entropy and chaos.

The Coherence of the Manifest Dimension

In the general case, through the action of the holotropic attractor, processes in the universe are oriented toward wholeness, complexity and coherence. "Holotropism" (the dynamic tendency toward wholeness) is a subtle but effective orientation. It creates a universe of staggering coherence. We review here some particularly striking aspects of the coherence discovered in physics.

In the middle of the twentieth century, Arthur Eddington and Paul Dirac noted some curious "coincidences" among the basic physical constants of the universe. The ratio of the electric force to the gravitational force, which is approximately 10^{40}, is matched by the ratio between the size of the universe and the dimension of elementary particles: that ratio, too, is approximately 10^{40}. It is not evident how these ratios could have been produced, and then maintained, by random processes. The ratio of the electric force to the gravitational force should be unchanging (as these forces are constant), whereas the ratio of the size of the universe to the size of elementary particles should be changing (since the universe is expanding). In his "large number hypothesis," Dirac speculated that the agreement between these ratios, one variable and the other not, is more than coincidence. Either the universe is not expanding, or the force of gravitation varies with its expansion.

Contemporary cosmology unearthed an entire array of similarly mind-boggling forms of coherence. The mass of elementary particles, the number of particles and the forces between them display harmonic ratios. Many of the ratios among basic parameters can be interpreted on the one hand in reference to the relationship between the mass of elementary particles and the number of nucleons (particles of the atomic nucleus) in the universe, and on the other in reference to the relationship between the gravitational constant (the factor of gravitation in the evolution of the universe), the charge of the electron, Planck's constant (a unit of measurement used to calculate the smallest measurable time interval and physical distance) and the speed of light.

Also, the microwave background radiation—the remnant of the Big Bang—turned out to be unexpectedly coherent. When we map its sequence of values, we find peaks and troughs in a non-random sequence. There are large peaks followed by smaller, harmonic peaks. The series of peaks ends at the longest wavelength physicist Lee Smolin termed "R." When R is divided by the speed of light, we get the length of time that independent estimates tell us is the age of the universe. When we divide the speed of light by the value of R (c/R), we get the frequency that equates to one cycle over the age of the universe. When R is squared and divided by the speed of light (R^2/c), we get the value equal to the acceleration of the expansion of the distant galaxies.

The coincidence of these values is not likely to be fortuitous. The universe is coherent beyond the range of mere probability. Its coherence is the explanation of the presence of living organisms, including human beings. Life is only possible in a universe of which the physical constants are precisely correlated. Variation of the order of one-billionth of the value of some of these constants (such as the mass of elementary particles, the speed of light, the rate of the expansion of galaxies and two dozen others) would have resulted in a sterile, lifeless universe. Even a minute variation would have prevented the creation of stable atoms and stable relations among them, and thus, would have precluded the evolution of the complex systems that manifest the phenomena of life. Yet, living systems are found in more and more places in the universe, under more and more diverse conditions.

Not only is the universe coherent as a whole, it is also the ground or template for the evolution of a vast array of coherent systems, ranging in size and complexity from atoms to galaxies. That these complex and coherent systems would have come about by a random mixing of their components is astronomically improbable. The statistical analysis of the complexity even of relatively simple biological systems tells us that to produce them by a random interaction among their components would take longer than the age of the universe.

The complexity of the DNA-mRNA-tRNA-rRNA transcription and translation system precludes the probability that living systems would have been produced by random processes within the known time frames. According to mathematical physicist Fred Hoyle, the probability of a living system having been produced by random interactions is equal to the probability of a hurricane blowing through a scrapyard assembling a working airplane. The 13.8 billion years for the evolution of physical entities and four billion years for the appearance of living systems are not sufficient to account for the presence of stars and galaxies, and for the web of life on this planet. Yet, there is a nonlinear but definite progression in the universe toward higher forms of complexity and coherence.

The idea that evolution is governed not only by the known laws of motion, but also by a dynamic attractor, contrasts with the view held by mainstream scientists. According to the received concept, evolution occurs as a succession of states where each state produces the conditions for the next. The progression from one state to the next is governed only by the classical laws of motion and interaction. The order and complexity that arises in the course of evolution is a consequence of this "march" from one state to the next. According to the mainstream concept, the emergence of coherence in the universe is fortuitous.

But could the evolution of the coherent, complex systems that manifest the processes of life be due to the random mixing of quantum particles and their ensembles? Or are the processes responsible for the evolution of such systems not entirely casual? The latter is likely to be true. It suggests that the laws of nature are not mere mechanical laws: they jointly constitute a universal coherence-orienting attractor. This is far more plausible than the assumption that the order and coherence present in the world would be the product of random interactions.

The Holotropic Quantum Universe

As noted, the observed universe is highly, indeed amazingly, coherent: it is precisely in-formed. The universe is an in-formed, super-quantum system, oriented toward complexity and coherence. For the dominant paradigm in science, this finding is new and surprising. It calls for an explanation.

As we also noted, the simplest and most logical explanation of the holotropism manifested in the universe is the presence of a wholeness-orienting attractor. This "holotropic" attractor expresses the ensemble of the laws of nature as they act on processes that create being (existence) as well as becoming (evolution) in the universe. The laws of nature are not the classical mechanistic laws of motion; they are universal algorithms that orient existence and evolution in space and time. We have reason to believe that a holotropic attractor in-forms the universe. The tropism created by this attractor is a drive or tendency toward wholeness, expressed in consciousness as universal, unconditional love.

Wholeness is not a descriptor of the state of being of things. It does not describe a condition of being, but rather a goal-state of becoming. Although it is a noun, in actual usage, it suggests a process—a drive or tendency toward a state: the condition of being whole. It derives from the same etymological root as "hale," "heal" and "health."

Levels of spiritual evolution can be gauged by degrees of wholeness. Highly spiritual individuals exhibit a high level of wholeness. Spiritual leaders, as well as mature philosophers, scientists and artists exhibit a similar mindset, characterized by empathy, compassion and unconditional love. Wholeness and love are correlated: love serving as the instrument, or basis, of striving for wholeness. Authors Judy Rodgers and Gayatri Naraine, who carried out an in-depth survey of "great" individuals, noted that love is the foundation of their greatness. They wrote, "We listened to sociologists, biologists, mystics, educators and politicians, and regardless of whether they referred to the inspiration of the Divine or to our biology as human beings to explain such behaviors, love all appeared as the foundation."[4]

Tom Freke, a philosopher who both studied and had spontaneous experiences, noted that in the altered state in which such experiences occur, one finds oneself profoundly connected with all that is, overflowing with the unconditional compassion the spiritual traditions called "awakening" or "enlightenment." This experience, he noted, is that of all-consuming oneness and all-embracing love.[5]

The experience of connection and love are not limited to members of our species: they are present in nonhuman species as well. This is the finding of Frédérique Pichard, a dedicated explorer of the intelligence of dolphins, based on her prolonged and intensive interaction, first with the dolphin called Doni, and then with the dolphin Aladin.[6]

It appears that the mammalian brain, a supersensitive information decoding and transmitting system, displays in the consciousness associated with it an orientation toward wholeness through love. When not distracted by irrelevant or countervailing information—by "noise" overriding "signal"— the human as well as animal brain transmits the holotropism that "informs" the universe into consciousness. This explains why leanings toward wholeness appear in the consciousness of children, as well as of Indigenous people. Their brain, the same as the brain of artists and spiritual people, resonates with the universal attractor that brings particles together in atoms, atoms together in molecules and stars together in galaxies.

The striving toward love and wholeness is not an arbitrary or artificial attribute of the human mind: it is rooted in the nature of the universe. Ours is a wholeness- and love-oriented dynamic entity: a holotropic universe.

The holotropic attractor is a subtle and fundamental disposition or drive affecting complex and coherent systems in the biosphere. It is the imprint of the universe on living systems, and it affects the perceptions of the systems and their response to their perceptions.

In systems such as our human organism, the effect of the holotropic attractor can reach waking consciousness. But whether it actually does that is not immediately evident: it calls for overcoming the beliefs and the experiences that block and mask the relevant perceptions. The holotropic attractor is a subtle lure. We are not ordinarily aware of it. Yet, when we feel attracted to and perhaps at one with another person, with a culture or with a tree and a forest, we manifest the influence of the attractor on our consciousness. We resonate with the wholeness that is present in the world. The manifestation of holotropism in our consciousness is natural, even when it is not a conscious leaning toward connecting with others and with the universe—with The Source.

The connectedness lure appears in consciousness in various forms and to various degrees and levels of intensity. It ranges from a subtle "feel" of being one with people and with nature to the highest, deepest and most intense love we can experience for the human family and for the whole universe. But regardless of what form and to what intensity our holotropism is manifested, it is testimony to our inherent connection to the world. This connection may be seen as "spiritual," since it comes to the fore in the thinking, the consciousness and the behavior of spiritual people. But it is not esoteric—it is not outside our real experience of the real world.

As shown by the practice and the experiments of psychologists and parapsychologists, spiritual experiences are not especially rare, and they are certainly not supernatural. They are relatively frequent occurrences in the lived experiences of sensitive persons. They occur mostly in meditative, exalted or otherwise altered states, where the "chatter" of the everyday world is no longer dominant. Then this fundamental element of human experience can come to the fore.

The recognition that we are in-formed by a holotropic attractor is a radical departure from the view held by most people in the contemporary world. The mainstream view, that our sense of oneness, belonging and love is mere imagination is false. It needs to be challenged. The realization that in light of the findings of the quantum sciences we have good reason to affirm that the universe is in-formed as a whole, and that its in-formation carries a holotropic lure, makes for a powerful challenge.

We open our eyes to the fact that the world around us is shaped, "in-formed," by a fundamental holotropic lure. The challenge is to connect, more exactly to reconnect, to the holotropic foundation of the world. This reconnection is feasible, and it is important: it changes us, and it changes the world around us. This change may be our salvation. It could orient a critical mass of people toward sustainable, humanistic, life-friendly behavior before the unsustainable world we have created collapses around us.

This is the crucial question of our time. We approach it by reviewing holotropic developments in the contemporary world and asking, "How can we become consciously holotropic ourselves?"

CHAPTER 4
A HOLISTIC DESIGN AND BIOMIMICRY APPROACH TO CATALYZING A REGENERATIVE WORLD

by Brian Russo, Sheri Herndon & Eli Kline
with special thanks to Tamsin Woolley-Barker, PhD,
Harry Uvegi & Kurt Krueger

Universal principles and the natural laws of living systems are the essential frameworks for the regeneration and renewal of our civilization in crisis. As we have learned from the patterns of evolution, crises precede transformation. These patterns have been at play in the rise and fall of civilizations before, and we will need to take these lessons to heart if we are to positively progress in our sacred evolutionary story. By using our growing understanding of the holographic universe to inform and embody our comprehensive set of holistic design principles, we can implement the solutions that guide our species towards harmonious relationships with nature and each other.

In the journey of co-creating our shared regenerative vision with our allies and aligned organizations, we do so in conscious partnership with the holomovement itself: the dynamic wholeness-in-motion in which everything moves together in an interconnected unfolding. When we consciously tune into this universal design, we see that it is the Source of all life which flows through all things. By remembering this essence and being in service to all life, we are well-positioned to embrace our role as a guardian species for this time of great transition. On a 'local' level, our partnership is between humanity, life, and the Earth: a conscious being in her own right who has been in the business of ecosystem design for over 3.7 billion years. In that time, nature's intelligence has found solutions to more problems than our species can comprehend. Understanding these foundational designs and evolutionary processes allow holistic designers to develop systems that work with and for all life.

Aligning Our Design in Cosmic Patterns

In intimate collaboration with Earth's patterns of living systems, we can more intelligently develop a new 'operating system' for humanity that will restore the dynamic equilibrium that allows all life to thrive. This new operating system is powered by an engaged and embodied collective intelligence that remembers nature's wisdom. Thus, we see the emergence of new governance protocols arising out of this 'natural law.' Nature's structures, like the mycorrhizal fungi networks, provide the basis for mapping and embodying our own synergy map through which each of us exquisitely fits into the grand design of our Holomovement. While this operating system could remain on the theoretical level alone, we must now activate our community into a deeper, sacred dance in rhythm with life and the pulse of creation.

Aligning with these patterns is foundational to create a movement of wholeness. Through rigorous scientific inquiry, we now know we have exceeded multiple 'planetary boundaries' (Wahl, 2016), thus creating even more of an urgency to find the wisest ways forward. At the heart of the metacrisis is the story of separation leading to a culture of division and conflict hindering the critical coordination needed for a truly regenerative and awakened civilization. A culture that cannot dialogue and resolve conflict through peaceful means will never be capable of evolving the social systems around us, let alone having sufficient social unity and alignment to implement the already existing regenerative solutions on a planetary scale.

The silver lining in the dissonant story of separation is that it gives rise to the yearning for harmonic resolution, true belonging, community and collaboration. We can begin to engage with the patterns of life in ways that serve and inspire a collective response based on wholeness. By embodying the Principle of Unity, the foremost principle of holistic design upon which all the others are derived, we can see that "Everything is interconnected and interdependent, and as such has purpose, functionality, and a reason to be. Our sustenance and the nature of our experience corresponds directly with the health of the greater whole" (UFHD, 2020).

With this principle firmly grounded in our thoughts and actions, everything we design is in service to all life. Once we begin to embody this new operating system, we will discover collective capacities that are emergent and waiting to come fully online. Thus, we create the conditions conducive for the highest expression of humanity.

Clarifying Our Shared Vision

Our shared vision to regenerate the Earth and humanity is based on holistic principles taken from observing and studying living systems and how they evolved. Yet, our shared holographic vision, or "collective image," will appear hazy and undefined without a clear and embodied understanding of how these principles work in our human designs. Therefore, to clarify this vision, we utilize the concept of an "Image of The Future," a framework developed by futurist-sociologist Fred Polack. He discovered that there is one causal factor that enables a shift out of the dark ages and into a regenerative civilization, and it depends on a "small minority of people at the edge of culture holding a sufficiently coherent positive Image of the Future."

Coherence, which etymologically means "sticking together," always implies "harmony, connectedness, stability and efficient use of energy" in the dynamic equilibrium between order and chaos (Welss, 2022). At this time, we are still cultivating the sufficient level of coherence necessary to enable more effective social organization and coordination through our global movement.

In the words of American author Joseph Chilton Pearce, "Passionate intent and unconflicted behavior alters the structure of the Universe." Therefore, the deep passion in our vision, underpinned by the coherence of unconflicted behavior, can seriously uplevel our collective capacities to have a powerful impact on the cultural transition underway. Our Holomovement Image of The Future is beginning to take form on the 'holographic plate' of our collective consciousness. The idea of a holographic plate (encoded with beams of light to project a 3D image) projecting our collective consciousness is a helpful metaphor for how we can inform that image to come into greater alignment with our shared vision. In this sense, the very language of our Holomovement is an invitation to encode our life-centered patterns on this 'plate' to invite humanity to a higher level of coherence and activation of our evolutionary potential.

The "Magic Canoe," as created by social architect Juan Carlos Kaiten, and its tales of synergy iteration, further developed by Jon and Sommer Joy Ramer, is another useful image of how we deepen the alignment of our vision by rowing together in a state of heart and mind coherence. While humanity's resonance with these intentions is not evenly distributed, our Holomovement can bring these intentions into greater alignment as we activate our collective capacities on an unprecedented scale. Anneloes Smitsman from the EARTHwise Centre reminds us that "Evolutionary Coherence is a dynamic state of harmonic resonance and spontaneous collaboration between the diverse elements and relationships of complex living systems [and] a natural state of attunement to the innate wholeness and unity of life" (Smitsman, 2020). The coherence of this transmission itself contains the emerging new 'social DNA' that supports us in solving these crises.

Our Frameworks for Stewarding Earth

Our frameworks for stewarding the Earth are focused on creating shared understandings and are underpinned by the golden rule for regenerative cultures: "Life creates conditions conducive to life."

This life-centered principle was espoused by biologist Janine Benyus as the foundation of the discipline of biomimicry. Biomimicry is defined as "imitating or taking inspiration from nature's forms and processes to solve human problems" (Benyus, 1997). We also hold bio-reintegration, as developed by Jeff Clearwater and VillageLab, as the evolution of biomimicry. In this manner, we intend to redesign our social systems to support life through a stewardship model that not only regenerates Earth's land, water, and species, but also supports those social dynamics that allow humanity to thrive. In the spirit of this foundational aspiration, we share the following aligned frameworks that can serve as the basis for regenerating our world.

The Wheel of Co-Creation and the Sacred Story of Creation, as initially developed by American futurist Barbara Marx Hubbard, provide one of our most integral frameworks for mapping and organizing our Holomovement. The Wheel and Story together are a living blueprint for coordinating ourselves through collective behaviors that lead to wise action. The Wheel is embedded within The Sacred Story, which reminds us that we always begin with Source, and through that connection with Source, we discover and unite with others in what we call a "Communion of Pioneering Souls." By using the Wheel of Co-Creation as inspiration for the design and framework of the Holomovement, we can lessen the fragmentation seen through the silo effect in the sectors or domains of human life such as arts, media, education, environment, health, science, relations, justice, infrastructure, economics, governance and spirituality. This evolutionary community of the Holomovement could be seen as the core of the fractal that can influence vital leverage points that can deliver real change through meaningful and metric-based intentions and goals, which can then scale through the integration of conscious technology.

The Participatory Commons framework, developed by Jeff Clearwater and VillageLab, offers insight into how our aligned organizations can initiate a purpose-based commons that enable scalable, collaborative ecosystems of coordinated action. The Universal Foundation for Holistic Design (UFHD) provides whole system designs along with in depth principles to help guide the process of restructuring societal systems to work in concert with natural life sustaining ones. Sheri Herndon's MetaTao Whole System Design Framework also contributes many of the key framings behind our organization of this chapter and many of the underlying concepts as featured throughout this chapter. The Rainbow Circle, developed by Brian Russo, provides a meta-organizing wholistic design system for coordinating synergistic action by aligning people and organizations within our universal design.

Additionally, we integrate other relevant frameworks such as the one developed by David Sloan Wilson and his collaborators for the Prosocial Commons based on Elinor Ostrom's 8 Core Design Principles. The Alignment Beyond Agreement framework developed by philosopher Yasuhiko Kimura also informs our social architecture for serving the Holomovement by making visible a core distinction that can elegantly increase our common ground. The key principle is that "Alignment is a congruence of intention, whereas agreement is a congruence of opinion. Alignment does not require agreement as a necessary condition" (Kimura, 2004).

Therefore, we can move beyond agreement and the question of 'who is right' to align our collective intentions with the proven strategies and innovations that will more easily manifest the implementation of shared visions and projects. So often our social innovations get stuck in the early stage of development because there is priority given to opinions rather than finding the solid ground of intention.

"When a complex system is far from equilibrium, small islands of coherence in a sea of chaos have the capacity to shift the entire system to a higher order" (Prigogine, 2017). When we implement this strategy along with frameworks and distinctions, we discover that we can become what Meg

Wheatley calls "a system of influence." In her seminal paper called "Lifecycle of Emergence: Taking Social Innovation to Scale," Meg and her co-author Deborah Frieze tell a compelling story about the emerging communities of practice around the planet, our "small islands of coherence." It's time to create the designs that link and coordinate these "islands" so that they become a 'system of influence' that transforms our system. The conditions of our system approaching maximum instability can cause our quantum jump to happen quickly to "trigger [the] re-patterning of a higher order" (Carter et al., 2002). The unitive narrative, another of our esteemed frameworks, also tells the story of this quantum leap forward.

Toward a Coherent Energetic Architecture

From the perspective of a deep systems design awareness, the holistic design for our new social systems integrates three layers: energetic architecture, social architecture, and technology architecture. In the Holomovement, this energetic architecture is a combination of our personal biofield, as well as the capacity for collective social coherence. Our energetic architecture includes the Noosphere: the "thinking layer" of the planet that many people refer to as our global brain. Since love is "the principal driver of 'noogenesis,' or the evolution of mind," we must also embrace the role of heart coherence in our energetic architecture (Goddard, 2022).

Claudia Welss, citizen scientist and the Board Chairman of the Institute of Noetic Sciences (IONS), gave a key insight around this process of how we can cultivate our coherent social synergy to effectuate a more strategic impact. To this end, Claudia states:

> "Conscious mastery in creating coherence is the inner technology that represents a supra-sector of the Wheel of Co-Creation, one that lifts the whole system and supports the integrity of the natural patterns emerging from the synergy of the parts. Attention to this energetic architecture

is as important as attention to the social architecture in designing for social synergy. In fact, the success of the social architecture seems reliant on the quality of the energetic architecture, or container, from which it arises" (Welss, 2008).

The integrity of this container and the energetic coherence of our community are key, as they hold the ethical principles and regenerative values upon which our civilization is being redesigned. Integrating both the energetic and social layers into the technology layer also becomes essential for the integrity of the emerging Web 3.0 models that underpin our technological architecture.

In order for the new enlightened tech stacks to serve a regenerative vision and to be able to ultimately achieve mass adoption by millions of people, it must be authentically encoded with the codes of Life in her most beautiful expression. A good example of this is the evolutionary social web of CoreNexus, created by Adam Apollo and Harlan Wood, which utilizes the internet as part of our emerging Noosphere to connect and coordinate at both a local and global level to regenerate our world.

Digitally mapping the Holomovement through semantic analysis can demonstrate the interrelationships within its emerging architecture. Words and concepts can be graphed within a harmonic geometrical structure in a way that correlates them to sectors, colors and archetypes to reveal the universal patterns in which we weave our movement. This digital structure can begin to access the inherent and intuitive wisdom and knowledge aggregated in its nodes and their relationships to enhance synergy across all sectors. Such a platform can act as a representation of our emerging noosphere through the World Wide Web. CoreNexus, Rainbow Circle and other systems provide various approaches to mapping the whole, and the Holomovement's mapping will need to have the interoperability capabilities to use various mapping technologies in how it holds the Whole in an expansive, resonant and inclusive manner. Utilizing a mapping technology to create a "digital Earth" is also vital for our ability to visualize how our efforts are changing the world in real-time through linked data and metrics.

With this kind of energetic, social alignment architecture at the core of our Holomovement, it could convene and connect with the global network of regenerative organizations working with natural patterns to bring forth the deep systems change we need.

We must continue to align with life's regenerative patterns, natural laws, and cosmic principles of how life creates, composts and regenerates. Peoples from Indigenous cultures have passed on regenerative practices from generation to generation and have done so in intimate relationship with nature. To align with these regenerative patterns transcends survival needs and activates our human potential, which we call thrivability. As humanity becomes more aware of the utility and beauty of regenerative designs that have real world application, we can accelerate systems transformation with the wisdom of the ages and dormant collective intelligence waiting to be activated.

The Superorganism Strategy

Following nature's patterns to regenerate our world requires us to align with nature's largest and tiniest patterns that appear at every scale in our world. For example, the fractal-like arm of a galaxy is reflected in the same fractal design of a tree and its leaf veins. Dr. Tamsin Woolley-Barker has been studying superorganisms and their patterns for over two decades and provides us with the insight that the design is the strategy for how a superorganism is able to be resilient, thrive, and generate abundance (Woolley-Barker, 2017).

All kinds of superorganisms perform an elegant dance of adaptation to change their steps with the music of time, yet they retain the core strategies on which their success is built. Humans are superorganisms, which can be defined as "communities of genetically distinct individuals who belong to the same species, where members take on different tasks and whole classes of non-sibling adults help others raise their young" (Woolley-Barker, 2022). While these strategies remain to some extent in Indigenous cultures and the family unit, their true power has been largely forgotten in the relentless pace of modernization.

As we rekindle our collective capacities, we can adopt the winning superorganism strategy of meaningfully banding together in greater numbers around a shared purpose to best serve our future. If we are to embody the best strategies of our ancestors, synthesize them with our modern innovations and technologies and integrate the understanding of living systems, then we need to be well acquainted with how a superorganism thrives and creates abundance from its shared identity. This shared identity is built around a common purpose, without which there can be no coordination, co-creation, or collaboration between organisms to achieve mutual benefits.

Through the eyes of the superorganism, we learn to see that "separate" parts are unified in their reciprocal relations. This reciprocity, which informs the superorganism's shared identity, is "our way of giving and taking for mutual benefit. Indigenous peoples of the Andes refer to this reciprocity as *Ayni*" (Dyer, 2020). It is the giving and receiving of *Ayni* which forms "an unbroken circle—a unifying force that binds together All That Is" (Dyer, 2020).

This principle is at work in nature as "sharing is fundamental to the superorganism strategy. Termites and leafcutter ants share their underground nests, honeybees share defenses, and swarm-raiding ants flush out prey together. All superorganisms jointly construct and defend their nests, and all share the group's reproductive success" (Woolley-Barker, 2022). These stories are vital for making visible the lessons of nature and evolution that we can now apply at a deeper level in the designs of all our social systems.

The superorganism's sense of shared identity drives swarm creativity: the confluence of self-organized behaviors that solve the survival needs for the good of the whole superorganism by accumulating the right resources and investing in symbiotic partnerships. This strategy is applicable to our Holomovement, as we can take these insights from nature to design our systems to make resources more readily accessible where needed and synergize partnerships for the long-term benefit of the Whole.

"Upcycling" is another superorganism key strategy that we can use to design more regenerative systems. It is a natural extension of swarm creativity as organisms transform waste products/byproducts of their symbiotic partners into value-added resources. The payoffs generated by long-term cooperation lead species to continue their win-win-win strategies that support themselves, other species, and the entire ecosystem. This commitment to "designs that work" informs their strategies and collective intelligence and ensures that it is applied by the next generation. In our own ecological designs, this upcycling is reflected in the circular economy and cradle-to-cradle design thinking that can drive civic innovation.

While nature's most common superorganisms are "around a family structure," ours can function through a higher order 'property of thought' "which can bind genetically unrelated individuals into functionally organized groups" (Wilson, 2021). This "brain of brains" of our collective superorganism enables us to see through the eyes of wholeness.

From this perspective, we can then embody 'Holopticism,' a concept developed by Jean-François Noubel, which derives from the Greek roots 'holos' (whole) and 'optikè' (see). Holopticism is "the capacity for an individual to see the whole as a living entity in the collective in which he/she operates" (Noubel, 2022). Imagine if we developed holoptical protocols where any person in any system could easily have access to the information from the whole, just like a healthy ecosystem operates at a level beyond thought. With this kind of protocol in place, there is a structure of belonging that allows us to have a relaxed nervous system and drop into heart coherence with others in the superorganism of which we are a part. This felt sense of connection and collective knowing allows us to intuitively take our place within the movement of our superorganism.

Such a seamless synergy is possible when we envision our organizations as the organs of a shared body that each have their specific function and relation to the Whole. Embodying reciprocity in all these interdependent relations ensures the health and good of the Whole, thus spurring on creativity and innovation in our systems that have yet to be seen.

Teeming up for the World Game

In "Teeming: How Nature's Oldest Teams Adapt and Thrive," Dr. Tamsin Woolley-Barker explores how superorganisms "live and grow value faster than any species has done before us" through mutual cooperation and collective intelligence (Woolley-Barker, 2017). Teeming, which refers to an ecosystem being filled with wildlife, is also our capacity to coordinate our collective intelligence in teams to achieve our greatest dreams and vision.

Thanks to our ever-increasing digital interconnectedness, what has now been described as Holomidal collective intelligence has emerged. "Local and global, decentralized and distributed, agile, polymorphic, [this intelligence] based on leadership, individuation, open source, integral wealth and mutualist economy, this young form of collective intelligence still lives through its infancy phase. However, we can already see its huge impact on humanity where more and more people in civil society self-organize in order to address societal issues that pyramidal collective intelligence cannot address and even provokes" (Noubel, 2022).

When we "teem" up to put this collective intelligence into practice, it is founded on the deep knowing that "each member of the group is smart enough to know that he or she has something of vital importance to contribute to the whole—and that the group does too" (Dyer, 2019). It is a living process wherein "every individual action modifies the whole which in return informs the [collective] about what to do next, and so on. An unceasing feedback loop allows for the individual and the collective to communicate with one another" (Noubel, 2022). This understanding has profound implications which need to be explored in dialogue with members of the Holomovement.

This superorganism strategy of collective intelligence gives us a new way to play Buckminster Fuller's World Game, with its goal to "make the world work, for 100% of humanity, in the shortest possible time, through spontaneous cooperation, without ecological offence or the disadvantage of anyone" (Wahl, 2016). When we can use our collective intelligence to create the data modeling structures that inform how we play this game, we can effectively organize to collaborate in solving our challenges. One of the greatest of these challenges lies in how we play the financial game, as "much of our day-to-day behavior and cultural activity is structurally determined by our monetary and economic systems. Their redesign is a crucial enabler of the transition towards a regenerative culture" where sustainable action is incentivized and nature-backed currency can shift the paradigm and change the rules (Wahl, 2016).

In teeming up for this World Game, we can gamify our Holomovement in order to engage people in all the "games" we are playing for the good of the whole. Gamification pioneer Yu-kai Chou's "Octalysis Framework" is one example of engaging people through intrinsic motivation by having them answer an "epic" calling that empowers them to creatively solve our most difficult challenges. Lucian Tarnowski's "UP Game" is another example of making regenerative planetary transformation a sport by "unleashing the collective intelligence and action of teams to develop narratives, strategies and solutions to solve some of the world's biggest problems" (Tarnowski, 2022). They do this by unleashing community potential, activating collective intelligence, and unlocking cooperative advantage. This is our path forward for scaling culture that is in harmony with life.

CoreNexus' evolutionary social operating system is also highly resonant given its mission to "Gamifying regenerative impact through turning digital creators into philanthropists, and then getting people involved (and paid) to collaborate in real world missions. Perhaps more importantly, this social system connects people with aligned purpose around real-world connection, action, and regeneration, while helping them take back their personal social network information from the existing global centralized platforms" (Apollo, 2022).

In the past, our human superorganism has been too fractured to solve our planetary and intractable problems on this scale. Yet, now we are empowered to align in wholeness and put our superorganism strategy into action as we playfully embark on our quest as heroic stewards to regenerate the Earth and re-humanize humanity in the process.

WEvolution

Michael Petrakis states, "The purpose of an evolutionary leader is to understand and leverage the infinite power of love and the holographic structure of reality for making evolution effortless, irresistible, irrefutable and therefore inevitable." Yet, even the concept of "evolution" is moving beyond itself to "WEvolution"—the collective transformation of our species. This cosmic truth imparts the knowing that we all light up each other to shine the brightest colors of our souls.

Following our WEvolutionary impulse allows us to become part of the new emerging species: Homo Luminous, or humans of light. This light is figurative in the sense that we are embodying a higher ethic toward wholeness, and literal in the sense that our bodies can have a greater capacity to hold electrical charge and to allow the light of consciousness to penetrate our bodies and unwind the sacred wounds (*sanskaras*) in our DNA. This is a key to our longevity as well as our spiritual development.

Medical anthropologist Dr. Alberto Villoldo invokes the term Homo Luminous as a quantum shift in consciousness where we are capable of dreaming our new world into being. Alternatively, Barbara Marx Hubbard used the term Homo Universalis and proclaimed that we were becoming members of a new species, as further described in the next chapter. We are now crossing a threshold that has been upon us for eons as we quantum jump toward our "Mass Maharishi Effect Omega Point" moment.

Our Invitation

Our intention with this chapter is to be an invitation to not just experience these new emerging personal and collective capacities, but to embody them at a whole new level. We also extend this invitation to each of you to integrate these profound insights and understandings for how all of our gifts can be more fully activated and synergized within a larger whole. It is essential in this moment of history and looming existential risk that we apply the principles of the Holomovement and the reality of our ecological interconnectedness to catalyze local and global transformation, and the kind of wise collective sense-making and healing that can create the conditions for a phase change.

Throughout this chapter, we have planted the seeds of an invitation that is actually a species-wide initiation into who we are becoming as members of a new species and as a glorious movement. First starting close in, and then growing globally, we weave all these islands of coherence together through a beautiful alignment process. We are ready to activate our community into the sacred dance of life as we stand on the threshold where our crisis truly is our birth. We want to invite each of you into our greatest human and social potential, as we stand on the verge of actually igniting true global coherence.

We have to imagine it's possible before we can step into that infinite and wild potential. Activating our collective capacities is the next step of our shared action. Are we open and willing to step into this reality together on an unprecedented scale and put these principles and practices into full expression in service to all life?

As the Hopi Prophecy reminds us, "The time of the lone wolf is over... [It's time] to look around and see who is here with you and celebrate." We are the ones we have been waiting for. Let this be a celebration of who we are becoming together.

References:

Benyus, Janine. *Biomimicry: Innovation Inspired by Nature.* New York, NY: Harper Perennial, 2002.

Edmondson, Amy. *A Fuller Explanation: The Synergetic Geometry of R Buckminster Fuller.* Pueblo, CO: EmergentWorld, LLC, 2009.

Wheatley, Meg and Frieze, Deborah. "Using Emergence to Take Social Innovation to Scale." margaretwheatley.com, 2006. margaretwheatley.com/articles/using-emergence.pdf.

Welss, Claudia. "Subtle Realms in Social Synergy: Toward World 2.0." 2008.

Kimura, Yasuhiko. "Alignment Beyond Agreement." Genku World. Vision-In-Action LLC, 13 Dec. 2004. genkuworld.com/consulting/alignment-beyond-agreement.

Carter, et al. *Global Ethical Options: In the Tradition of Gandhi, King., and Ikeda.* Weatherhill, 2002.

Woolley-Barker, Tamsin. *Teeming: How Nature's Oldest Teams Adapt and Thrive.* First Edition. White Cloud Press, 2017.

Smitsman, Anneloes. "Into the Heart of Systems Change." Maastricht University, 2018.

Wilson, David Sloan. "Reintroducing Pierre Teilhard De Chardin to Modern Evolutionary Science." humanenergy.io, July 2021. humanenergy.io/wp-content/uploads/2021/07/Reintroducing-Pierre-Teilhard-de-Chardin-to-Modern-Evolutionary-Science.pdf.

Dyer, Dery. *The Return of Collective Intelligence: Ancient Wisdom for a World out of Balance.* Bear and Company, 2020.

Prigogine, Ilya. "Islands of Coherence: A Safe Harbor in a Sea of Chaos." Islands of Coherence, 2022. www.islandsofcoherence.network.

Goddard, Andy. "Living with the Mystics Day on Pierre Teilhard De Chardin." WCCM in the UK, 1 Aug. 2022. wccm.uk/living-with-the-mystics-day-on-pierre-teilhard-de-chardin.

Noubel, Jean-François. "Holopticism," Collective Intelligence Research Institute, 15 July 2015. cir.institute/holopticism/?fbclid=IwAR2gObMMnUixz B9ooGxn_uta9wspZA1-2rsCz3JuwGDQ_oaWE-xblJUIq4c#:%7E:text=1%2 0Related%20Posts-,Definition,and%20knows%20what%20to%20do.

Teilhard De Chardin, Pierre. *The Future of Man*. Collins, 1964.

Chou, Yu-Kai. *Actionable Gamification: Beyond Points, Badges and Leaderboards*. CreateSpace Independent Publishing Platform, 2015.

Tarnowski, Lucian. "UP Game." up.game, 2022. www.up.game.

Tarnowski, Lucian. "Celebrating Earth Day with the United Planet Game." Medium, Medium, 3 May 2022. https://luciant.medium.com/celebrating-earth-day-with-the-united-planet-game-6fb74d298e29.

Universal Foundation for Holistic Design, 2019. www.ufhd.ca.

Wahl, Daniel Christian. *Designing Regenerative Cultures*. Illustrated. Triarchy Press Ltd, 2016.

Apollo, Adam. "CoreNexus - 3D Social Dashboard and Regenerative Operating System Experience." CoreNexus. corenexus.is.

CHAPTER 5
SUPERCOHERENCE AND THE INTELLIGENCE OF THE COSMOS

by J. J. Hurtak, PhD, PhD, Desiree Hurtak, PhD
& Elisabet Sahtouris, PhD

We are living in exciting times with NASA's James Webb telescope looking into the origins of life, while other scientific endeavors explore the very microstructures of amino acids and organic molecules in our universe. If physics and biology are the product of a greater design of life, from an implicate order of existence, then the universe must have a purpose. The evidence of modern biology suggests strongly that the purpose includes us. In fact, our research suggests there is a blueprint connecting our biological systems to a higher reality and purpose underlying the whole process of life.

"Mach's principle" famously states that the mass of a single particle is determined by the mass of the entire universe; therefore, local behavior of any particle is influenced by the greater process of the universe. From the sounds of the smallest sea shell to the greatest whirling galaxies, it can be argued that the whole of the universe may be contained in every part. All of life is a beautiful reflection of a holomovement.

Despite the infinite opportunities to experience our connection to a purposeful order of existence, many scientists would argue the universe is nothing but a cold, unknowing place in which human beings are accidents of evolutionary particles. Yet, several centuries of development in physics and mathematics have taught us that information is a crucial player in physical systems and the processes of life.

Since the late 1950s, American physicist David Bohm (1980) began to develop a unique, conceptual framework of physics, which showed how relativity and quantum theory come together through undivided wholeness as a hologram. The challenge then was to develop a "new approach" to describe such undivided wholeness. He started with the concept of an interconnected Universe, knowing that our Universe was not formed merely as a "blank sheet of paper." Bohm proposed that underlying it all is the existence of an implicate order that manifests into an explicate order. He claimed that it applied not just to stars in the universe or atomic structures, but to the biological domain, including cognitive processes and consciousness experiences.

Still, the Western world generally regards the external world as primary, paramount and ultimately knowable. Yet, centuries ago, Plato said that our world is a shadow-like representation of a deeper realm of archetypes and ideals and that the basic building blocks of existence, matter and energy are mere representations of something more refined and subtle—something that we could call consciousness.

One of the major tasks of science is choosing the appropriate metaphors to convey scientific models. Scientists always have relied on metaphors to offer context to the unfathomable. For example, in referring to how our brains function, we often use computers as a relatable metaphor. The choice of such necessary metaphors depends on scientific concepts of the domains studied, from the whole universe to our Earth, to our human selves. World-renowned physicist Ervin Schrödinger, in his essay "Mind and Matter," first published in 1958, pointed out the strange fact that scientists can only build models of the universe in their conscious minds, but then leave that consciousness out of their models.

By employing the metaphor of a keyboard, we can better understand our universal connection and coherence. This metaphor, often used by evolution biologist, futurist, and this chapter's co-author, Elisabet Sahtouris, came out of a series of formal symposia to identify fundamental concepts in different sciences developed in different cultures, specifically how Western quantum physicists turned to Vedic science to make sense of their early findings. Both standard and quantum physics recognize vibrations as somehow fundamental to the universe. As a keyboard is a small set of frequencies, we can easily imagine extending it to make it infinite. In the lowest octave, we can associate the deep sound with the lowest frequencies in the universe—matter. Moving up the keyboard, into the mid-range octave and notes, we can assign electromagnetic energy and then, on up the scale to the highest frequencies, we can associate mind, soul and pure consciousness.

This universe of vibrations also represents each one of us. We are not bodies with minds and souls, but rather body/mind/spirits—just as is the whole universe. Taoist science reflects a similar matter/energy/spirit continuum, and while this two-dimensional model is clearly simplified, it is useful for several reasons.

First, we can visualize Western science approaching from the "matter" end of our metaphorical keyboard defining reality as anything that is measurable by physical instruments. Thus, it is limited to the measurable aspects of electromagnetic energy, unable to perceive mind and consciousness symbolized by our keyboard's high-frequency notes. Although, with new theories such as the M-theory and superstrings, we are beginning to create a larger scientific network inclusion of resonance, depth and meaning. Eastern sciences, however, approach from the higher octaves of our keyboard, in pure source of "All That Is," in the universe thus, accessing the entire "keyboard" by slowing the vibrations through energy to matter.

Albert Einstein demonstrated that "energy is matter; matter is energy" through E=mc2 and that this vibrational music is accessible from any key on our universal keyboard. Therefore, vast and expanding levels of information might be said to be associated with the Universe, and this could be linked to "Consciousness" or what could be called the "quantum consciousness field" that exists within and beyond our local realm. If the consciousness field truly exists, then vast amounts of active information would exist and could be found throughout our reality. Here, Consciousness is suggested to be the nonlocal, all-prevalent field and may be the hidden variable that determines the cause of multiple quantum transitions.

Bohm defined this reality as an energy plenum that provides a superposition of possibilities as it is a key part of the implicate order, and we are part of the plenum, connected by the consciousness field. The human mind, according to David Bohm (1952), would be an integral part of that field. And, although there is Free Will, we could say we have access to the "Quantum Mind" and function as biotransducers operating on a micro scale within the macro scale of holographic processes.

Since everything that occurs in the living universe is ultimately the result of one or more quantum mechanical events, the universe is inhabited by a greater consciousness field that collectively is responsible for its detailed workings. We further see that the mind and its relationship to the consciousness field does not simply come out of materialism or simply evolve out of the lowest of physiological strata. Nor is consciousness to be defined in the dualistic sense of Western science, where matter is in opposition to the mind or consciousness is in opposition to the material, but rather we should see a transcendental monism where the mind sets order to matter and can even transmute the very nature of matter. We may well discover that we are living in a world of both real-time events of external objects, as well as in an advanced or implicate world of super-mental events that are not physical, but embedded as theoretical possibilities in the surrounding consciousness field that can ultimately become manifest.

Our textbooks tell us that our brain is the source of all thought and that, like a computer, we learn to react and make decisions based on past programming and what we have learned from our environment. However, scientists like Henry Stapp (2007) from Lawrence Berkeley National Laboratory and Stuart Hameroff (Hameroff and Penrose, 2016) from the University of Arizona, in researching brain functions, no longer see thought merely as chemical processing of neurotransmitters, as stated in classical physics.

In Karl Pribram's book, *Languages of the Brain: Experimental Paradoxes and Principles in Neuropsychology* (1971), he too looked beyond the paradigm of limited brain mechanics and the flow of sodium ions into holistic levels of information processing. His research, along with that of David Bohm, allows us to see the electrifying details of the whole universe arranged as a system of vast information levels that can be used by the world community and, thus, realize our Mind experience is something more than simply the inherent workings of the brain. Emerging from this research are theoretical proposals that the brain's processing of information takes place through quantum mechanical processes where consciousness itself is seen as part of the nonlocal quantum field, equated to a type of hologram, where the total information of the system is available in every part and information exists in a "nonlocal" environment. The concept of the Holographic brain is where quantum effects formed by neurons affect human consciousness. However, we want to go one step farther to say the consciousness field effects not just the brain, but the mind; hence, the more appropriate term would be Holographic Mind.

So, what about individual consciousness? There are aspects of Self or "I" within the physical neurological network of the brain. Nevertheless, the consciousness field exists throughout all life as a super-holographic field. Henry Stapp's work (2007) shows a quantum inter-connectedness—the "web" concept.

The human brain receives information from the existing super-holographic quantum field that relates most to human consciousness. Humans draw from parts of the field that relate mainly to their own individualized thoughts, while birds in flight, for example, seem to work with more of a collective field. Ultimately, each person has access to the field, but our association to the field varies from person to person, based on our unique attunements and choices. Thus, the existence of consciousness thought is a field of resonance that is all-prevalent, possessing aspects of individual consciousness within the collective consciousness field.

Consciousness connects us with all surrounding energy fields. The beginnings of this understanding were gleaned, in part, by the research of Einstein-Rosen-Podolsky in 1935, through their thought experiment, which concluded that hidden variables must exist in order to explain certain phenomena. But if consciousness is the hidden variable and multiple dimensions exist, we also may be multi-dimensional beings capable of building bridges, not only non-locally to any object in the universe, but to any thought throughout the myriad dimensions.

It is one major step to go beyond the unique chemical substratum to the basic software language of the mind in the understanding of life; it is quite another quantum leap to see the languages of science and religion, logic and God, factual reality and Spirit, local evidence and the eternal, as a holomovement of "being and becoming" within the Mind. Certainly, our body has its own specific inner architecture, but it also connects with a larger network of consciousness fields within and without that facilitate for us a greater awareness of Life. As we approach the holistic understanding that we are more than just a body, we discover that we are a network of Life and Consciousness.

This shows the enormous power that can be awakened within the sleeping mind. The implications of nonlocality in thinking and communication reach deep beyond the "wet-ware" of the brain into that most intimate aspect of a cosmic vision.

Ecosophy: A Philosophy of Harmony and Equilibrium Within the Cosmos

Evolutionary biology was long stuck in the concept of evolution by natural selection through competition among individuals. Gradually, through the work of biologists such as E.O. Wilson, George Wald, Lynn Margulis, Stephen Jay Gould, David Sloan Wilson and Tamsin Woolley-Barker, we discovered the way individuals learned to cooperate early in evolution led to a second tier of selection that was far more important. As Margulis put it, "Life did not take over the world by combat, but by networking." This networking often led to cooperative symbioses, merging even the most unlikely partners into viable new creatures and ecosystems.

We also gained enormously from the partnership between Margulis and James Lovelock in bringing the concept of a living Earth, long recognized by countless Indigenous cultures, into the world of Western science as the Gaia hypothesis, later to become theory. A living Earth is a concept just as is a nonliving Earth. The latter, however, has long been assumed to be fact by Western science, while the former is still questioned, or at best, still considered a theory. Theories are formal proposals and cannot be made in a conceptual vacuum. To theorize about how the universe or cosmos or anything within it is formed and works, we must begin, then, with a concept of what these entities are.

Once we conceptualize Earth as a living planet, our focus shifts from 'rabbits in habitats' to 'rhabbitats.' In other words, to ecosystems, ranging from Type 1 (comprised of fairly competitive species) to Type 3 (highly cooperative) with Type 2 some mixture of both. However, we can also see these distinctions as representing sequential steps from competition to cooperation. Such a maturation cycle begins with youthful competition, sometimes creative, sometimes hostile, then moves into negotiations that eventually lead to new cooperative entities at a larger scale. Thus, ancient bacteria eventually formed nucleated cells, which in turn matured to produce multi-celled creatures. These in turn formed ecosystems that matured from competition to the most highly evolved cooperative systems of mutual benefit for all, as in prairies, coral reefs and rainforests.

Many early humans lived in harmonious bands and tribes that worked out sustainable relationships within their ecosystems, seeing themselves as related to other species, cooperating with them in the mature mode, and working out reciprocal trading relations with neighboring human groups. As agriculture led to larger and denser human populations that built ever more technological habitats, they began seeing themselves as superior to other species, as well as to each other's cultures. We are now at the unsustainable end of around 6,000 years of competitive empire building, some so competitive that they became dangerously hostile. Thus, we now face the need for our own maturation into a cooperative global society in harmony with the rest of nature.

As long as we see the ecosystems of Nature simply as resources for our human economy (the acquisition, processing, distribution and consumption of those resources) and then the dumping ground for what we do not consume, we become increasingly unsustainable, which literally means 'cannot last.' The solution is actually simple: turn this whole enterprise upside down, fitting our human economy into our ecology, our ecosystems, which naturally recycle everything. This would lead us to what I, Elisabet, call an Ecosophy: a wise society.[7]

Whether the nation states we evolved in our empire building phase can last into a better future is not clear. Nations were too often formed by scratching lines across land without regard for ecosystems, such as watersheds or human cultures they crossed. Cities that grew naturally from smaller villages and towns, on the other hand, resemble nucleated cells when seen from the air, and are highly cooperative entities. Nations, especially as they gain competitive power, have military defenses; our further rationale is that networked cities may be better suited to a cooperative world than nations.[8]

If we think it impossible to organize our global population of billions of people into a harmonious whole, consider our bodies made of some 50 trillion nucleated cells and ten times more than that of essential bacterial cells making our vitamins, repairing our guts, running our immune systems and generally keeping us healthy. The politics and economics of these bodies of ours are superbly organized, with continual negotiations between the self-interest of every individual cell and its organs and the whole body. The ethics of this holarchic living body are profound, as if each cell deeply knows its wellbeing depends on the wellbeing of the whole.

We would do well to note that Nature is profoundly conservative with what works well, and radically creative in addressing and changing what does not. These two endeavors are not in competition, but are a wondrous cooperative rebalancing process that must always be practiced simultaneously in our linear time physical reality. Our very evolution as a species depends on getting this right.

Experiments in Connecting with the "Consciousness Quantum Field"

As we grow into an awareness of the power of co-operation and begin to understand the interconnections within the quantum consciousness field, we can begin to comprehend some experiments of Remote Viewing, which began in the early 1970s, at Stanford Research Institute (SRI). Much of the revolutionary work in this field was done by Russell Targ, Dr. Harold Puthoff, astronaut Edgar Mitchell, Andrija Puharich, and J.J. Hurtak. These experiments in remote viewing demonstrated the mind's ability to "reach" global targets, in violation of traditional rules of science. More work is needed in this area to understand the mind's role in consciousness, although consciousness is not limited to the physical mind.

Remote viewing is the study of viewing objects or events at a distance beyond the five-sensory range. In 1995, comprehensive studies in remote viewing were declassified by the CIA and released to the public. Not only did their research provide "accurate remote viewing results" in terms of images transferred across long distances of space, but it also demonstrated no-degradation of information retrieved instantaneously from thousands of kilometers away (Targ and Rauscher, 2001). In some cases, however, this is not just a spatial phenomenon of viewing objects in Russia from a place in California, for instance, but also one that can be based on viewing near-future events as well.

Scientists Hal Puthoff and Russell Targ found in their studies of "remote viewing" (Tart, Targ and Puthoff, 1980) that a remarkable energy in human consciousness flows immediately without "any" loss of time from a unique and powerful reality, which makes consciousness itself part of the biogravitational field. These events, or "occasions of experience," could be considered actual quantum state reductions of events in physical reality that were picked up nonlocally from the quantum field (Targ and Hurtak, 2006). This further suggests that the quantum field is also a consciousness field that does involve quantum state reductions, e.g., in a form of quantum computation, whereby the larger mind functions as an "encyclopedia galactica" in the universe. Of course, there have been sensitives and spiritual thinkers all throughout history who have been able to tune their mental antennae a little bit, but the majority of us have existed on an unconscious or semi-conscious level without accessing the vast information available.

Drs. J. J. and Desiree Hurtak have studied shamans in Africa, the Pacific and South America, Christian mystics, and Buddhist and Hindu sages and found that they are amongst those who have always understood that we are all multi-dimensional beings and that part of our psyche exists, or has existed, in other quantum fields of information.

Studies ranging from Stanford Research Institute in the 1970s, to the Global Consciousness Project at Princeton University today, and in various other institutes around the world, have revealed that a "consciousness quantum field" exists, which acts to order and create harmony in living systems. While our day-to-day awareness has been limited to only one reality plane, this research into consciousness is beginning to explain how there are also many planes of reality that simultaneously function together. This includes such diverse phenomena as mind-over-matter, telepathic communication, and remote viewing. The research suggests that higher states of consciousness are not merely a product of environment, training or habit, ethnic impressions or education, but instead work with the Consciousness field available to all humanity.

Consciousness extends into space-time becoming manifest in an indefinite number of ways and perceptions; for some, it is seen as Teilhard de Chardin's Noosphere. For us, it is the Holographic Mind that is omnidirectional and omnipresent. If we live in a supra-consciousness realm where facts and objects are universally interconnected, this means we are able to reach all levels of Understanding and Wisdom when we become aware of how to tap into the many layers/levels of the quantum consciousness field, especially beyond that of the local realm.

As we evolve into the consciousness functioning, we can ultimately experience the fullness of the universe. It shows that actually everything can be everywhere at the same time. What the mystics discovered thousands of years ago, and what is being understood now, is the understanding that the basic aim of the Holographic Mind is to experience Life in all dimensions and in all of its myriad realities. Physics itself is starting to accept the importance of the observer which relates to the consciousness field, entanglement and nonlocality.

The Book of Knowledge: The Keys of Enoch (Hurtak, 1973) speaks about a very unique relationship that is given to everyone who seeks to understand the nature of life that comes through an "inductive linkage"—energy arrangements which reach down to the subatomic level of organization and all the way up to the vastness of the Universe. Speculatively, there can literally be millions of ways that consciousness can be synthesized by different human beings. What was once the greatest mystery of biology—the human mind—is gradually yielding its secrets. We see that humanity is more than flesh; it is a continuous transducer or "biotransducer" of energies.

We are part of consciousness and the collective field that causes us to move beyond our separate selves and be filled with greater feelings, emotions and thoughts of collective Oneness for understanding how we are all interconnected through Consciousness. This neutralizes the separation between the personal "I" and the collective. This transforms our thoughts into positive and not negative events in life. The vast realms of consciousness also allow us to turn our mind, heart and feeling to the great mystery and awesome wonder of universal existence and to feel the profundity of reality that is the majesty of the Cosmic and Pre-Cosmic domains of life.

Eastern thought, quantum physics and parapsychology combine to demonstrate how ill-advised Western science has been in ignoring consciousness for the greater part of the present century. Physically, this unconsciousness can be seen in the pollution and destruction of the environment, the massive weapons of war, and extensive poverty throughout the world.

Bohm realized consciousness is not limited to mechanistic processes. Inspired by this understanding, we can begin to reactivate our spiritual nature and re-stimulate our inherent powers of consciousness, such as universal awareness, intuitive perception and universal love. This will lead us—individually and collectively—to a New Being, an awareness of inherent immortality, the power of self-regeneration and healing, creativity and the direct awareness of Life.

As discussed in the previous chapter, it starts by sharing common goals and vision. The actual ability to share begins to define a path of self-realization and build a meaningful language for the wide range of perceptions as to the "true Nature" of things. Then we may see how consciousness is eminent in the universe and is inseparably connected with all phenomena and matter, just as the mind is inseparably connected with the body and spirit. With the growing understanding of how our system is aligned with a greater energy system, we will soon come into the awareness of the total harmony of Life that is inherent within each of us and that connects us with the greater universe.

In reaching the 'Age of Holism,' we have begun to feel and experience through our collective inner resources the evolution of the evolutionary process itself. In this mosaic, we recognize new realizations of the interplay of consciousness, the mind and the universe, and these can be spelled out as three unique realities:

1. Our physical reality consists not only of one physical reality, but a harmony of interactions of dynamic movements of a vast number of consciousness realities connected with the implicate order, whereby, human intelligence is a cosmo-physical event in the universe.

2. Our physical, as well as the consciousness universe, are not separate from our individual thoughts. We are continually in touch with universal consciousness, and we co-create with one another as our consciousness becomes aware of the larger collective field.

3. The laws of contemporary three-dimensional science and physics are transcended or superseded by the physics of consciousness, as matter is subordinate to consciousness which stems from the higher dimensions of universal existence.

Thus, we see that advances in both physics and the studies of consciousness reveal a more intricate interworking than we had once thought possible. What remains is to apply ourselves to the Work that we may become worthy of living in the greater universe. Through this quickening, we will experience the future mind of the human race as a holographic process, where every part is part of every part. This process works not only within the global mind of humanity, but also meets with the pluralistic nature of the Absolute.

References:

Bohm, David. "A Suggested Interpretation of the Quantum Theory in Terms of 'Hidden' Variables, I and II." *Physical Review*, (85):166-193, 1952.

Bohm, David. *Wholeness and the Implicate Order*. London: Routledge, 1980.

Hameroff, Stuart R. and Penrose, Roger. "Consciousness in the Universe: An Updated Review of the 'Orch OR' Theory." *Biophysics of Consciousness: A Foundational Approach*. eds. Roman R. Poznanski, Jack A. Tuszynski, Todd E. Feinberg. Chapter 14. World Scientific, 2016.

Hurtak, J.J. *The Book of Knowledge: The Keys of Enoch*. Los Gatos: The Academy For Future Science. 1973.

Mancuso, Stefano and Viola, Alessandra. "Brilliant Green: The Surprising History and Science of Plant Intelligence." *Perspectives in Biology and Medicine*, 57(4):569-574, January 2014.

Pribram, K.H. *Languages of the Brain: Experimental Paradoxes and Principles in Neuropsychology*. New York: Brandon House, 1971.

Rauscher, Elizabeth A. and Targ, Russell. "The Speed of Thought: Investigation of a Complex Space-Time Metric to Describe Psychic Phenomena." *Journal of Scientific Exploration*, Vol. 15, No. 3, pp. 331–354, 2001.

Schrödinger, Erwin. *Mind and Matter*. Cambridge: University Press. 1958.

Stapp, Henry P. *Mindful Universe: Quantum Mechanics and the Participating Observer*. New York: Springer Science & Business Media, 2007.

Targ, Russell and Hurtak, J.J. *The End of Suffering: Fearless Living in Troubled Times … or, How to Get Out of Hell Free*. Charlottesville: Hampton Roads, 2006.

Tart, C., Puthoff, H. and Targ, R. "Information transmission in remote viewing experiments." *Nature*, 284, 191, 1980. https://doi.org/10.1038/284191a0.

CHAPTER 6
VALUES, CONSCIOUSNESS AND THE HOLOMOVEMENT: GROUNDING THE NEW PARADIGM

by Joni Carley, DMin & Phil Clothier

Bohm described "holomovement" as an undivided wholeness that is expressed in every seemingly separate entity, event and action—the fractal reality Dr. Jude Currivan so beautifully unpacks in Chapter 2 of this book. "Holo," though, implies more than the tangible entities, events and actions of our reality. Within our wholeness, as a collective world population, there also includes the divine flow of the intangible essence that fuels our sense of purpose and connects us to our inner selves, to one another, to Gaia and to the mysterious spark of the human spirit.

While more difficult to quantify than entities, events and actions, it is the intangible factors that often determine the tangible. The paradigm that we are arising from places heavy value on the what we can measure, for example, our ever-escalating funding of weaponry, material- and growth-based economic norms and reliance on data-driven metrics, while it holds relatively little value for the intangibles people value most like connecting with others, being well and happy and having a sense of being part of a greater whole.

In this chapter, we explore the field of values, culture and consciousness, a field that holds the potential to transform life conditions on planet Earth. How the Holomovement progresses is dependent on how we manage the current cultural context of today's challenges and on creating a more fertile cultural context in which holocracy can thrive. Our evolving cultural context is determined by the values and consciousness we choose to uphold.

Accounting for Values

A teacher of an accounting course once said, "Finance is the stories we tell about money." Likewise, a holocracy comes down to the stories we tell about our values and our way of life. Just like there is a rich and sometimes complex language to express the many aspects of money management, values provide the rich language and the range of complexity needed to tell the story of a holocratic culture.

While no one doubts the need for financial accountancy, cultural accountancy is all the more important because culture determines outcomes to a much greater degree than dollars do.[9] Many systems exist for measuring values and culture. Through these kinds of metrics, we are able to understand the personal beliefs and priorities of individuals and groups, and to explore the current values and behaviors that describe life conditions now, what is working well and what is undermining quality of life. Using data-based, values-driven measuring tools, we can clarify the specific, authentic desires, needs and aspirations of groups. Truly achieving wellbeing for people and for all other life on Earth requires better data on who specific groups are, what they actually need and want, and how they see themselves involved in creating their desired outcomes. Values-based data provides accountancy for the things that matter most to distinct groups of people and for how their needs and aspirations fit with those of other groups and with the rest of the world.

Just like financial data is key to old paradigmatic norms, values-based data is key to achieving holocrative norms, otherwise we risk trying to build something new on the very same metrics that underlie our current cultural norms. We measure what matters, and adoption of holocratic values matters more than ever. Values-based cultural measurements have the added benefit of creating a highly accessible language to explore multidimensional aspects of human life, including what bonds us together, our diversity and our innate drive to expand.

While there are many systems for measuring values and culture, the experience we bring and the stories we tell in this chapter are largely based on the Barrett Model and measurement tools created by Richard Barrett. This approach is being used to measure and transform teams, organizations, communities and entire countries all around the world, having been administered over decades in 50+ languages, to over 10,000 organizations in 150 countries.

Values and the Holomovement

Moving toward "cultural good" is both a reflection and a result of values that are playing out not just within each person, but within the culture as a whole. Values are the common denominators between individuals and collectives and, as such, they are the building blocks of cultures. The operative values in any given culture are a reflection of how much equanimity there is in the system. The paradigmatic shift we appear to be living through is a meta movement from separation-oriented to holo-based values, which are emerging as we-centered, compassionate, cooperative, eco-conscious and holistically-grounded.

We value what we need, and we are motivated accordingly. Values determine behaviors, and they transcend demographic differences. The groundbreaking work of Abraham Maslow's Hierarchy of Needs revealed two main types of needs: (1) deficiency needs are basic needs arising from being deprived of something; and (2) growth needs arise from a desire to grow as an individual. According to Maslow's original theory, a person must fulfill her deficiency needs before she can move on to fulfilling growth needs. Although we now know that values-fulfillment is not quite so linear, Maslow's hierarchy of needs still provides an important lens on personal and social development.

We see this dynamic of shifting values and priorities happen as people have life-changing accidents or a diagnosis of life-threatening diseases. In this sense, our basic human fears give us a clue to the universal values that we all share, like being safe and having enough resources to survive, belonging and being loved and feeling a sense of self-worth and recognition or appreciation from others. Once these basic needs are met, they provide the foundation for our growth needs, including self-development, a sense of purpose in life and contributing to something greater than self.

Barrett took Maslow's work to the next level in revealing how all of our needs are expressed as values, how values correlate with Maslow's Hierarchy of Needs and how accounting for values allows us to manage a much larger spectrum of the human experience than merely tracking material gains and losses. Barrett defines values as "the energetic drivers of our aspirations and intentions," a definition that points toward the role of values in achieving the aspirations and intentions of holocracy and, ultimately, the Holomovement.

Universal Values

We tend to gravitate toward people whose values are most aligned with our own. When peoples' values align, cultures thrive. Because they are our primary motivators, even more primal than genetics according to twins studies,[10] values are foundational attractors in part because they are universal. Universal values transcend gender, geography, race, age, political and other demographic differences, and remain consistent throughout time and across religious and philosophical teachings. On a national level, values can be made visible by explicitly accounting for them and then used to provide the cultural pillars for building a country that works for everyone.

For example, in a 2010 statistically relevant National Values Assessment of the United States of America, the data revealed new depth and insight in our understanding of universal human values. Among the many demographic questions in the survey, they inquired about political affiliation. The data showed that nine out of the top ten personal values were exactly the same for American citizens who identified as "Republican" versus those who identified as "Democrat." The common values for both groups were caring, family, humor/fun, honesty, friendship, responsibility, respect, accountability and positive attitude. The only difference among both groups' top ten values was that Republicans chose "integrity" and Democrats chose "compassion."

So, if we all hold the same fundamental, universal human values, what are we arguing and fighting about? The answer lies in a simple principle: *Beliefs divide and values unite.*

When we dig beneath the belief layer that divides so many groups and fractures society to the point of violence and war, we find fundamental human values that can unite us. Not only can attending to and accounting for values help our leaders and politicians better understand each other and the true needs of their people, values accountability can help us to consciously establish the intangible infrastructure necessary to effect holocratic transformation.

The Holomovement reflects an emergent global urge toward more unity-based values, but there is considerable conjecture and assumption around what those values actually are. Given that science is demonstrating that our wholeness is not merely an aspiration but rather our existential reality, holo-directed cultural development needs to accommodate that reality by establishing cultural accountability.

Values Accountancy

Accounting for our actual coherence and divergence by tracking and developing specific, stakeholder-determined values would lay meaningful groundwork in establishing and developing synergy among diverse stakeholders. Accounting for values alignment among stakeholders is a means for both drilling down into the nuances of coherence that make and break collaborations and for tracking cultural development progress over time and across sectors and demographics. Using values-based metrics would support the Holomovement of movements in establishing accountability for its diversity by quantifying authentic alignments and divergences and by clarifying shared vision. This accountability would support development and establishment of holocratic norms because values are the interface between each of us and whatever group or culture of which we are each a part.

We saw this in 2021, during some difficult days of the Covid-19 pandemic, when we were working with a global aid agency. During one of many Zoom meetings, everyone experienced a collective "aha! moment" when a team member shared a profound truth: "You are never not contributing to shaping the culture." Every thought, word and action make a difference, either positively or negatively. Nothing is neutral. Even on a very small scale, our thoughts (or thoughtlessness), words and actions make a difference and have ripple effects far beyond what we can see. It is our values that guide these actions.

Values Over Time and Where We are Now

What have we learned about how personal values relate to the Holomovement? Beginning in 2012, the data and observations from the 1.5 million Personal Values Assessments completed on the Barrett Website, and from 27 countries' National Values Assessments, some of which were conducted over multiple years, reveal that our top ten values show clear and consistent patterns from year to year.

Firstly, people prioritize foundational relationship values: family, caring, respect, friendship and trust. The second largest grouping of values, which are higher order values, include humor/fun, enthusiasm, creativity and continuous learning, revealing the human spirit and the desire to enjoy life, grow, have a sense of purpose and make a positive contribution.

There is one more highly common value that indicates resilience, persistence and maybe even the fundamental desire for life to survive and thrive, even in the face of existential or psychological challenges. That is the value of *commitment*. As Rabindranath Tagore, Nobel Literature prize winner in 1913 wrote, "The fundamental desire of life is the desire to exist."

Given that the Holomovement is about the inter-relatedness of all things and the emerging desire to create new levels of wellbeing for all life, the collective values of humanity shown in this research offer a data-based starting point for creating the cultural infrastructure necessary to support holocratic norms, which build on our basic drive to exist by recognizing our higher-level values for thriving. But if human beings have such wonderful values that seem to align so perfectly with the Holomovement, why haven't we figured this out already? Why aren't we living in a new state of wholeness? What is getting in the way?

In 2012, the results of a Singapore National Values Assessment, done in partnership with National University of Singapore and shared with government policy makers, politicians, academics and the national media, showed the top personal values of the Singapore people were: family, friendship, health, happiness, caring, honesty, responsibility, well-being (physical/ emotional/ mental/ spiritual), respect and balance (home/work).

They also showed the negative or regressive values and behaviors that people perceived and experienced in Singapore society: *kiasu* (taking extreme measures to achieve success), competitive, self-centered, material needs, *kiasi* (taking extreme risk-avoidance measures), deteriorating values, elitism, blame, uncertainty about the future and security. A journalist in the back of the room when results were being revealed raised his hand to ask a simple and profound question about the difference in the data sets between individual and current collective values: "If we are the wonderful people shown in the personal values list, who are the people behaving so badly in the current society picture?"

This question is at the heart of the dilemma we face in transforming society, and the answer is critical to solving the current global crises. Twenty years of research and dialogue with thousands of people make the answer very clear—both the light and dark exist in each of us.

Our personal values are a reflection of our needs and aspirations and are usually expressed in very positive terms. However, when our individual and collective fears show up at family, team, organization or societal scale, the data tends to reveal our darker side and how that creates life depleting, life exhaustive energy. Fears are expressed as limiting or negative values like control, greed and dishonesty. These words, which we normally consider to be behaviors, are values too. They never show up unless there is a perceived individual or collective benefit. Let's take "blame" for an example. If I blame you, at that moment, I probably feel a little safer because I have shifted the negative focus away from myself. So, the unconscious intention, need or value may be "safety," but the behavior emerges as blame.

At the risk of massive oversimplification, all human fears can be grouped into three categories, and part of the human condition is that we all experience some or all of them throughout our lives:

1. I don't have enough. I do not have enough money, safety, protection, health, food, etc. to satisfy my need for survival.

2. I am not loved enough. I do not have enough love, care, attention, etc. to satisfy my need for belonging.

3. I am not (good) enough. I do not have enough recognition, power, authority or respect to satisfy my need for self-esteem.

For some people, the fears come from real threats. For example, many people around the world live in war zones, where basic survival needs are barely available and there is a real risk of death. For others, these feelings emerge from inner fears that may have developed during childhood like, for example, someone who has a very large bank account may still hold fears about not having enough money.

When we are able to identify the fears holding us back, the next stage is to become aware of when these fear-based thoughts arise. This awareness empowers us with a choice: to be held prisoner by fear or to acknowledge its existence and continue forward with agency. This makes sense at an individual level when overcoming personal limitations, but understanding these values and fears at a societal level is equally important. This brings us to a principle that can be expressed as a formula: $UF \times P = DI$, meaning Unconscious Fears x Power = Devastating Impact. The more that unconscious fears (UF) dominate someone's life and the greater power (P) they hold and exert over others, the more negative, life-depleting and devastating impact (DI) they will have on the organization, society and environment. It is only through this awareness and the choices we make through our thoughts, words and actions that we can start to heal ourselves and make a contribution to healing the societal and environmental needs of the Earth. Confucius understood this principle 2,500 years ago and is quoted as saying:

> "To put the world in order, we must first put the nation in
> order; to put the nation in order, we must first put the family
> in order; to put the family in order; we must first cultivate
> our personal life; we must first set our hearts right."

Our awareness of our personal values allows us to account for the interchange between nations, families and individuals, and, when measured and consciously managed, accounting for values provides a mechanism for allowing what is in our hearts to be expressed in our nations.

Values accountability provides a powerful bridge between individuals and the whole, which is critical to a holocratic approach. Creating new patterns for humanity needs to be done by reaching into higher level values while staying mindful of the personal survival and relational values that we all need to have fulfilled.

Connecting the Tangible with the Intangible

Moving from the divisive approach of the old paradigm to incorporate the understanding that we are fractals and not fragments of the whole, requires a shift from focusing on horizontal development to putting more emphasis on the usually ignored vertical development necessary to achieving a healthy holo-society. The educational, social and economic systems of the world are primarily focused on horizontal development with emphasis on math, engineering, accounting, management theory, etc., which are all valuable skills for getting tangible stuff done.

However, there is a growing recognition that horizontal development is only part of the story—that we need to balance the outer, skills-based work with inner development to not only be a human "DO"ing but to also slow down and attend to the inner, intangible, vertical development to truly become a human "BE"ing, which is a matter of consciousness. The way to a holo-world includes developing the unity consciousness necessary to create it. Just like the atrocity and suffering we witness today is first and foremost a crisis of consciousness, transitioning into a holo-paradigm is a matter of individual consciousness and of alignment of consciousness within and among populations.

Alignment of consciousness can be determined by measuring alignment of values. Because values bridge the gap between the tangible and intangible, and values are quantifiable, accounting for consciousness by way of tracking values is an inclusive means for clarifying and developing coherence among stakeholders that not only simultaneously embraces and transcends diversity and individuation, but it also addresses the multi-dimensionality of our existence.

The degree to which collective consciousness aligns in every dimension is the degree to which there is harmony in a system, and we can measure that harmony by quantifying values alignment. As we move from a paradigm driven by transactional and competitive consciousness to a paradigm founded in the existential reality of our unity, attending to values and consciousness is a way to navigate what Bohm calls the "multi-dimensional reality of oneness." Managing the multi-dimensions involved in organizing ourselves in accordance with our existential unity requires a radical shift in consciousness. Accounting for values is one of the few easily accessible methods to explore consciousness. Values accountancy would provide commonly determined guardrails for navigating the way forward, and it would help to link metaphysical factors with three dimensional results. Building values and cultural quantification metrics into new paradigm social structures would help to demonstrate authentic unity among diverse people and would provide clarity on alignment and divergence around priorities and shared vision.

Holocracy will become the norm if and when a critical mass of people align such that holo-values become their norm. At the same time, values-based metrics would provide commonly grounded scaffolding for co-creating holo-cultural structures. When values provide the basis from which projects and actions are determined, studies show that the alignment of collective consciousness that results is far more powerful than equally good projects and actions done from the basis of fear, competition and division.[11]

Measuring and tracking commonly generated, values-driven metrics would facilitate and enrich the quality of dialogue necessary to bring the eight core unifying principles of the Holomovement into manifested reality.

The Holomovement's Eight Core Unifying Principles and Relating Values

1. *Interconnected Wholeness*: Tracking values reveals specific intersections between us as individuals, communities, nations and as a global citizenry. Values can be thought of as cultural pixels,

as constant building blocks that create the infrastructure of our fractalized wholeness. While standard demographic instruments primarily measure differences among groups, values accountability provides a means for reflecting the individual within the whole, as well as a means for reflecting how people want their interconnectivity to play out.

2. *A Conscious Living Universe:* As we gain greater confirmation and clearer recognition of our interdependent co-arising with the whole of Gaia, we are compelled to expand our consciousness to accommodate new ways of knowing ourselves and our place in the universe. Addressing the consciousness of the universe requires establishing holocratic valuations for consciousness itself.

3. *Purposeful Evolution:* Accounting for values provides a means to pinpoint collective vision and shared will in the midst of our complex and interconnected evolution. Much of the work in the space of conscious evolution is based on subjective assumptions and conjecture about what a peaceful world would look like and how we should get there. Cultural accountability by way of values measurements would support inclusive, transparent, data-based determination of how people are actually aligned, or not, for evolutionary transformation.

4. *Wholesomeness as our Natural State of Being:* The cultures we live in are both determinant of and reflective of the vitality of our wholesomeness. Without accountability for collective values, even the very basis of what constitutes the whole is subjective. Paying attention to values develops conscious awareness of our inherent wholesomeness.

5. *A Self-Healing Cosmos*: If healing is the awareness (consciousness) of all aspects of self, we can see the vital importance of utilizing values to understand our individual and collective needs. The natural path of the cosmos toward self-healing may be paved by projects, but it is lit by the consciousness of those who are walking it. Attending to consciousness itself is an act of self-healing. Accountability for consciousness in holo-development is critical to understanding the link between values, beliefs and behaviors and how they are experienced and confirmed.

6. *Embodying the Holomovement*: Values are one of the few easily accessible methods for exploring our embodiment of wholeness. As we grow in consciousness, our awareness and identity expand in its cosmic connection. This growth in awareness can lead to a shift in values and behaviors, which naturally becomes a force for healing self, others and the planet.

7. *Unity in Action*: Groups unified in values have shown to be more effective than those acting solely on rules and standards. Values metrics are unity metrics. Divergences in values can reflect the unity in our diversity, and they can also reflect dysfunction and negativity that is undermining good work. Values accountability allows individual purpose and good of the whole to be tracked in accordance with each other.

8. *Self-sustaining Development of Unity Consciousness:* In the human spirit's quest to expand truth, beauty and goodness and to embody its inherent unity, values provide a way to bridge the individual journey with the collective will. Values quantification would specifically provide a means to account for unity consciousness, for alignment with that consciousness among any particular group of

people and for nuances in how unity plays out in diverse situations. At the same time, it would also identify values digressions, which reflect dysfunctional, separation-based, fear-oriented consciousness. A culture's unique values reflect its innate sense of the good of the whole, and they provide guide-lights on the evolutionary path of cultural consciousness toward holocracy.

Values are superchargers for bringing purpose to life in the present while also supplying commonly grounded scaffolding for building shared vision for the future. As we sort our way through our civilizational meta-crisis, humanity is recognizing that we are both physical and spiritual beings and that our inner beings matter greatly. We are allured by our values, and they draw us toward harmony. They connect the intangible with the tangible, the metaphysical with the physical, and so help us to access the inner space that sources possibilities from the infinite, quantum space and moves them into probabilities and finally into manifest actualities. Values are the lanterns on the path of our evolutionary return to oneness.

As the miracle of motion that is our existence goes forward, values-based metrics will provide a collectively determined roadmap for navigating the Holomovement and our conscious evolution. Even more than mapping, clarity and alignment around authentic values would help to deeply stake the compass points of a road so new it requires a completely new paradigm to name its destination.

SUPPORTING A UNITIVE AND TRANSFORMATIONAL AGENDA FOR GLOBAL CHANGE

by SDG (Sustainable Development Goals)
Thought Leaders Circle members:
Joni Carley, Scott Alan Carlin, Richard Clugston,
Jude Currivan, Gordon Dveirin, Kurt Johnson,
Heidi Sparkes Guber & Daniel J. Stone

In 2021, a Thought Leaders Synergy Circle of the Evolutionary Leaders network was convened to support, promote and address a transformational agenda building from the spirit and intention of the United Nations Sustainable Development Goals (UN SDGs). It is work motivated by the infusion of innovative, unifying and uplifting visions, values and strategies, co-creative partnerships and heart-based service for the good of the whole.

The SDG Thought Leaders Synergy Circle consists of a wide range of individuals who stand ready and are equipped with the vision, understanding and skills to help foster the achievement of a future of peace, sustainability, equality and democracy. And since this responsibility should be shared universally, we anticipate supporting achievements both within the context of the United Nations, as well as with other sectors working toward this shared vision. Ultimately, our commitment is to act as agents of change in alliance with those who are likewise committed to the evolution of our species and the protection of the planetary home we share, amplifying and helping to manifest a vision that ensures a healthy, vibrant future for all life.

In this regard, before the initiation and subsequent naming of a Holomovement, our intention has been to enact an integrative and unitive approach that is the modus operandi of this emergent 'movement of movements.' And we welcome dialogue, discussion and exploration of synergies with already existing public organizations which are also dedicated to implementation of the SDGs.

We promote a life-affirming approach to regenerative and sustainable development. Without addressing the underlying beliefs and conditions of the past, it will be impossible to make significant and sustained progress toward these goals. The approach must be based on an understanding of the unity of all people and beings on the planet and our planetary home in its entirety. It must also be based on an understanding that while the technical solutions to these issues might differ, the problems are all inherently interconnected. Therefore, approaches to solving global challenges must adopt new wholistic paradigms that recognize and account for the inter-relatedness of the issues to one another.

Fortunately, there are approaches to addressing the major issues of the 17 SDG categories that are embedded with this new unitive paradigm; these approaches tend to promote practices such as dialogue, diversity, power-sharing and cooperation. And there are now many examples where these approaches have achieved significant success. We therefore are advocates for critically examining assumptions that are driving these various issues and for using methodologies that embody the values of unity rather than separateness.

Finally, the role of leadership cannot be underestimated. But rather than the traditional, top-down, politicized nature of leaders that have currently controlled these issues, the nature of this leadership must be different. Leaders for the essential transformation must recognize that real and lasting solutions to these problems require widespread sharing of responsibility and power with other responsible parties to act with agency. Therefore, those in leadership roles must be visionaries acting as facilitators. And they must recognize that any real progress requires a commitment to the long-term focus on the achievement of the goals.

We shape our mission, frame our vision and empower our strategy in the evolutionary context of a unitive narrative. As referred to in Chapter 2 of this book, our members drafted this narrative "to provide an emergent cosmological, planetary, interspiritual and societal foundation to serve and support the conscious evolution of humanity and heal our collective worldview from separation to a perspective of unity in diversity."

The synergy circle members, many of whom have worked with the United Nations, global governments and organizations and civil society for many years, recognize that such a unitive narrative, founded on the latest scientific evidence across all scales of existence and numerous fields of research, is essential to underpin and frame a unitive worldview to inspire and empower transformational change in the world. Our hitherto fragmented worldview, with its flawed paradigm of materialist separation, has engendered dysfunctional and unsustainable behaviors and social structures. Because the UN SDGs are global responses to these symptoms of our collective dis-ease and distress, approaches to their implementation are often founded on, structured and compartmentalized by, the same fragmented narrative and so, in and of themselves, are inherently limited.

The emergent unitive narrative heals our individual and collective psyches from the illusion of separation to a communally lived wholeness. In expanding a circle of empathy from "me," to inclusion of the shared "we" and the universal "all," our focus transcends from an ego- to an eco- and evolutionary perspective. In revealing the innate meaning and purpose of our existence and our evolutionary potential, it naturally embodies universal principles of unity in diversity; empowering us to envision and offering guidance on action steps toward a regenerated, compassionate, peaceful and just world.

This wholistic perspective approaches the 17 SDGs as an interconnected whole, each one interdependent with each other and essential to achieving an inclusive, prosperous and thriving global society and living in planetary harmony with Gaia.

Instead of solely quantitative goals based on economic growth, and recognizing and including qualitative goals of development based on increasing and co-creative learning and competent growth toward wholeness, its unitive approach also resolves their apparent contradiction in advancing the commitments of the SDGs.

Regarding the UN's Agenda 2030 particularly, such unitive consciousness can radically reframe and empower our collective approach and actions by emphasizing calls to be in service for the good of the whole and guiding us in how we wholeheartedly participate in this vision.

In addition to drafting a unitive narrative, which can be used with specific reference to the SDGs, it is also a universally foundational underpinning and framing which can support and be applied to other unitive approaches. In this approach, our aims to speed up and scale up its impact includes initiating a Unitive Thematic Cluster under the NGO Major Group of the United Nations to provide a platform for like-minded ECOSOC accredited NGOs to partner in UN SDG processes.

Recognizing and appreciating there are already many exemplars of successful multi-level unitive aware projects for interventions and capacity building, we are also building an extensive and interactive online compendium as an open resource to learn from and co-develop best practices. In doing so, instead of choices founded in fears and scarcity, engendered by the illusion of separation, we can come together, learn from each other and co-create a future affirming shared life, love and hope in action. Through this collaboration and shared work, we can realize a reality where the SDGs and Agenda 2030 resolutions are natural outcomes of a world that works for the good of the whole.

Resources:

See Evolutionary Leaders / SDG Thought Leaders Circle / Unitive Narrative

https://www.evolutionaryleaders.net/unitivenarrative

https://sdgthoughtleaderscircle.org/unitive-new-narrative/

https://sdgthoughtleaderscircle.org/

CHAPTER 7
THE SOPHIA CENTURY: DIVINE FEMININE RISING

by Lynne Twist & Mary Earle Chase

There is a beautiful teaching that comes from the Bahá'í faith called "the bird of humanity." The Bahá'í believe in the unity of all religions and all humanity and in the equality of men and women. The Bahá'í scriptures say that the bird of humanity has two great wings, a male wing and a female wing, but for centuries, these two wings have not been of equal strength. The male wing has been fully extended, fully expressed, while the female wing has been folded in, not fully extended.

In order to keep itself afloat, the bird's male wing has become overdeveloped, its muscles strained and shaking violently. Without its balancing counterpart, the bird of humanity has been continually flying in circles, unable to reach the heights of real attainment. When the female wing of the bird of humanity is fully expressed, the male wing can then relax, and with two wings fully extended and of equivalent strength, the bird of humanity will soar to new heights. The time for the fulfillment of this teaching, when men and women come into balance in equal partnership, is the 21st century. We call it the Sophia Century.

Sophia is the Greek word for wisdom, which English has inherited through words like 'philosophy' or "love of wisdom." From ancient Greece to early Christian mystics to twentieth-century philosophers, traditions across the world have understood wisdom as beyond information or knowledge, but something deeper, even enlightened, and often describe it as a feminine characteristic. In this Information Age, as humanity careens toward a future filled with ever more facts but not enough wisdom, the concept of the Sophia Century illuminates how the rise of feminine values can heal and rebalance a patriarchal world, bringing forth a future that is environmentally sustainable, spiritually fulfilling and socially just.

The Sophia Century is not about feminism and women's rights—or rather, it is not *only* about those things. It is about saving humanity, as well as all life forms now threatened by the misguided values of the patriarchy. This century is the time to think bigger, to free both men and women from systems and structures based on masculine values that are not inherently bad but, lacking counterbalance, have wreaked havoc on the planet. Benign values such as control, assertiveness, competitiveness and ambition, *when taken to the extreme*, have led to domination, exploitation, greed, overconsumption and corruption. That imbalance has led to the ugly legacies of centuries of racism, sexism, colonialism, capitalism, nationalism, militarism and white supremacy. It has laid the groundwork for existential global crises: accelerating climate change, global pandemics, and the extinction of half the world's species. Overbearing masculinity also has led to obscene economic inequality, the decline of civil discourse and grave threats to democracy.

The Holomovement aims to support our re-awakening to the wholeness and interconnectedness of all life at all levels of being, from the atomic to the cosmic. Just as the holomovement represents the flow between the implicate and explicate orders, it also exemplifies the flow between masculine and feminine—similar to the symbol of the interconnected swirl of yin and yang and the bird of humanity.

The rather unfortunate terminology of a "big bang" as the initiator of our universe has in part led to a masculine interpretation of our universe and many of the cultures on planet Earth. However, as Dr. Jude Currivan previously shared in this anthology, it was neither big nor a bang, but rather a breath of love coming from the womb of consciousness.

If we are looking to transform our future, we need to uplift and enliven feminine values, ideals and characteristics that are heart-centered: compassion, empathy, nurturance, diversity, equity, inclusion, humility and love—to charge both women and men with bringing about balance and interdependence. The Earth, our societies and our institutions are crying out for the rebalancing of feminine and masculine energies so that empathy, insight, nurturing, collaboration, compassion and gratitude can combine with logic, reason, technology, initiative and power to build a world that works for everyone.

Challenging the Patriarchy

Patriarchy is the system of beliefs, values and relationships that has structured gender inequality into society such that men dominate in both the public and private spheres. It exaggerates and amplifies unhealthy masculine qualities and justifies domination, discrimination and all sorts of societal and personal injustices, including a woman's right to control her own body.

Patriarchy is the water that we swim in—so enveloping that we often barely recognize it, and so pervasive that we take it for granted. There was a time prior to 1500 B.C. when the Great Mother was the primary deity in many cultures, with all creation emerging from her womb. Many Indigenous cultures share mother-centered origin stories, but ever since Eve was blamed for getting Adam thrown out of the Garden of Eden, the Great Mother was replaced by the Great Father in the Western worldview. Patriarchal religion, materialism, secular science and technological progress have robbed us of our sense of the sacred. Unmoored from our divine origins, we are adrift in the narrative of a lifeless universe without purpose or meaning.

As a mindset or worldview, patriarchy derives from three key tenets: separation, scarcity and domination. It sees humans as separate from each other, from the natural world and from the divine source of life. This illusion of separation has infected all of our human systems, creating consequences that threaten all life on Earth.

Our cultural embrace of separation is coupled with a belief in scarcity— the fear that on Earth there is not enough to go around, requiring constant struggle and competition for scarce resources. Thus, success depends on power and control. This myth of scarcity has shaped our institutions and our interactions for centuries, with devastating results. Worth is measured by productivity that produces a certain kind of wealth based on commodification and accumulation. If something isn't a commodity—if it doesn't create money—it has no value, and whatever can't be measured and quantified is undervalued. More is always better! The patriarchal system that has dominated humanity for thousands of years has focused on individual wealth rather than community well-being, resulting in vast financial inequality and the pillaging of the planet for individual enrichment.

Inhabiting a worldview of separation and scarcity, women and men alike are often trained to cultivate the masculine values and qualities of ambition, assertiveness, focus, strength and orientation to action and achievement. These are admirable qualities. Unfortunately, in this current system, they have been distorted, resulting in violence, war, greed, exploitation and a willingness to sacrifice people and the environment for dominion and profits. We inhabit a "you *or* me" world, when what is being called for now is a "you *and* me" world.

Now in the first two decades of the Sophia Century, we can see progress being made toward a world that works for everyone. Long left on the sidelines of a male-dominated world, the feminine nature of the Holomovement is now taking its place as the birthplace and deepest nature of our existence. The

Divine Feminine is now in ascendancy and promises to bring the love, nurturing care and true compassion of a human consciousness that we so desperately need to make life whole once again.

In many countries, more women are running for—and winning—electoral office, increasing female representation in government. The corporate and business world is offering more opportunities for going beyond the glass ceiling. The #MeToo movement has catalyzed truth-telling among women as well as a new consciousness among men about sexual harassment and unwanted sexual encounters in the workplace. As with the painful legacies of racism, sexism is being exposed in our culture, opening the way for healing and transformation.

At the same time, no country in the world, rich or poor, has achieved gender equality, and women and girls continue to be discriminated against in education, in health, in the home and in the workplace. The coronavirus pandemic disproportionately burdened women, pushing mothers and caregivers back into confined roles and rolling back some of the precious momentum of progress. In an almost unbelievable reversal of basic human rights, a woman's right to choose childbearing on her own terms is threatened in much of the United States.

Sophia Values for a Changing World

What is needed in this new century are the values of feminine wisdom to be upheld in equal admiration—Sophia values based on interconnectedness, respect for nature, deep relatedness, community, spirituality and love. The Sophia values are present in all humans: we care for our children and elders; we nurse and heal; we teach; we feed; we birth and mourn; we value peace and justice; we are inclusive and caring. Collectively, however, women's deep understanding of these values offer us an opportunity to bring forth the feminine qualities to create a balanced flow of energy, of emotion and of love.

Flow itself is feminine. Arkan Lushwala, a Peruvian shaman and ceremonial leader, likens the male and female energies to fire and water.

They can work together beautifully, he says, but when out of balance, the more masculine fire energy consumes and destroys through war and violence. Fire needs the energy of water to be tempered and controlled— although too much water can flood or drown. Water calms the fire, cleanses and nourishes growth. The feminine water energy wants to flow. When the masculine disrupts this flow by suppressing or controlling feminine energy, life processes are hampered and diminished. In economic terms, when financial resources are accumulated primarily by the few, the flow is dammed up, and the many are left out. Unblocking the feminine allows for the flow of emotion, tenderness, generosity, intuition, inspiration and insight.

It seems that vulnerability and humility are also critical drivers of leadership effectiveness, both fundamentally feminine traits. A recent article in the *Harvard Business Review* entitled "7 Leadership Lessons Men Can Learn from Women" analyzed studies of leadership effectiveness. It found that rather than encouraging women in business to act more like men, the opposite should be the case. Leadership behaviors such as leading through inspiration rather than domination are more likely to establish an emotional connection with colleagues and transform people's attitudes and beliefs, aligning with them according to meaning and purpose.

Let's be clear, however, that the values we identify as masculine or feminine are not consigned to males or females only. Women share masculine characteristics such as ambition, assertiveness, focus, and orientation to action and achievement, and men exhibit feminine characteristics of nurturing, spirituality, empathy and compassion. We are not advocating replacing male chauvinism with female chauvinism, but rather a co-equal partnership of men and women that incorporates and balances both the masculine and feminine qualities in us all.

The elevation of female leadership and feminine values is up to both women and men. If women don't step up and exercise their power, then we bear responsibility for the continuing degradation of the planet along with men who aren't willing to change and align themselves with a more feminine future. Sophia wisdom and feminine ways of being that are alive in each of us are crucial to our survival in the Sophia Century.

The Divine Feminine and the Sacred Masculine

The Sophia values are at the heart of the Holomovement reflecting its deepest source of love, compassion and connectedness. In this global movement, the Divine Feminine is rising in individuals as well as in society. What we call divine or sacred calls forth guidance from our highest selves, and archetypes can help us understand and connect with these inner realities—the psychic counterpart of instincts.

An archetype, as conceived of by psychologist Carl Jung, is a theme that humans live by, a pattern of behavior or thought that is inherited unconsciously and is universally present in individual psyches. The ancient Greeks, Romans, Indians and Chinese imbued their gods and goddesses with archetypal qualities. Although modern-day folks may not accept such mythology, we nevertheless have much to learn from them. Recognizing and valuing these attributes as *divine* enables us to see that they belong to all of us and can teach us how we might inhabit and express them.

There are various versions of the female archetypes, and according to Jung, these are the simplest ones: the Queen is feminine power; the Mother is the source of love, acceptance and nurturing; the Wise Woman is the source of knowledge, intuition and spiritual insight; and the Lover is sensual, sexual and devoted to beauty, pleasure and the expression of joy. The Divine Feminine encompasses all of these qualities; they are our birthright awaiting our embrace.

In the past few decades, the Goddess Movement has run parallel to the traditional women's movement, promoting the ascendance of the Divine Feminine in modern Western culture. Unfortunately, this movement also has been co-opted and mischaracterized as "New Age-y" and spiritually suspicious. Its true intention of female empowerment is often lost in translation.

Masculine archetypes are also sacred and worthy of spiritual respect or devotion. The male counterparts of the female archetypes are: the King, whose power brings order and safety; the Warrior who protects and fights for the higher good; the Magician, a combination of priest and sage who channels inner and outer wisdom; and the Lover, who is devoted to sensuality, beauty and healing.

There are many masculine traits worthy of respect, the primary one being able to provide for and protect family, which is so critical today. Yet, it is clear that the Sacred Masculine has been distorted by the patriarchy, robbing men of their emotionality and imposing the need to conform to "macho" standards.

A great tragedy of the patriarchy is the cultural convention that men and boys are deprived of experiencing and expressing emotions other than anger. They are not allowed to cry. In Africa, it is said that the souls of the American people are dry because we don't water them with tears—tears of grief, tears of being moved or touched, tears of joy. The ability to feel grief and to mourn is related to forgiveness and the ability to make amends. In fact, we cannot "fix" things without first acknowledging them and feeling their impact if we are to learn from experiences.

Rev. Deborah L. Johnson says, "We must feel—to deal—to heal." In speaking about the mass extinction of life forms that is happening now on our planet, cosmologist Brian Swimme said, "Perhaps we haven't deepened our hearts enough to make possible the grief that is wanting to be felt."

That comment holds true for all of the tragedies unfolding now, and often, it is women who are more likely to confront and hold that grief. It is this emotional intelligence and empathic experience, feminine qualities to be valued and honored, that will energize the eradication of injustice, economic exploitation and ecocide occurring today.

The Divine Feminine and Sacred Masculine live in all of us, and now is a crucial time to seek the balance of those energies in order to navigate and transform an uncertain future. Our expression of these archetypal energies can empower our own lives as well as release new forces into the world: power that flows and is win/win; love that is both fierce and unconditional; wisdom that derives from both knowledge and intuition; and sacred sensuality that honors beauty and joy as well as Mother Earth and all her creations.

Fortunately, there is a 21st Century Men's Movement working to define and teach healthy masculinity—integrating feminine values while celebrating the unique gifts of maleness. One such example is The ManKind Project, a worldwide network of groups offering programs focused on modern male initiation, self-awareness and personal growth aimed at strengthening true masculine power. Their New Warrior Training Adventure is a modern male initiation and self-examination that roughly follows the "hero's journey" of classical literature and myth. It offers a new vision of what it means to be a conscious, nonviolent "warrior" in today's world.

Birthing a New Future

We are being called on to hospice the death of the old systems built on patriarchal violence and destruction and midwife the birth of new ones based on an entirely different relationship with our Mother Earth—what Thomas Berry calls "a mutually-enhancing human-earth relationship." This is where the values that we call 'feminine' hold such promise. We have the capacity, responsibility and privilege to realize a new civilization. It is precisely the wisdom that is held in the Divine Feminine that is needed to give birth to this transformed world.

The birthing process is a great metaphor for our times. If you came upon a woman giving birth and did not know what was happening, you might think she was gravely injured or dying. Birthing is a harrowing process for the mother as well as witnesses. Author and activist Valarie Kaur, the creator of the Revolutionary Love Project, correlates the birthing process with our sometimes terrifying world. She asks, "Is this the darkness of the tomb or the darkness of the womb?"

To give birth, the midwife tells us to breathe and then to push. Breathe and push. Kaur goes on to say, "In all of our labors, the labor of raising a family, or making a movement, or birthing a new nation, we need people to help us breathe and push into the fires of our bodies and the fires in the world."

The great eco-philosopher Joanna Macy urges us to feel into our pain of these current times to reveal and motivate our love. She says, "The anguish we feel for what is happening to our world is inevitable and normal and even healthy. Pain is very useful. Just don't be afraid of it. Because if we are afraid to feel that, we won't feel where it comes from, and where it comes from is love, our love for this world. That's what is going to pull us through."

We are midwives in this great transition, this evolutionary leap, where men and women must come together to keep breathing and pushing for what Charles Eisenstein calls, "the more beautiful world our hearts know is possible." We don't know what time we have left, how long we are able to endure this birthing process, but we do know the clock is ticking.

We're at the culmination of what Buckminster Fuller talked about 50 years ago, a time when every single institution of humankind is dysfunctional and failing us and needs to be re-imagined and re-created. Some believe that we have already run out of time, that runaway climate change and global pandemics are proof. Others hold onto hope for our transformative potential. Peruvian healer Arkan Lushwala had these words at the beginning of the Covid-19 pandemic:

> "In a deep, primordial part of ourselves, many of us have been waiting for something like this to happen. Someone or something powerful and sacred enough had to intervene in order to stop the destruction of the sources of life. The Earth herself, she has now done so ... With deep compassion for those who are suffering, I have to say that the Earth is still being kind and gentle, that her way of defending

herself could be much worse … *Pachamama*, our mother, wouldn't be doing what she is doing right now unless there is time to change. The capacity that nature has to regenerate is extraordinary, extremely powerful and in some cases surprisingly fast. But we have to listen. The Earth is telling us that the moment is now. Change is now."

Mother Nature can regenerate herself, and we humans can regenerate our societal systems, yet, we have not mobilized the global mass movement needed to transform the structures that maintain the status quo. If the current institutions are created and maintained by the patriarchy, leadership must come to the fore with a new movement based on the life-giving energy of the feminine and empowerment of women.

Embodying the Sophia Warrior

We stand today on the shoulders of courageous people who have come before us seeking to expand women's rights and influence of the Divine Feminine. We are guided by the Indigenous people of the planet who are deeply rooted in the natural world and in the interconnection of all life and the divine inspiration that flows to honor the spirits present in all creation. What will it take to have a movement be large and strong enough to solve our current crisis?

It is time for a powerful movement to transform the patriarchy and elevate women and feminine values. A movement arises when people are moved! It is time to rise in service of wisdom, to become spiritual warriors, which we choose to call 'Sophia Warriors.' In the past, a warrior was a brave and experienced fighter—almost always male—but now the term 'spiritual warrior' has come to describe someone who is fighting *for* rather than against something, someone who is strong and dedicated, unwilling to give up. The Sophia Warrior does not fight to win, but rather to preserve life. S/he lives according to the noble warrior creed of integrity, honor, courage, compassion and mastery of the mind/ego.

Sophia Warriors come from the heart and take action out of love, the kind of love that is a well-spring for justice and social change. As Will Keepin says in his profound "Twelve Principles of Spiritual Leadership,": "The first principle is that the motivation underlying our activism for social change must be transformed from anger and despair to compassion and love."

The movement that is creating the Sophia Century is a nonviolent battle for the future. We will not save humanity out of fear for the future; we will save ourselves out of love for the human family and for this beautiful, life-giving planet. All the great social movements of our time have been led by leaders steeped in love—Gandhi, Martin Luther King, Jr., Nelson Mandela—men whose strategies were nonviolent but unrelenting. Martin Luther King, Jr. famously said, "Power without love is reckless and abusive, and love without power is sentimental and anemic." So, this is not sentimental love—this kind of love incorporates audacity, strength and bravery. It lives in the hearts of all women and men everywhere. Each of us are essential to making a movement powered by love.

We all have a role to play in creating a new future where masculine and feminine values and energies are balanced in true partnership. We cannot escape into denial, depression or hopelessness about the future. Yes, we face an uncertain future: yet what a time to be alive! Let us dare to dream and enact a world where we are empowered to have open, honest communication about our feelings and share in the work of raising families and where work in the home would be considered an essential part of the economy. Women would be paid equally with men and thrive in family-friendly work environments. Access to health care would be a basic human right, and women would have unchallenged choice over childbearing. The power structures—governmental, corporate and institutional—would proportionately represent both sexes, as well as communities of color. Our justice system would focus on healing and changing behavior and on reparation and restoration rather than punishment. Our educational system would instill a love of learning and provide equal opportunity to all. Fundamentally, we would have a society based on equality, respect and love. The Sophia Century is about wholeness not just for women but for everyone. This quote from the late author bell hooks says it well:

> "The soul of feminist politics is the commitment to ending patriarchal domination of women and men, girls and boys. Love cannot exist in any relationship that is based on domination and coercion. Males cannot love themselves in patriarchal culture if their very self-definition relies on submission to patriarchal rules. When men embrace feminist thinking and practice, which emphasizes the value of mutual growth and self-actualization in all relationships, their emotional well-being will be enhanced. A genuine feminist politics always brings us from bondage to freedom, from lovelessness to loving."

Our current times, though daunting and often overwhelming, ennoble us and give us the opportunity to live the most meaningful lives any generation has ever lived. The bird of humanity can soar only with two fully-developed wings, and soar we must if we're to survive and thrive for years to come.

CHAPTER 8
ECOLOGICAL CIVILIZATION: THE HUMAN TRANSITION FROM DOMINATION TO PARTNERSHIP

by David Korten, PhD & Riane Eisler, PhD

On June 8, 2022, David Korten and Riane Eisler presented a program— "Illuminating the Challenges"—to the annual meeting of the Evolutionary Leaders Circle and further elaborated upon the topic at The Global Oneness Summit in October of 2022, where they were joined by renowned thought leader Duane Elgin. The following exposition is a further expansion of this message for The Holomovement: Embracing Our Collective Purpose to Unite Humanity. Their pieces are presented sequentially and with each further cross-referencing the other and the Holomovement.

Illuminating the Challenges
David Korten, PhD

It is an honor and privilege to share this chapter essay with Riane Eisler, whose work—especially her framing of the human choice between domination and partnership—has had a profound impact on my own work for nearly three decades. This topic continues to become even more relevant since Riane and I first connected.

As choice-making, living beings with distinctive potential, it is now within our human means to create a world of peace, material sufficiency and spiritual abundance for all on the living Earth that birthed and nurtures us. We are failing to achieve this long held dream because our collective denial of our nature and needs as living beings is leading us down a path to self-extinction.

Science now warns that we must dramatically transform how we relate to one another and Earth, or risk unrecoverable disruption of Earth's ability to sustain life. Meanwhile, we have reached unprecedented global inequality, and institutional credibility is evaporating.

With humans gone, Earth may eventually recover and perhaps birth a new—possibly wiser, less ego-driven—species that will actualize the potential we seem intent on denying. That recovery, however, may take millions, even billions of years. We bear a deep responsibility to our descendants, our ancestors and creation to avoid this needless set back.

We are dealing with a deep, systemic failure of values, institutions, our choices and use of technology and the design of our urban-rural infrastructure. Ours is not a broken system in need of repair. We have a failed system designed to serve an imperial civilization of domination and exploitation. It is disrupting Earth's ability to sustain the regenerative processes by which our planet maintains the clean air and water, fertile soils, stable climate and much else essential to our existence and wellbeing.

A viable human future depends on replacing this failed system with the culture, institutions, technology and infrastructure of an Ecological Civilization dedicated to partnership and the wellbeing of people and the living Earth—the primary theme of Riane Eisler's work. To secure our future, we must learn to live in partnership as mutually interdependent living beings on a finite living Earth.

Our hope lies in embracing a basic insight of our early ancestors that is now affirmed by leading-edge science. South Africans call it *ubuntu*, which translates: "I am because you are." The implications are both profound and obvious: "I depend on you; we all do best when we all do well." Using modern-day tools of science, to which our ancestors had no access, we are coming to a profoundly deeper understanding of life and this philosophy.

Take our most intimate experience of life, our own body. This vessel of our consciousness and the instrument of our agency is composed of 30 to 40 trillion living cells. These cells, in turn, depend on the support of comparable trillions of microbial cells, including wondrously varied forms of bacteria, viruses and fungi. In an extraordinary demonstration of the power of partnership, each cell of our body's trillions of cells makes constant decisions essential to our body's ability to serve our consciousness.

Extrapolate outward from our individual bodies and consider the vastly larger and more complex organism that is Earth. It too, survives as a living being only for so long as its countless individual organisms self-organize in partnership as a living community to create and maintain the conditions on which planetary life depends.

As science has discovered, it did not just magically come to be. It was a long and difficult journey of mutual learning over some 3.7 billion years. During this time, life evolved from rudimentary microbes to living organisms of ever greater physical and cognitive abilities and capacity for creative partnership.

Creation continues to unfold. Life continues to learn through collaborative, bottom-up, self-organization. We, the human species, must learn to do the same. Our distinctive human ability to shape the future of life on Earth with conscious, collective intention is a defining aspect of our distinctive nature. We have yet to acquire, however, the wisdom to use this ability responsibly.

The frontiers of science are rapidly deepening our understanding of creation's extraordinary complexity and interdependence. Quantum physics tells us that relationships, not particles, are the foundation of what we experience as material reality. Using instruments of observation never before available, science is achieving similar advances in our ability to observe the inner workings of life's capacity for and dependence on partnership.

Biology is finding that intelligent life exists only in diverse communities of choice-making organisms that partner to create and maintain the conditions essential to their individual and collective existence and wellbeing. The social sciences are finding that the most equal human societies are the healthiest and that humans get their greatest satisfaction from caring for other living beings.

Planet Earth is our ultimate example of a living entity composed of interconnected communities of life. Among all the planets we know, Earth is distinctive in its achievement of this miracle. Its diverse living beings learned to self-organize to exchange nutrients, water, energy and information. Through these partnerships, they create and maintain the conditions on Earth in which all of life depends.

How does life achieve this miracle of decentralized, bottom-up, self-organization? We are far from answering this question. Yet, our survival depends on learning to partner with Earth to support, rather than disrupt, these processes.

We humans are members of the living Earth community—not its masters, conquerors or owners. Yet, rather than honor our responsibilities to the community on which we depend, we speak only of our personal rights. We divide Earth into individually managed plots owned and exploited by their owners, who are allowed to disregard their impact on the interdependent regenerative systems on which our collective existence and wellbeing depend. This dishonoring of our responsibilities to Earth's larger community of life gains authority from mainstream religion, law and economics which position us as masters of domination rather than as partners in caretaking.

In the opening pages of the Christian Bible, Genesis 1:26 sets the tone with these words: "Then God said, 'Let us make man in our image, after our likeness; and let them have dominion over the fish of the sea, and over the birds of the air, and over the cattle, and over all the earth ...'" By this reckoning, we were created to dominate and exploit Earth in whatever way might please us. We now face the ultimate consequences of that deeply misguided belief.

Similarly, much of contemporary law is focused on securing and protecting the property rights of individuals, with no limits on the amount of property a single individual can own and exploit. Economics celebrates those who profit from destroying our living Earth in the name of numbers we call "money" posted on bank ledgers. In that process of domination and exploitation, we commit the ultimate sin against creation and ourselves—destruction of Earth's capacity to sustain life. Extreme inequality dehumanizes us all. There will be no winners on a dead Earth.

An essential, first step to our survival is to confront the seriousness of our crisis and embrace the potential of our true nature and the extraordinary opportunity now at hand. Riane speaks of this in her four cornerstones of the continuum from domination to partnership: childhood, gender, economics and story/language. An Ecological Civilization will structure each of these cornerstones consistent with a partnership society:

1. *Childhood*: It truly takes a village to raise a child. Full development of the human brain requires diversity in caring relationships. Organizing society with strong families and communities to provide an optimal childhood experience will be a defining priority of a partnership society.

2. *Gender*: In the typical dominator society, men are raised to kill as hunters and warrior protectors. Women are raised to be mothers and caretakers of family, community and garden. Men dominate. Women partner. In the partnership society, deep collaboration will be the standard irrespective of gender.

3. *Economics*: Economics is the field of study to which we look for guidance in organizing to produce our means of living. The economics of a dominator society values life only for its market

price. The economics of a partnership society will value money only for its use in serving life.

4. *Story/Language*: By the defining story of a dominator society, it is our human nature to compete to dominate. By the defining story of a partnership society, it is our nature to partner in the care of one another and other living beings.

"I am because you are." We thrive together, or we expire together. Rich and poor alike—irrespective of gender or race—now have unprecedented reason to join in common cause to create an Ecological Civilization—a true civilization of peace, equality and care for one another and living Earth. This is our time to take the step from domination to partnership and bring into being the Ecological Civilization of which we and those who came before us have so long dreamed and which the Holomovement embodies.

The time is now. The choice is ours.

Meeting Our Challenge: Four Foundations for a Partnership Civilization

Riane Eisler, PhD

I have a great passion for this work of building a more just, caring, and sustainable world—a passion rooted in my experiences as a child refugee fleeing the Nazis with my parents. These traumas led me to questions many of you probably have asked: When we humans have such great capacities for consciousness, caring and creativity, why has there been so much insensitivity, cruelty and destructiveness? Is this inevitable? Or is there an alternative?

These questions eventually led to my multidisciplinary research identifying the core components of societies that support our positive human capacities and how to build these societies. It also showed, as Einstein famously said, that we cannot solve our problems with the same thinking that created them.

We can, and must, use new thinking to shift to a civilization dedicated, in David Korten's wise words, to partnership and the wellbeing of people and the living Earth. This is why I invite you to look at our world through the lens of the domination system and the partnership system—or rather, because it's always a matter of degree, the partnership-domination social scale.

Using these new categories, we can see that all the modern, progressive, social movements actually challenged the same thing: a tradition of domination. The Enlightenment challenged the so-called divinely-ordained right of kings to rule their "subjects." The abolitionist, civil rights, Black Lives Matter movements challenged the "divinely ordained" right of a "superior race" to rule "inferior ones." The feminist movement challenged the "divinely ordained" rule of men over women and children. The environmental movement challenged our once-idealized conquest and domination of nature.

However, and this is vital, these movements focused primarily on dismantling the top of the domination pyramid: politics and economics as conventionally defined. They paid little attention to four interconnected foundations or cornerstones of our social systems.

It is on the four cornerstones of childhood, gender, economics and story/language that domination systems of strongman rule and violence have kept rebuilding themselves in regression after regression, be it Eastern or Western, religious or secular, rightist or leftist. As David Korten writes, to build foundations for a system that will support human and planetary well-being, we must structure each of these cornerstones to be consistent with a partnership system rather than a domination system.

The First Cornerstone: Childhood

The first cornerstone of critical importance we will examine is *childhood*. We are not yet used to thinking this way, but neuroscience shows that children's experiences and observations, especially in their first five years, shape nothing less than the architecture of our brains, and with this, how we feel, think, and act—including how we vote.

The issue is not genes, but gene expression. And gene expression is the product of the *interaction* of our genes with our environments, which for humans are primarily our cultures or subcultures.

So, how children are raised is not only a family issue; it is a key social issue. Families do not spring up in a vacuum. Like education, religion, politics and economics, families are embedded in the larger social system—and are very different depending on the degree of orientation within the partnership-domination social scale.

Authoritarian systems recognize the integral connection between families and other social institutions, like politics and economics. These rigid domination systems reflect the strongman rule and violent values they advocate. For example, Vladimir Putin, Russia's current president, has recently reduced the penalty for family violence, making it substantially less than a crime against a stranger. Why? Because of the link between an authoritarian, male-dominated, punitive household and an authoritarian, male-dominated, violent State.

Fortunately, there is movement toward a more partnership-oriented approach to child rearing and care. For instance, the American Psychological Association condemned spanking as not only ineffective, but also psychologically and physically harmful. Yet, there is still much work to be done in how we nurture and support the cornerstone of "childhood." Studies continue to document the global prevalence of not only spanking but also of beatings, genital mutilation, child marriage, child labor, and child killings.

We cannot move to a more peaceful world if our future generation of leaders are being raised and shaped by systems of domination and discrimination. Likewise, we cannot realize a partnership society unless we change dominator gender stereotypes and male-dominated relations in both the public and private spheres.

The Second Cornerstone: Gender

This takes us to the second cornerstone: *gender*. It is a common assumption that gender roles and relations are secondary matters. In fact, they are central social issues. To begin with, ranking the male human form over the female human form is a template for equating *difference* with superiority or inferiority, dominating or being dominated, being served or serving—a model for other in-group versus out-group prejudices, be it racism, anti-Semitism, homophobia, and so-forth. This connection is clearly visible in regressive and violent regimes like Nazi Germany and Stalin's USSR. Whether this model informs a Western, secular, rightist society, a leftist one, or religious societies like the Eastern Taliban and ISIS or the would-be Western rightist-fundamentalist regime, a top priority is subordinating women along with other out-groups, such as immigrants and people of different ethnicity, tribal affiliations, religious beliefs, and/or sexual orientations.

A key element of systems of domination is also associating "real" masculinity with conquest and domination. These traits are given much more value, funding priority, and economic rewards than those stereotypically associated with femininity, such as caring, caregiving, and nonviolence.

By contrast, more partnership-oriented nations, such as Finland, Norway, Sweden and Denmark, have caring policies: universal health care, high quality accessible childcare, generous parental leave and support for a carbon-free natural environment.

Again, not coincidentally, these nations have more gender equity in *both* the family and the State. Indeed, in these nations, which regularly rank highly in the world Happiness Reports, about half of national legislatures are composed of women. As the status of women rises, so also does the value of traits and activities stereotypically associated with women, as does the number of men engaging in these essential "feminine" activities.

These nations are *not* socialist societies. They are more partnership-oriented, and hence highly value caring, compassion, and equality.

The Third Cornerstone: Economics

This partnership-oriented approach also has a very positive effect on the *economic system*, the third cornerstone. Current economic systems, both capitalist and socialist, fail to adequately value and reward the work of caring for people and nature in ways that put food on the table and a roof over people's heads. These models originated in the early industrial times of the 1700s and 1800s. But they are not only antiquated economic operating-systems; they perpetuate the distorted values of more rigid domination times.

While capitalism challenged the top-down economic control by kings and "nobles" and socialism challenged the top-down control of the bourgeoise, there is nothing in capitalist or socialist writings about care for nature, which was seen by both Adam Smith and Karl Marx as only there to be exploited. Moreover, for both these men, caring for children, the sick, and the elderly and keeping a clean and healthy home environment was to be done for free by women in male-controlled households. In fact, in Marx's time, a wife could not sue for injuries negligently inflicted on her. Only her husband could sue: for loss of his wife's services.

This devaluation of care is still reflected, and perpetuated, by our commonly used measures of economic health: Gross Domestic Product (GDP) and Gross National Product (GNP). For example, these metrics only give economic value to trees, which provide us with oxygen so we can breathe, when they are dead: logs. Similarly, they fail to include the care work performed in households, even though studies show that this work (still primarily done by women) would constitute between 30 to 50 percent of GDP/GNP.

Supporting an economics where we value money as a service to life is urgently needed. My book *The Real Wealth of Nations: Creating a Caring Economics* proposes a *caring economics of partnerism* that rewards caring for people, starting at birth, and caring for nature through both business and government policies. To support this shift, the Center for Partnership

Systems (CPS) is developing new metrics that show the enormous economic value of caring for nature and for people through "Social Wealth Indicators."[12]

The Fourth Cornerstone: Story/Language

All of which takes us to the fourth cornerstone for a more equitable, caring, and sustainable world: *story/language.* We need new stories that reflect what we now know about our past, present, and the possibilities for our future. We inherited many false stories that present domination systems as our only alternative. For example, normative stories, whether religious like original sin or secular like selfish genes, present violence and domination as normal and inevitable—despite the evidence from neuroscience to the contrary. Not only that, we are still taught false stories about our past that ignore the powerful archeological evidence and linguistic and DNA studies about human cultural evolution, showing that, for millennia, human cultures oriented to the partnership rather than domination side of the partnership-domination continuum.[13]

In addition, we need an evolving language that supports the social movement toward consciousness, caring, and creativity, starting with new social categories that no longer fragment our consciousness. Old social categories such as capitalist/socialist, right/left, religious/secular, Eastern/Western, and Northern/Southern marginalize the majority of humanity: women and children. Not only do they fail to include the whole of society; they also fail to tell us what is needed to build a more caring and sustainable future since there have been repressive, regressive, violent societies in all these categories. We urgently need the holistic social categories of the partnership system and the domination system.

Neuroscience shows that it is our nature to seek collaboration and relationships for the care of one another and our planet. In focusing on the four cornerstones of childhood, gender, economics, and story/language, as David Korten also urges, we can each play a vital part in the urgently-needed family, economic, and social transformation from domination to partnership—and build solid foundations for a more equitable, peaceful, and sustainable world. *Let's do it for ourselves, our children, and generations to come.*

SPOTLIGHT FEATURE
POLITICS OF BEING

by Thomas Legrand, PhD

The systemic crisis we are facing points to an overall obsolescence of our current model of development focused on economic growth. It is also a civilizational crisis as this model is itself embedded in a specific cultural program: the modern paradigm and its set of values: materialism, reductionism, individualism, humanism, anthropocentrism, scientism, etc.—that set us apart from one another and nature.

A New Development Paradigm

In fact, the United Nations Development Programme in its 2020 Human Development Report calls for "a wholesale shift in mindsets." This evolution is in essence spiritual, "a change of mind and heart," as the Earth Charter said at the beginning of the new millennium. This evolutionary crisis we are facing results from an imbalance between humankind's material and technological power and the relative underdevelopment of the consciousness, wisdom and ethics we need to manage this power and the increasing complexity it has brought to our world. Humanity has seen its power multiply, to the point that many scientists consider that human beings have become the dominant influence on climate and the environment, characterizing a new geological epoch called "Anthropocene." But our development path has not allowed the kind of human growth necessary to build a wiser society that makes good use of this power.

The Earth Charter proposes a new vision of progress, which can support this human evolution. It affirms that "when basic needs have been met, human development is primarily about being more, not having more." I call this new development paradigm the "Politics of Being," which acknowledges that all living beings have the right to be. It recognizes that life is a spiritual journey and aims at aligning our institutions with our true reason for being here on Earth: becoming who we are, the best and most complete version of ourselves. Because of our interbeing nature, "being" leads us to nourish the connections not only to ourselves, but also to others and nature, and fosters both human flourishing and sustainability.

The primary objective of governments should be to provide the means for each being to express its full potential, achieving its deepest healthy aspirations, while cultivating human qualities and virtues. The latter echoes the conclusion of American political economist Elinor Ostrom, who is arguably the most influential scholar at the moment in institutional analysis. In her lecture for the reception of her Nobel Prize in Economic Sciences in 2009, she summarized the most important lesson she drew from fifty years of research:

> "Designing institutions to force (or nudge) entirely self-interested individuals to achieve better outcomes has been the major goal posited by policy analysts for governments to accomplish for much of the past half century. Extensive empirical research leads me to argue that instead, a core goal

of public policy should be to facilitate the development of institutions that bring out the best in humans."

Spiritual Values as the Foundations of the Politics of Being

Cultural development is about cultivating higher values, which are at the core of our nations' projects as reflected in most national mottos such as France's "Liberty, Equality, Fraternity" or India's "Truth alone triumphs." The 1776 American Declaration of Independence also recognizes "Life, Liberty, and the pursuit of Happiness" as unalienable rights which governments are created to protect. They are the North Star(s) of our nations, which help us collectively thrive.

The seeds of the Politics of Being can be found in new fields of scientific research, as well as social change and political initiatives rooted in some of the highest values, which lie at the core of spiritual teachings. They constitute different communities, organized to promote these values as new lenses through which to look at our current challenges or new paradigms to transform our societies. These values include: the understanding of interdependence (systemic and complex thinking), life, happiness, love or empathy, peace, mindfulness, and mystery. Together with Plato's transcendentals—Truth, Goodness and Beauty—as well as freedom and abundance, these highest human values constitute the foundations of the Politics of Being.

Science can tell us how to cultivate these values at the individual and collective level, allowing us to identify an agenda for action in all sectors, with clear priorities, as well as many concrete public policies based on existing examples. All which can embody the Politics of Being and bring about the cultural evolution—as well as the human, social and environmental regeneration—so desperately needed. In closing, I offer the following core messages to support this way forward.

Ten Core Messages Within the Politics of Being

1. *We need a collective shift of consciousness, a cultural evolution of a spiritual nature, to address our current challenges.* It is already ongoing, and we are currently facing an evolutive crisis, which requires individuals and societies to look inward and transform.

2. *As a wisdom-based, science-informed approach, a Politics of Being can support this evolution.* Its main goal is to support the fulfillment of all beings, that is to say the realization of our truest and highest being. "Being" is a wiser and more adequate development objective than "having"; it applies to the whole Earth community.

3. *Cultivating our fundamental "interbeing" or relational nature is instrumental to allow us to live in harmony with one another and the Earth community.* Our spiritual nature makes us interconnected at the level of being with everything that is. Only by recognizing their interconnectedness and sustaining the whole can each part thrive.

4. *Societies progress as they increasingly honor the highest values, qualities, and ideals, such as freedom, goodness, beauty, truth, understanding, life, happiness, love, peace, etc.* These are spiritual qualities in the sense that they reflect an awakened human being or divine perfection. Science and practical initiatives shaped around these universal values can help us design a Politics of Being. Cultural development relates fundamentally to an evolution of our values, which shape our worldviews and institutions.

5. *The focus on being and the highest values provide a simple conceptual framework for a Politics of Being, which can integrate all relevant*

claims and initiatives. As such, it can help unify this vision and strengthen this movement.

6. *Our institutions should help cultivate human virtues.* They should acknowledge and facilitate the expression of our potential for goodness, cooperation, and intrinsic motivation.

7. *Concrete and actionable policy recommendations supporting this agenda already exist in many sectors.* A Politics of Being can bring them together and scale them up, articulating them in a coherent and meaningful narrative.

8. *Spiritual teachings and wisdom traditions, through dialogue among them and with science, have much to bring to inspire, help design, and implement a Politics of Being.* They are our most valuable common heritage, able to offer a profound understanding of human nature, as well as practical knowledge and tools for inner, and ultimately social, development.

9. *Each nation needs to reconnect to its own soul and wisdom to develop its version of a Politics of Being that can support its development and help it bring its unique contribution to the world.* Unity in diversity is the key to harmonious coexistence of nations in a globalized world.

10. *Healing trauma is, for individuals and societies, the gateway to being.* It is fundamental in order for new ways of being and living together to be possible, and for the whole Earth community to flourish.

Reference:

Source of Contribution: Legrand, Thomas. 2022. Politics of Being. Wisdom and Science for a New Development Paradigm. Ocean of Wisdom Press.

INTERVAL

INTERVAL

THE WHOLE IS ALL THERE IS: PART I SPOTLIGHT

by Robert Atkinson, PhD

H aving read how the Whole organizes and exerts agency over the parts, we can now take time to reflect on the divine essence of this Wholeness and look ahead to how we can integrate this knowledge to live in harmony. As an octave wave, with its interval between peaks and troughs, connecting the overall flow as one motion that fulfills its unified purpose, this is the book's turning point. With the current state of the whole, we need to be proactive in bringing this wholeness-in-motion back into balance, as we put into action all that we understand to be true about Wholeness.

This is Our Moment of Choice to Harmonize the Whole

In 2020, 43 Evolutionary Leaders, a dozen of whom are also contributors to this pathfinding anthology, laid some of the groundwork for this book with *Our Moment of Choice: Evolutionary Visions and Hope for the Future*. That award-winning book was built upon a holistic view of all parts working together in harmony. With humanity facing multiple interconnected crises, it is also true that the unfolding global shift in consciousness is harnessing our collective power to consciously choose a flourishing, life-affirming future.

In seven thematic circles, creative solutions to our global challenges were offered illustrating how there is a power to achieve the unimaginable through a common purpose. This makes it clear that we are each the co-creators of a just, peaceful and thriving world, acting in the best interests of the Whole.

A few of those unitive visions in *Our Moment of Choice* serving as a foundation and framework for *The Holomovement* include: from Barbara Marx Hubbard, "In this synergistic social convergence, we work toward cooperation through attraction that fulfills our unique potentials;" from Eben Alexander and Karen Newell, "We all seem to be connected through the binding force of pure, unconditional love;" from Claudia Welss, "Just as our hearts orchestrate greater inner coherence, our own coherence helps orchestrate coherence in the external world;" and from Deepak Chopra, "The road to wholeness begins by knowing what's at stake: a complete shift in how we relate to reality."

Our Moment of Choice and the visions and solutions of *The Holomovement* give us a comprehensive map of the terrain we need to cover to complete the transformation of consciousness underway and ensure the integration of all parts of the Whole. Realizing a unitive consciousness is where the Holomovement takes us, and how the evolution of consciousness will unite humanity.

Reflecting on How We Understand Reality in its Wholeness

The Introduction to *The Holomovement* offers an understanding of the Whole. One of the truths of the Holomovement we've seen already, in Chapter 1, is that the Whole has been observed and expressed from many different angles and traditions throughout the ages. Not only has the Nameless, the One, been broken into "10,000 pieces," but the language used to name and describe both the parts and the Whole is so imprecise that confusion and contradiction characterize all things. Yet, even this results in an intricate dance between the parts and the whole that maintain the inherent balance of the wholeness-in-motion, which is always unfolding and enfolding.

Starting off with the Whole itself, as in Chapter 2, there is no confusion that we are seeing the fundamental wholeness of all existence. Though science has taken a narrowed point of view for centuries, the latest scientific breakthroughs not only confirm Bohm's holomovement insights of nearly a half century ago but also extend those to describe a universe that exists *to* evolve, not just from simplicity to complexity, but to ever greater levels of cooperation and unity. Leading-edge science is finding that the evolution of consciousness is directed toward collaborative relationships that reflect, support and embody the unified wholeness existing all around us.

We are now witnessing the emergence of a new story, one that recognizes the whole first. A unitive narrative is needed now to underpin this emerging consciousness, frame a holistic and transformational approach, and embrace the unity in diversity that characterizes every system and sub-system within the Whole.

Evolution is happening on all levels at the same time, all parts interdependent with the whole. As shown in Chapter 3, the holomovement can be understood as the transfer of information from the implicate order to the explicate order. This means the implicate order "in-forms" the explicate order, creating complex and coherent systems at all levels of interaction. The force guiding this wholeness-in-motion, referred to as the "holotropic" attractor, keeps all things moving toward coherence and wholeness through a nonrandom, purposeful ordering of all things. This energy, known as an *elan vital, syntropy, prana,* the *etheric force* and other names, drives the evolutionary process. A grand movement taking place around the world aligns with this cosmic attractor at the heart of the laws of nature, governing all the processes in the universe.

This point is made even clearer in Chapter 4, as the way of Nature is shown to be governed by the coherence of balanced and centered systems throughout existence. All movement within this whole is interconnected and interdependent, a living, dynamic energetic flow expressing patterns that keep all things aligned. From this organic design are derived universal principles that form the framework for the regeneration and renewal of our planet. This allows us to apply holistic design principles to implement solutions that guide us toward harmonious relationships of conscious partnership with nature, each other and the Holomovement itself. By putting into action an "operating system" for humanity that mimics nature's wisdom, we can embody collective intelligence, restore the dynamic equilibrium and allow all to thrive. Aligning all we do with these patterns found in nature is foundational to a movement of wholeness.

Consciousness itself is vital as a holotropic force, but even more so is the interplay of consciousness on all levels from micro to macro, as described in Chapter 5. This interaction and flow is seen in the keyboard metaphor, as the evolution of consciousness moves naturally from the lower keys, or denser frequencies of matter, to the higher keys of mind, soul, spirit and pure consciousness. While a range of forms and functions exist within the body of the whole, the deep interaction and interplay of consciousness on all levels is what maintains the needed harmony and balance with universal consciousness. This creates a chain linking all levels of existence in one energy field of wholeness. The keyboard metaphor shows the inherent unity in diversity of the whole as well as the essential unity of science and spirituality.

The consciousness that pervades the entire energy field holds the potential for universal values, or value-driven interconnectedness that transcends gender, geography, race and age, as shown in Chapter 6. Holocratic values support the good of the whole and move the evolution of cultural consciousness toward unity. We-centered, compassionate, cooperative values, as the common denominator between the individual and the collective, are the building blocks of harmony within communities of all sizes. Consciousness determines the values we live by; the values we live by determine the degree of harmony and unity within each sub-system and within the Whole. Attending to both values and consciousness is a sure way of navigating what Bohm calls "the multi-dimensional reality of oneness." Values are the lanterns on the path of our evolutionary return to wholeness.

In Chapter 7, we see the value of understanding the wholeness of the human family in the metaphor of the bird of humanity flying with its two wings balanced, where the feminine and masculine wings are of equal strength, both fully extended and fully expressed. That is the only way humanity as a whole can soar to the heights of its collective potential. The time has come to save humanity from the threats of imbalanced values, to rebalance the entire wholeness-in-motion, to enable women and men to come into equal partnership, heal the world and usher in an age of maturity, characterized by sustainable, spiritually fulfilling, and socially just values and principles. This is not only possible, but inevitable, as the Divine Feminine and Sacred Masculine live in all of us.

This principle of equal partnership is explored further in Chapter 8, as it is what underlies a holistic, ecological civilization built upon an ever-expanding energy of Oneness that will birth a new species of human being. Partnership consciousness is critical for humanity to evolve into. In this time of necessary cooperation, it is essential to understand the very basics of the laws of nature, such as that this consciousness is what propels and directs every single one of the 30 to 40 trillion cells of the human body. The degree to which all systems within the Whole organize, partner, and cooperate to maintain the necessary conditions of planetary life is unimaginable. Just as with the wholeness-in-motion of the Holomovement itself, the story we tell is critical to shaping the systems we depend upon. A civilization-in-partnership is a unitive narrative in action.

As we now arrive to this current stage of this book, we might consider the nature of intervals and their energetic flow, as when a pendulum changes direction. This is a moment to pause and reflect on the diverse perspectives shared in the first part of this book.

In the following piece by Doug King, Dr. Kurt Johnson and Nomi Naeem, we delve deeper into the need for an integral perspective in the framework and embodiment of this unifying vision. Following their "Holomovement in an Integral Vision," is Ken Wilber's Interval piece "Waking Up, Growing Up, Opening Up, Cleaning Up and Showing Up," further explaining the critical need for clarity in *how* we grow and ascend the stages of integral development to truly participate in the Holomovement.

HOLOMOVEMENT IN AN INTEGRAL VISION

by Doug King, Kurt Johnson, PhD & Nomi Naeem, MA

A "Google" of the word "integral" yields some 1.25 billion entries; a similar "search" at Wikipedia produces over 500 categorized entries. This propensity reflects the word's literal definition—"necessary to make a whole complete; essential or fundamental."

Closer studies of these online entries concerning "integral" also identify several hundred influential global leaders, organizations, NGOs and/or networks that use the word in some "official" way as part of their branding. This obviously reflects a general realization today that, in the face of myriad global challenges, a new era of *adaptation* by our species, for better or worse, is clearly afoot —a viewpoint echoed throughout this book.

The Nature of Integral Vision

The history, or lineage, of "integral ideas" springs from multiple decades of inquiry and scholarship by what are often generally called "developmentalists" (or "structuralists") or "developmental thinkers." Popularly today, the most well known of these include the "Integral Vision" of Ken Wilber and "Spiral Dynamics" (or "Spiral Dynamics Integral") of Don Beck and Chris Cowan (both further developed by numerous contemporaries, many of whom are now also well-known in modern literature).

Academically, this vision stands on the background of diverse developmentalist scholars, a short list here (mingling both foundational scholars with others who have applied their work) would include, alphabetically: James Mark Baldwin, Erik Erikson, Michel Foucault, James Fowler, Howard Gardner, Jean Gebser, Carol Gilligan, Daniel Goleman, Clare Graves, Abigail Housen, Lawrence Kohlberg, Jane Loevinger, Abraham Maslow, John Perry, Jean Piaget and Robert Selman, among others. In turn, this literature is often also contexted with that of various other religious, academic or popular icons ranging from Sri Aurobindo and Pierre Teilhard de Chardin to Willis Harman and Barbara Marx Hubbard. From all of these spring innumerable writings in our global literature concerning the "story" or "message" of our time.

Imagining Integrally

One of the best ways to conceptualize the landscape of these myriad elements of global visioning is to think of them as a grand, cosmic, board game striving to contain, and comprehend, everything going on in the world. Regarding such a grand game board, the first thing you want to know is everything that is participating—everything that is "in play"—(hopefully) not leaving anything out. Hence, think of the basics of an integral concept of life as first pouring all the pieces in play in the world onto the board as you begin the game—so you can see "everything that's at play."

Considering the long history of integral thinking, the variety of pieces on the game board is vast, but could be suggested to include fundamental elements and activities, below as identified by integralists, about which, some further comment will follow in this needs-be-brief article. Listing these in this way is also apt to the game board metaphor since core to the definition of a board game is both "the pieces and their movement."

Elements of an Integral Vision

At play first are our distinctive First-, Second- and Third-Person experiences of reality (common to all languages) which, along with Third Person Plural, comprise what Integral calls "the *quadrants*" (more on this important basic in a moment). Next is the universality of "inner" and "outer" dimensions in all elements or experiences (inner/outer "*zones*").

Further at play are major "typologies" —chiefly like masculine/feminine, but others as well, as distinguished across sociology, psychology, etc., even astrology—("*types*") and the simultaneity of all the distinguishable kinds and varieties that comprise everything ("*lines*"). Rounding out the basics on the game board are the relation and dynamics of shorter term phenomena (short-term "*states*") and longer term phenomena (long-term "*stages*" or "*structures*").

Lastly, with this seen all at once, the observed *general patterns* are at play—thus recognizable developmental histories, patterns and emergences. Yes, it may seem complex but, remember, we are trying to be aware of everything going on the "game board of life" all at once.

A little reflection, even about any day in your own life, will show how all these elements (often called "the Integral Map") are at play. They are certainly all at play in the texts of *The Holomovement: Embracing Our Collective Purpose to Unite Humanity*.

What is the Game About?

With all this in mind, and making a big jump, some important conclusions also emerge from an integral vision. Today, thousands, if not millions, worldwide now understand life as a process which needs, ideally, to include these integral results, all fundamental to the Holomovement, and further described in the following *Interval* piece by Ken Wilber: "Waking Up" (to our divine nature; our full moral capacity); "Growing Up" (creating a world that reflects these Heart values); "Cleaning Up" (healing, reconciliation, dealing with shadow); and "Showing Up" (activism and speaking Truth to power).

Two additional contributions to this process also include "Linking Up" (creating cooperative and synergized work together) and "Lifting Up" (co-energizing and co-inspiring)—these latter two processes being added by colleagues and not Wilber himself.

Function and Fulcrum Points from Integral Vision

Let's conclude with some brief function and fulcrum points for the Holomovement that distinctly arise from integral vision. Let's return a moment to the insight of integral philosopher Ken Wilber that the intertwining of all these elements is contained, and expressed, in the structure and dynamics of *all of our human languages*. This must reflect a very important reason, and fundamental underlying construct—as will be clearly illustrated in our simple example below.

First-, Second- and Third-Person Experience

Consider all the "court drama" TV shows you've watched over the years—from *Perry Mason* to *Law and Order* (I, II, etc.) or whatever your choice might be. Thinking of all the drama elements of the plot, plus the ever-present effort by the series' character(s) to resolve "what really happened"—notice how it is always resolved.

The elements of the court drama, which always concludes the show, are consistent with the Integral Map: the "eye witnesses" and their First-Person testimony from their "direct experience *of*" what happened (to use Integral terminology)—and then, the forensic data (ballistics, DNA, etc.), the Third-Person (verified scientific "knowledge *about*"). Then, here is the kicker—it's the Second-Person (dialogue between and about) among the parties that leads the jury to actually *vote to determine what they've decided is true*! They actually vote on what is true [free will and the role of the observer!]. We often don't think of it this way, but it clearly illustrates the elements that are in play, consistent with an Integral Map of players and process.

The Lesson: Our human future will be determined by the balancing of our "direct experience *of*," our "knowledge *about*" (our two primary ways of knowing) and the results of our dialogue about what is true, both as to problems and their solutions.

Historical Inflection Points Generate Win-Win Solutions

Today's global challenges, fostering the emergence of a Holomovement, clearly mark a historic convergence or *inflection point*—in dictionaries defined as "a time of significant change in a situation; a turning point."

Such crossroads are always characterized by a peculiar confliction of universal realizations. On one hand, there is realization that the old paradigm is dismantling, lacking the coherence or interconnection to satisfy the authentic needs of all the components at play—thus, "Things aren't working. Things are falling apart."

This realization itself, however, reflects the *other* universal realization arising—recognition of the fundamental interconnectedness underpinning everything in the first place. But having not been seen or heeded—we see, "We really messed it up."

Thus, both a universal sense of potential *and* a universal sense of having fallen short simultaneously arise—and this predicament obviously calls for new solutions. In evolutionary process, this is called "opening a new adaptive zone," and in integral, an "emergent meme"—a new potential. Obvious examples abound. When the opportunity to add "flying" to how our world's animals live, flight opened to insects, dinosaurs (from which we have birds), also mammals and even fish. Humans also learned to fly, and it revolutionized how we live.

At historical inflection points, people run to where they perceive "safety." Depending on their level of consciousness (in integral, their level of "Waking Up") and behavioral development (their level of "Growing Up," etc.), they will run to either unity or division (that is, to an integral view based on interconnection, or an old paradigm view based on separation and division). This is pivotal because whereas unity can produce win-win solutions, division by nature nurtures win-lose.

The Lesson: Fortunately, reflecting biological process itself (group and multi-level natural selection toward "the good of the whole") and the integral maxim that's "it's an all-quadrant phenomenon all of the time," a hidden blessing in universally tough times is that, generally, historical inflection points are so threatening they tend to produce desires for win-win solutions. That's the good news, and it brings us to our last point from integral vision.

Whose, or Which, Solutions Will We Choose?

The difficult news is: whose? or which? solutions will we choose? Here, there are several universal elements, or variables, at play. We'll put technical terms for them in parentheses here and there (as needed), but they all illustrate why integral vision is essential to the Holomovement. Wise decision making will especially have to take into account the following variables:

1. What solution "works" in one time, place or circumstance may "not work" (or even drastically backfire) in another (the adaptive/ maladaptive maxim in evolutionary theory and various systemic "the only way fallacies" pointed out in integral vision).

2. Globally proposed solutions vying for selection will inevitably come from differing (sometimes drastically differing) worldviews, or leaders, and each will be offering *their* unique win-win solution(s) based exclusively on that, or those, worldview(s). Thus, all of these panaceas will be, by nature, incomplete. This reflects a nuanced element in integral vision—"Myth of the Given" (the mistaken notion that the "download" or inspiration given to *you* [or this or that individual or leader] is *the*, one and only, answer etc.).

Successful solutions will more probably require collective, synergetic approaches.

3. If one doesn't persevere to see the details of their vision or goal (which likely came to them as a short term "state"—inspiration, insight, epiphany, etc.) unfold and be nurtured into a more permanent "stage" or "structure(s)," their vision will likely dissipate, their goal(s) never achieved. Examples abound. The American Revolution not only involved initial revolutionary actions "on the street," but its leaders also persisted to create new structures and new norms (the American form of government, etc.—yet it still could be lost, even now!). With both "The Arab Spring" and "Occupy Wall Street," for instance, an initial sense of "victory" was won on the streets but, by whatever circumstance, no one stuck around to create new structures and norms. In those cases, and many others like them, conditions then returned to the original status quo, or something quite like it.

4. There may be an underlying element that is not seen (like "the apple rotting at the bottom of the barrel") that may only be discovered later, or not at all, when it is too late. In "hard science," this stems from what is often called the "Double-Standard Fallacy" (mistaking one thing for another), or in common parlance—re: facing world challenges—"thinking the problems are the solutions." The most common occurrence and recognition here regards elements of the status quo being so embedded one cannot distinguish the causes of problems from the symptoms. The most prominent example of these in the world today is embedded "dominance hierarchies," in dictionaries defined as "social hierarchy that arises, creating an inherent ranking system." In these challenging times, this is a discussion in itself. Assumptions concerning social hierarchy are often communicated from birth, regarding what group, gender

or other fixed identity has superiority and, thus, must dominate another. Only partnership consciousness, not domination, will serve a globally salvific Holomovement.

As we are now able to be the observers of our past, we can see the evolution of life's meaning. We are now aware of our co-creative potential that can manifest greater and deeper understanding of diversity, complexity and unity. Our moments of choice today will define the next stage of the Holomovement process. Integral pioneers like Ken Wilber propose even greater possibilities into realms previously unimaginable, as long as we are able to become intentionally aware of our growth and development into our higher stages of integral development.

INTERVAL
WAKING UP, GROWING UP, OPENING UP, CLEANING UP AND SHOWING UP

by Ken Wilber

This book has wonderfully focused on the general Wholeness—or the Holomovement—that marks the entire universe, uniting everything in existence, and driving it all toward a greater holotropic Wholeness, while emphasizing the connection of human consciousness to this unity. For example, author Ervin Laszlo states in his chapter:

> "The challenge is to connect, more exactly to reconnect, to the holotropic foundation of the world. This reconnection is feasible, and it is important: it changes us, and it changes the world around us... This is the crucial question of our time. We approach it by reviewing holotropic developments in the contemporary world and asking, how can we become consciously holotropic ourselves?"

Another states, "Collective purpose directed toward the good of the whole may be the most critical need of our time. Shared purpose is what makes the Holomovement the Holomovement." Of course, a shared purpose means a shared consciousness or awareness.

So, this becoming aware of the Wholeness or Holomovement of our universe seems especially important. But what hasn't been much dealt with in these early chapters is exactly how do human beings become aware of this Holomovement? How can they share consciousness of it? After all, it doesn't do much good to have a universe run by a Holomovement if few people are even aware of it.

What is being overlooked is that human beings grow and develop, and that growth and development has very carefully been looked at and investigated. What researchers have found is that our growth and development—in cognition, in emotions, in aesthetics, in sociality, in spirituality and up to a dozen overall areas—all grow and evolve through around a dozen stages. Not surprisingly, each of these stages get larger and more complex and, most importantly, more whole—they all follow a type of Holomovement. But this Holomovement cannot be seen from the lower stages. In fact, it takes several higher stages before this overall Wholeness can even be seen or understood. So simply talking about the Holomovement as it applies to the universe will do no good if we haven't grown enough to even be able to be aware of it. You can't talk about the "collective purpose" of humanity if well over half of the people can't see the purpose in the first place.

That's the area that I want to cover in this chapter. Researchers have studied these stages of growth and evolution in considerable detail and have discovered that each of the areas in a human consciousness goes through around 12 levels or stages of awareness; however, only at the upper fifth, or so, of them can anything like a Holomovement even be seen or conceived.

I want to briefly go through each of these areas of growth carefully to show what is involved in being able to think fully and perceive anything like a real Wholeness or Holomovement or Holotropic drive. In this understanding, we can successfully transmit ideas about a genuine Holomovement, including our collective purpose toward bringing that awareness into being, with a large number of people.

Let me start by mentioning that I divide the overall area that has been found to contain growth and evolution in human beings. These are the levels or stages that have been found to move in the direction of a Holomovement. I call them: Waking Up, Growing Up, Opening Up, Cleaning Up and Showing Up. I will take them one at a time.

Waking Up

"Waking Up" is fairly well known. Other terms for it are: Enlightenment, Awakening, Transformation, Satori, Fana, Spiritual Experience and so on. Namely, it's where a person has an experience of Waking Up to a totally holistic universe, where self and other, finite and infinite, whole and part, are seen to be completely and fully one. Or we could say that all opposites are seen to be nothing but two different perspectives of the same underlying reality. The Christian mystics call it the *coincidentia oppositorum*—the unity of opposites. This is quite obviously an experience of a very Whole, Holographic, Holomovement Universe.

Now, this experience of Wholeness might seem to be the total Wholeness of the entire universe. However, if we do indeed count consciousness, there turns out to be several different areas of Wholeness, counting all the ones that grow and develop through around 12 stages.

For instance, imagine it were 2,000 years ago and a Hindu was meditating and walking through the forest. He's aware of the sun, earth and trees in the forest, but after having a big satori, he would no longer be aware of the sun; he would be one with the sun. He would no longer be aware of the earth; he would be the earth. He would no longer see all the trees in the woods; he would be all the trees in the woods. That's certainly a profound experience of Wholeness, but notice that he would still think that the sun goes around the Earth and that the Earth was flat, and he wouldn't learn anything about the atoms, molecules and cells found in all of the trees. He has experienced Wholeness, but not a full and true Wholeness; it's not a total Holomovement. For that, he still needs to grow—including in cognitive and mathematical development, and he'd have to invent a telescope and study the skies very carefully, and so on. This area is particularly referred to as cognitive development, and he has around another six or seven stages to go before he could see the real and accurate Holomovement of the planets.

Growing Up

In that regard, an extremely important growth and development all human beings have to go through is what we call "Growing Up." I particularly want to spend some time on this, because it will show how in order to be able to see the real Wholeness or real Holomovement, several stages have to be traversed. Further, every single human being goes through all of these various stages.

There are several different ways to view these stages of growth and development. One of the best known ways is that described by Jean Gebser, who named these with the terms: the archaic stage (generally ages 1-2), the magic stage (usually ages 2-6), the mythic stage (generally ages 7-12), the rational modern stage (usually adolescence, or ages 12-20), the pluralistic postmodern stage (generally an adult stage, around ages 21-30) and finally the integral stage (which is the highest stage to emerge thus far in evolution, usually a highly developed adult stage, usually beginning around at least age 30).

This integral stage is particularly important because, as its name implies, it integrates or unites all of the previous stages. It provides a very sophisticated integration of all of our human potentials, as well as providing us a real introduction to Wholes or ability to have an understanding of the Holomovement. But notice how many stages that overall process involves, and notice the extra Wholeness that each stage creates—when you do so, you will see a Holomovement running through each of them.

This domain of Growing Up is so important, largely because it is almost totally unknown to even exist by the vast majority of the population. Most people have no idea that they go through more than a half-dozen stages in their own development, including cognitive intelligence, emotional intelligence, moral intelligence, spiritual intelligence, aesthetic intelligence, social or interpersonal intelligence and self or intrapersonal intelligence, among several others. The important point is that all of these lines of development grow through the same major levels or stages of development: archaic, magic, mythic, rational, pluralistic, and integral.

Thus, in the process of Growing Up, we have different lines (multiple intelligences) with the same levels (same stages that they all go through). The problem is most people have no idea they are moving and growing through these various levels of development. Thus, they aren't intentional about Growing Up—cognitively, emotionally, morally, socially, spiritually, or in any of the dozen or so different ways (or multiple intelligences) in which they can grow and develop in this lifetime.

This especially includes the higher levels of development, where the Holomovement can actually be perceived and understood. Most people will naturally grow and develop at least through the mythic stage of development, but since they are unaware of their Growing Up in general, they won't realize the higher stages of Growing Up available to them—including the rational, pluralistic and integral stages of development; thus, they won't tend to develop through those higher stages.

This is why Growing Up is one of the most important domains to draw our attention. We saw that these levels include, in developmental order, the archaic stage, which is the earliest level to exist and includes all the animalistic and instinctual sub levels of development. These are the levels Maslow called the "physiological needs" and Piaget called "sensorimotor"—the needs and drives for food, water, shelter, sex and so on. These are the levels of earliest development, starting in the womb and lasting through the first year or so of an infant's life.

At this early stage, the organism is not differentiated from its environment, so it can't tell, for example, where its body stops and the chair begins. It can't tell the difference between its mind and its body. Thus, it thinks that to alter the word or symbol representing an external object is to automatically and magically alter the thing itself. This "word magic" is the belief that to change a word will magically change the thing that the word represents. Remnants of this stage can remain into adulthood with superstitions and religious magic beliefs. Because the mind and the surrounding world (or the subject and object) are not yet differentiated from each other, the belief is that to change one will magically change the other—hence, magic!

This magical stage generally lasts through the first few years of life, at which point the subjective mind and the objective world will begin to differentiate and separate from each other. By the third year of life, this differentiation is largely completed. However, magical beliefs don't fully disappear at that point, but rather they are shifted to a whole host of supernatural beings—various gods, goddesses and elemental nature spirits.

Thus, there begins to emerge around age 3 or 4, and certainly by age 6 or 7, the so-called "mythic stage" of development, what Piaget called the "concrete operational stage" of development. The mind has effectively differentiated itself from the objective or concrete world. Thus, there will emerge simple arithmetic—addition, subtraction, multiplication and so on, which is the mind consciously operating on the world.

What is happening with this mythic stage is that "magic" has disappeared from the mind (because the mind has differentiated from the world), moving into all of the supernatural beings that emerge with this mythic stage. Thus, although I can no longer perform magic on the world, these supernatural beings have the ability and, if I approach them appropriately and correctly, will perform magical acts on my behalf. The mythic stage emerges and replaces the magic stage in Growing Up.

Notice how important these stages of development are in being aware or even able to conceive of any real Holomovement. The magic stage has nothing to do with a full Holomovement, and somebody at this stage of cognitive development could not even conceive of it. Nor can the next stage, the mythic stage, which tends to be very conformist. In fact, many developmental researchers, such as Jane Loevinger, actually name this mythic stage "the conformist stage" of development.

The magic stage tends to focus on first-person realities. A first-person perspective is grammatically defined as the view of the person speaking (or I, me, mine). The second-person is the view of the person being spoken to (you or thou). The third-person is the person or thing being spoken about (he, she, they, them, it, its and so on). The previous developmental stage, that of the magical, is mostly confined to first-person realities and is not focused on how society sees things. Instead, it is "me-centered," what is technically called narcissistic or egocentric or self-centered. This stage is pretty much the opposite of any awareness of a Holomovement. At this magic stage, the person cannot reliably take a second-person perspective, or the view from how another person would look at things.

A truly egocentric individual cannot clearly think what a "Holomovement" is or would consist of because it can only see its own "I." But if you wait until the child enters the next major stage of development—the mythic or concrete operational stage—the child has learned *to take the role of other*, or see through other peoples' eyes, and understands that everybody sees the world from their own view, and thus, society as a whole sees the world differently than them. This is a clear growth toward Holomovement.

Once in the mythic stage of development, the self is able to achieve second-person perspective and realizes that its surrounding world, especially the society around it, will act and think differently. It is also at this stage that major battles switch from within its organism (between instincts) to between organisms (between people). The child will generally decide that the easiest way to end these battles is to identify with what others are doing—and thus, it adopts the view of the other, or a you or thou, in a conformist stance and the uniting Wholeness of society at large.

At this stage, it is often the view of the mythic-literal religion that tends to define its particular society. Religion is a potent force in most societies because it is the major, social bonding force (a small version of the increasing Holomovement). This mythic conformist stage remains until the next major stage—that of the modern rational—comes into existence. This stage is often the launching point for mighty battles between science and religion, or secular and religious viewpoints—but set within the larger Wholeness that a greatly unified science can bring.

This rational stage tends to, in today's world, emerge and come into existence during the adolescent or teen years, which in overall human development, tended to be during the Middle Ages, or beginning around 1600 CE. This particularly involved the widespread emergence of the third-person perspective, which meant a great leap of the Holomovement. The human mind could begin to think in *universal* objective terms, generally referred to as "science"—and a science that could at least begin to think about a universal Wholeness or Holomovement. Historians have placed the beginning of the modern sciences (modern physics, modern astronomy, modern biology and so on) to around the year 1605, when Kepler and Galileo simultaneously and independently came up with the insight that "the laws of nature are to be best understood through measurement." Kepler measured the movements of the planets and came up with his laws of planetary motion; Galileo measured the movements of objects on Earth (such as, according to legend, objects falling off of the Leaning Tower of Pisa) and came up with his laws of earthly motion; and the super-genius Isaac Newton, in a real Holomovement action, brought them both together with his law of universal gravity.

This was all the result of being able to view the world in distancing, objective, universal, third-person, rational and holistic terms—a true beginning of a real Holomovement understanding. The emergence of rationality is often referred to as "formal operational cognition," because it is no longer the mind operating on just the world, but the mind operating on the mind, and thus producing objective, universal and holistic thoughts and ideas, often referred to as "scientific thinking" (and science is now taking the lead in pointing to the Holomovement).

This idea of measurement was a radically new idea, and hence evidence of a holotropic movement in action. Many philosophers had studied and categorized nature in empirical terms—such as Aristotle—but *none of them had measured* and, thus, none of them had come up with laws of nature, which was the true founding of science and the scientific method. So, with this stage, you could indeed begin to think of a Holomovement. But how it actually applied to the entire Holomovement and the entire universe wasn't very obvious, as we'll see—because higher stages of development were needed.

This scientific view had one specific problem, which kept it from a true and full Holomovement. It's very easy to measure *material* objects, but much harder to measure *mental* objects or ideas or psychological drives. Thus, virtually all of the areas that the new science focused on, as it began to measure its world, were material objects or material dimensions (physics, biology, chemistry, astronomy, geology and so on), and this gave rise to a strong mind/matter dualism, or mental ideas versus material nature, often called the "body/mind" problem.

This problem is not generally solved until the emergence of the next stage, the postmodern or pluralistic stage. Here, the mind and matter are understood as being two different dimensions of the same underlying reality (namely, a first-person or subjective view and a third-person or objective view, both understood to be merely two different views of the same underlying reality). This pluralistic view is arrived at from a fourth-person perspective, which rises above and transcends the third-person perspective of the rational stage, and at least starts to integrate the realms of mind and matter, thus moving even closer to realizing a Holomovement.

The postmodern, pluralistic view is not without its problems, however. Most severe is the result of taking the universal, systemic, objective view of rationality and dividing it into many separated, multicultural viewpoints. The main difficulty being this view has no idea how to bring all of these multiple viewpoints together into any sort of truly integral, unified or systemic world. Thus, it produces a very fragmented and dissociated worldview, which we see in most of the so-called postmodern philosophers (such as Foucault and Derrida).

This fragmented world is why the next major stage of development—the integral or systemic stage—is so important. The pluralistic or postmodern stage can be seen as the differentiating stage necessary for any higher integration, which is what the integral stage does and, thus, completes the emergence of a truly whole, complete and full Holomovement—at least in the understanding of human beings. This is the stage that is necessary to arrive at a "collective purpose" of human beings to see and bring a genuine Holomovement into widespread existence and awareness.

The integral stage is capable of looking at all of the multicultural fragments, or all of the different paradigms found around the world, and pulling them all together into genuinely integrated wholes and holistic worldviews—in other words, a real Holomovement. This is why this level is often called "cross-paradigmatic," because it takes real "paradigms" and cross-synthesizes them with other paradigms to create even greater Wholes, and to create new fields.

Opening Up, Cleaning Up, and Showing Up

Now that we have explored the stages of Growing Up, let me briefly turn now to the three additional ways necessary for us to awaken to our own Wholeness and a true conception of a real Holomovement—Opening Up, Cleaning Up, and Showing Up.

"Opening Up" refers to the nearly dozen multiple intelligences, or ways of knowing, that we humans have. If we want to know a full Holomovement, we will want to Open Up to all twelve intelligences. These include things like: cognitive intelligence, emotional intelligence, moral intelligence, aesthetic intelligence, spiritual intelligence, intrapersonal intelligence, social intelligence, values intelligence and several others.

Clearly, we need to Open Up to all of those. I mean, do we only want to see the Holomovement solely in cognitive terms and realities? Doesn't the Holomovement exist in emotions and drives, in moral realities, in beauty and aesthetics, in spiritual terms and realities (such as Waking Up)? The Holomovement, by definition, exists in the entire universe, so it must include all of those terms. Most people aren't even aware that they have these dozen or so intelligences, knowledges or awarenesses. Opening Up is crucial if we really want to see and understand the full and total Holomovement.

"Cleaning Up" refers to the area of the human psyche made famous by Sigmund Freud and his inner circle—Carl Jung, Otto Rank and Alfred Adler. In general, they discovered that the human mind can repress any number of its own capacities, knowledges, drives, emotions and virtually any other psychic ability. For every one of those capacities that are repressed, so too is the genuine capacity to see, feel or know the Holomovement. Cleaning Up these repressed areas is a necessary topic to address if we want to be fully aware of its totality.

"Showing Up" refers to being fully aware of all of the dimensions and perspectives that human beings have available to them. These dimensions and perspectives refer to the fact that humans can see things from the inside (subjective) and the outside (objective) views, as well as see them as individuals and as collectives. Putting these all together gives us four, major dimensions—the inside and the outside of the individual and the group. There is no inside without an outside and no individual without a group— anywhere in the universe.

Take, for example, a frog. It has an inside of its skin (which can be accessed by a surgeon), and it has an outside of its skin (which can be seen by pretty much anybody who looks). It exists as an individual and always as a group (there is no such thing as a single frog in nature; at the least, there are male and female frogs, and they exist as a group or collective).

So that gives us four, different dimensions or perspectives, which we call the "four quadrants" (sometimes called the Big Three, because the two outside or objective or material quadrants are often treated as one). We have the inside (or subjective) form of an individual and of a collective, and an outside (or objective) form of an individual and a collective—four quadrants:

1. *The inside of an individual*, what we call the "Upper Left" quadrant, includes thoughts, ideas, drives, emotions, and so on.

2. *The inside of a collective group*, the "Lower Left" quadrant, includes cultures, societies, worldviews and the group of individuals.

3. *The outside of an individual*, the "Upper Right" quadrant, includes quarks, atoms, molecules, complex molecules, a single-celled organism, a multicellular organism.

4. *The outside of a collective*, the "Lower Right" quadrant, includes atoms and molecules that have come together to form collective stars; complex molecules and crystals coming together to form planets; organisms coming together to form collective biospheres; great apes coming together to form families, and so on.

Clearly, the Holomovement is behind all of those realities. But they aren't always all included in our accounts. In consciousness studies, for example, about half the authorities believe consciousness is formed entirely by the brain (the Upper Right quadrant composed of the individual, objective, material realities, which the brain is), and about the other half believes consciousness is composed of mind—of the interior realities formed by the inside or subjective realities found in the mind (the Upper Left quadrant composed of the inside/subjective dimension of the individual). But clearly both of those areas or dimensions are included, and the Holomovement touches *all* of them.

We've already seen the holotropic growth of cognition from archaic to magic to mythic to rational to pluralistic to integral—a mental inside or subjective sequence if ever there was one, and it clearly forms part of consciousness. The brain, on the other hand, is an outside or objective reality—it can be fully seen by any brain surgeon (and anybody else watching). The Holomovement surely includes both.

This is why Showing Up for all four of these quadrants is so important. We don't want to see and include only first-person or only second-person or only third-person realities as we look over the full Holomovement. Yet, it is indeed what is often done, mostly because we aren't really aware of all four quadrants of reality.

Science, for one, often covers only the Upper Right quadrant—the quadrant made of material, objective, outside individuals—such as quarks, atoms, cells, multicellular individuals or individual plants and animals. Systems theory covers the Lower Right, or the collective forms of the individual in the systems Lower Right. Both of them leave out the entire Left-Hand or interior (subjective) realities, including consciousness, feelings, ideas, emotions, drives and so forth. This is why the Holomovement, which is largely a product of physics and mathematics, was first discovered in the material science Right-Hand quadrants—but then other people, seeing the importance of a Holomovement, extended it to include the entire universe, in both its scientific Right-Hand quadrants and its humanities Left-Hand quadrants, to form today's fully complete and total Holomovement, covering all quadrants. The Holomovement is indeed ever-present and all-present. So, including Showing Up is a very important part of seeing and understanding the entire and full Holomovement.

To summarize, we have seen at least five important areas that need to be included to fully understand the Holomovement:

1. *Waking Up* (or a spiritual Enlightenment, the wholeness of the entire universe). Although, as we saw, this is not enough itself to account for the total Holomovement.

2. *Growing Up* (an extremely important part of human beings that allows them to grow and develop through increasing Wholeness until they can actually see the full Wholeness of the entire Holomovement). Somebody at a magic or mythic or pluralistic stage cannot even conceive the true and full Holomovement.

3. *Opening Up* (to all of our multiple intelligences or ways of knowing so that the complete Holomovement can be seen). After all, the Holomovement is operating in the cognitive sphere, emotional and feelings sphere, moral and values sphere, truth sphere, aesthetic and beauty sphere, social sphere, and spiritual sphere, just to name a few of our multiple intelligences. In order to see the full Holomovement sphere, we would need to Open Up to all of our intelligences.

4. *Cleaning Up* (which refers to not oppressing or repressing some aspect of the brain/mind that is necessary in order to see or be aware of some aspect of the Holomovement). You need the Whole psyche in order to see the entire Holomovement.

5. *Showing Up* (which is being sure to include all of the important dimensions-perspectives available to human beings, so they all can be included when talking about or referring to the Holomovement itself). These include the four quadrants (or the Big Three), which show up in an enormous number of ways, from first-, second-, third-person pronouns, to Sir Karl Popper's three worlds, to Habermas's three verification claims for truth, to "the Good— second-person ethics and morals; the True—Right-Hand science;

and the Beautiful—Upper-Left Hand beauty in the eye (the I) of the beholder." The Holomovement has been extended to every one of these areas, so we definitely want to Show Up for all four quadrants when we speak of the Holomovement.

We want to be aware of and include these five major areas whenever we mention the Holomovement, since they are all required in order for human beings to be able to know, see and conceive the Holomovement itself. This is especially important since the Holomovement was first conceived in physics and largely explained in mathematical physical terms—which in itself includes only the Upper-Right quadrant of Showing Up, and doesn't really address anything in Growing Up, Opening Up, Cleaning Up or really even Waking Up.

Yet, it has been expanded as an idea to include all of those five areas, but often without any understanding of what those five areas actually are, or how they grow and develop and evolve over time (all following a Holomovement). So, it is my strongest conviction that all areas—Waking Up, Growing Up, Opening Up, Cleaning Up and Showing Up—should be included in any fully-baked discussion of the importance of the overall and total Holomovement as it truly appears in all areas of our life.

INTERVAL
THE WHOLE IS ALL THERE IS: PART II SPOTLIGHT

by Robert Atkinson, PhD

As we transition to Part II of the book, we can consider Ken Wilber's words as the challenge in bringing forth the reality of the Holomovement. As synchronicity would have it, the following chapters quite naturally fall into a sequence coinciding with Wilber's areas of development. In this second half of the book, our authors attempt to answer this call to action in how we evolve toward our highest purpose.

Previewing Our Actions Toward Maintaining Wholeness

Bohm identified the Holomovement as a natural, organic process of the Whole holding the parts together and the parts working in cooperation and harmony with the Whole. This wholeness-in-motion between the parts and the Whole keeps everything in balance. He called the Whole the implicate order, that field of consciousness keeping reality as One. The parts are the explicate order, the multidimensional, multileveled manifestations making up the material universe that have the responsibility of maintaining harmony and cooperation within the Whole. As a greater and greater complexity has evolved over millennia, it has become a greater challenge to maintain this balance. This is why Part II of this book is so important in showing the many ways we can support the Holomovement in maintaining its balance.

As we see in Chapter 9, there's a guiding story of the universe in which all things long for communion with other living things. This narrative is inspiring both those interested in an evolutionary view of spirituality and those in evolutionary science, who have acknowledged multilevel connections and cooperation with mutual benefit within and beyond common systems. This opens the door to worldwide cooperation and a global superorganism, as well as to humanity co-creating its own desired evolutionary future. Both science and spirituality agree that the evolving global mind has the capacity to unify around a common vision, and that this can be scaled up globally, for the good of the Whole. A modern narrative of this Whole, the Noosphere, or the Holomovement, needs to focus on the change in consciousness taking place, the integration of science and spirituality, the healing this is bringing about toward planetary cooperation, and the action being taken toward this outcome.

A most important avenue for action toward wholeness is how we learn about and relate to Gaia, our planetary home. In Chapter 10, we see how Holo-Education, the application of an understanding of the Holomovement to lifelong learning, nurtures our deep yearning to belong to the whole and inspires our natural attributes of curiosity and creativity toward the good of the whole. A system of learning built upon the whole employs a model of teaching designed to maintain a balance of the whole. In this "quickening Holism," we reflect on how the "task of education is to bring a better world into being through interrelated elements that are lodestars for transformative learning: gratitude and reciprocity, meaningful engagement with Indigenous traditions, a sense of wonder and place, reverence for life and intergenerational solidarity." Holo-education supports learning for the whole person while nurturing a unitive worldview that naturally evolves toward a unitive consciousness, which sustains wholeness.

A holistic education, built upon unifying principles, draws out our true nature and guides us toward acting in a way that benefits the whole. This is the focus of Chapter 11, how and why we can offer altruistic acts of generosity, kindness, nourishment, loving connection and support in everything we do. Altruism is a timeless, trans-species phenomenon based on the principle of "relatedness," which in both Indigenous wisdom and contemporary global consciousness communities is understood as taking in not only the entire human family but also our relationship to all life and Gaia herself. Altruism, our true nature, is a biological and spiritual imperative for manifesting our true identity. We become change agents and evolve because of our innate capacity to connect and care for each other. Altruism means not seeing any separation between the parts of the whole and living from our unitive nature. True altruism is being motivated by acts of service to both ourselves and the whole in a way that benefits all.

The principle of relatedness, upon which altruism sits, would turn punitive justice into unitive justice. In Chapter 12, moving personal stories reveal the healing of generations-long soul wounds. Healing into wholeness is accomplished by bridging diverse worlds through the adoption of universal spiritual principles, which unite the human family through the power of love. The systemic approach used to inspire action here is applying these unitive principles to build diverse communities, to create safe places for transformation toward conscious choice-making and the freedom to engage with all. This offers access to restorative justice through peace and forgiveness by transcending limited identities, joining with those having different stories, and acting in the world in ways that support and facilitate wholeness. The spotlight to this chapter adds a necessary context for fully understanding the concept of unitive justice.

Chapter 13 shows how unitive justice can be woven into a movement of movements by applying Bohm's concept of the holomovement to society.

With movements today for changing ourselves, changing our relationships and changing our systems and environments, what is most vital is how to bring them all together. The secret to harnessing them all into a Holomovement might be found in the heart of nature, where the root systems of fungi, called mycelium, connect to the roots of trees and plants. When mycelium thrive, its neighbors thrive, and the forest thrives. What's good for the part is good for the whole. Natural ecosystems evolve to support each other. Missing from humanity committing to the wellbeing of the whole seems to be common values and purpose. With unifying values, we could commit to the whole. Practicing and enacting unity is the task we have before us.

A common voice is also needed to serve the wellbeing of the whole. Chapter 14 provides just that, a way for the people of the Earth to communicate with each other. The technology already exists in the internet, a global network tying together nearly everyone on the planet. The only thing lacking, again, is the commitment to identify and live by the values that would benefit the whole. This is where the Holomovement, in the form of a citizen's movement with an Earth Voice, comes in, starting with a few key principles, to guide a collective conversation about our common future. This transformational path requires the whole of humanity coming together to make changes that will fulfill our collective potential. The spotlight to this chapter names the unitive pattern we are in the midst of, the collective voice already unfolding to benefit the whole of humanity and the planet, as the Holomovement.

On our journey returning to wholeness, we see, in Chapter 15, how this process is a dynamic of our essential reality. It is how we remember who and what we already are. This requires that we go through developmental stages of consciousness, ever evolving toward a unitive consciousness as we eventually experience a oneness with all life through a profound sense of peace and belonging. These experiences spread throughout the biofield, contributing greatly to the coherence of the whole, and we become agents of healing, far beyond what we might imagine. The hidden ways we are all interconnected become evident in the invisible connective tissue of the network of consciousness that holds the universe together. Coherence is the natural state of the Whole, from the smallest cells to the largest galaxies.

Every movement, especially the Holomovement, needs a soul, something that coordinates everything, serving as its rudder, sails and helm, all in one, and ensures its purpose is carried out effectively. In Chapter 16, purpose is seen as becoming increasingly collective, and increasing in power as it evolves. Collective purpose directed toward the good of the whole may be the most critical need of our time. Shared purpose is what makes the Holomovement the Holomovement.

We have the capacity to activate a deeper sense of purpose, step into a whole new way of living, bring about a new humanity and heal our home. Living out our inner purpose would create a new level of harmony in the whole ecosystem of the planet—and the universe. The Holomovement depends upon this, as it is the way of nature. Aligning the marvels of technology and its systems to the way of nature is critical, as well. Opportunities are unlimited for collaboration, trusted-sharing, synergizing and building abundance among and between existing and emerging networks.

As Bohm understood, there is an inherent mystery to wholeness: "I don't think we've ever captured the whole… rather, there is a quality of wholeness which is unbroken, seamless… the implicate order is ambiguous because of its potential…" This innate potential can inspire us, as it does all scientists, mystics and seekers who yearn for truth, to not only continue our search, but also, in the process, to strive to live in harmony with the unfolding mystery of the wholeness-in-motion all around us.

Avenues of action abound for living into this mystery of wholeness. These pages carry all the inspiration and tools needed to align our own personal endeavors with the harmony of the whole and keep our quest going strong. As we make our transition from an understanding of wholeness to its practical application in our everyday lives, may we remember a basic principle of the nature of reality and the Holomovement: consciousness evolves toward wholeness and unity.

PART II

Attributes of the Explicate Order—
Experience, Practice and Action
Towards Wholeness

CHAPTER 9
HEALING THE NOOSPHERE

by David Sloan Wilson, PhD & Jeff Genung

"There is almost a sensual longing for communion with others who have a large vision. The immense fulfillment of the friendship between those engaged in furthering the evolution of consciousness has a quality impossible to describe."
— Pierre Teilhard de Chardin

The term *Noosphere* was first introduced in 1922, by the French paleontologist, philosopher and Jesuit priest Pierre Teilhard de Chardin in his work *Cosmogenesis*, and later popularized by Chardin and his Russian-Ukrainian colleague and biochemist Vladimir Vernadsky. The word is derived from two Greek words that can be translated to mean *mind* and *sphere*, also relating to the atmosphere or biosphere. Teilhard envisioned the Noosphere seventy years before the birth of the internet and almost one hundred years before the emergence of Web 3.0.

His vision of the Noosphere, also referred to as the "Third Story of the Universe," after the story of the formation of the geosphere and biosphere, has largely been forgotten or ignored by science. It has, however, been kept alive in the modern day by those interested in consciousness and an evolutionary view of spirituality. In recent years, developments in evolutionary science based on cultural evolution have taken a renewed interest in Teilhard's view of the Noosphere, and his evolutionary cosmology maps closely onto the modern evolutionary concepts of Multilevel Selection (MLS). MLS theory establishes that natural selection can take place at multiple levels of a nested hierarchy, such as from genes to ecosystems in biological systems, and from individuals to global governance in human social systems. Under special circumstances, higher-level units such as a single-species society (e.g., a beehive) or a multi-species ecosystem (e.g., microbiomes) can evolve to be so cooperative that they qualify as organisms in their own right—a Major Evolutionary Transition.[14]

We consider the contemporary vision of the Noosphere as a global entity slowly coming into being, present at the beginning of human history and gradually increasing in scale. It can be sobering to consider that for most of our human history, the concept of worldwide cooperation, or a global superorganism, was beyond our species' imagination. Although highly cooperative human groups did exist, these human superorganisms were small and often in conflict with each other. Now, for the first time in human history, humanity can now be in the driver's seat of evolution. Moreover, given the nature of the existential crises we have created, we must begin to evolve consciously to ensure our very survival. Ensuring the health of the Noosphere supports the ever-evolving global mind to unify our vision and actions as a species for the good of the Whole.

To understand how to heal and protect it, it is helpful to reflect on the influences that have led to this moment of reckoning. By understanding the root causes of our dysfunction, we can better understand the antidote to our social and cultural ills.

Levels of Cooperation

Consider our origin as a species. Even though we share 99% of our genes with chimpanzees, our closest relatives, there is a night and day difference in the degree of cooperation. Naked aggression is over one hundred times more frequent in a chimpanzee community than a small human community. Cooperation usually takes the form of alliances competing against other alliances within the same community. The main context for community-wide cooperation is competition with adjacent chimpanzee communities.[15]

Small-scale human societies are different. Tyson Yunkaporta, author, researcher and member of the Apalech Clan in far north Queensland tells the story of the folk figure, Emu, in this excerpt from his book *Sand Talk: How Indigenous Thinking Can Save the World* to highlight our species' approach to naming of this bullying and aggression in our early beginnings of community dynamics.

> "Emu is a troublemaker who brings into being the most destructive idea in existence: I am greater than you; you are less than me. This is the source of all human misery. Aboriginal society was designed over thousands of years to deal with this problem. Some people are just idiots— and everyone has a bit of idiot in them from time to time, coming from some deep place inside that whispers, 'You are special. You are greater than other people and things. You are more important than everything and everyone. All things and all people exist to serve you.' This behavior needs massive checks and balances to contain the damage that it can do." (p 26-27)

If bullying and other disruptive, self-serving behaviors can't be controlled, expressing love and compassion can too easily be taken advantage by those with Emu-like behavior. This is why moral systems have a compulsory dimension (what we are expected to do, with consequences if we don't) and a voluntary dimension (what we want to do, motivated by the positive emotions). In chimpanzee society, Emu-like behaviors run rampant. In our species, we have evolved to oppose Emu-like behaviors—never entirely, but to a remarkable degree—enabling the group to function as a cooperative unit.

However, just as we pass down genes from one generation to the next, we also pass down shared stories framing a fundamental part of our cultural inheritance. Many of the challenges of our modern-day society are a result of an unhealthy story about the nature of our humanity within a narrative of separation and scarcity.

The story we are told most often of our behavior is that left unchecked, we will operate as self-interested individuals and groups to compete for resources without regard for the well-being of the resource or the interests of others sharing a common pool resource. Ungoverned competition typically depletes the resource, thus the story we call "The Tragedy of the Commons." Conventional economic wisdom held that the tragedy will always occur unless the resource can be privatized (which is not always possible) or top-down regulation is imposed.

Political scientist Elinor Ostrom, who received the Nobel Prize in Economic Science in 2009, was a researcher interested in understanding how diverse communities, with no clear contact with each other, were able to avoid the overuse and or overconsumption of resources such as pastures, forests, fisheries, and the groundwater. By studying common-pool resource groups around the world, Ostrom discovered that some were able to self-manage their resources in similar ways. In essence, she uncovered the playbook for cooperation through eight core design principles. This was the achievement that earned her the Nobel Prize.

We know how to cooperate and collaborate, but in our modern times, we have lost our way. Consider that individuals *never* lived alone throughout our entire history as a species. We have always lived within highly cooperative groups—even when those groups were warring with other groups. Within this context, we can appreciate how our cognitive processes are much more group-level phenomena than reductionistic science lets on. The concept of a group mind, which has become mainstream for the study of social insect colonies, is equally applicable for human groups. Perception, memory and decision-making all involve extensive social interactions, most taking place beneath conscious awareness. The most social of all is the human capacity for symbolic thought. Maintaining an inventory of symbols with shared meaning and transmitting the inventory across generations is an inherently cooperative process that cannot take place in isolation or among enemies. We are an ultra-cultural species because we are an ultra-cooperative species.[16]

In short, just about everything associated with Teilhard's concept of the Noosphere, which needs to be established at a global scale, *was already present at the origin of our species at a tiny scale.* This is a profound insight because scaling up something that already exists is much easier than building something from scratch.

Scaling Up Throughout Human History

Understanding our evolutionary framework as an ultra-cultural and ultra-cooperative species also requires an exploration into what evolutionary anthropologist Richard Wrangham calls the Goodness Paradox. Modern spiritual narratives are often uncomfortable with the fact that the same groups that successfully suppress fear-based behaviors among their members often collectively act like Emus toward other groups. Between-group competition need not take the form of violent conflict, but often it does, and it is something to acknowledge and understand within our own narratives if they are to be scientifically and spiritually balanced.

Evolutionary historian Peter Turchin writes about how between-group competition acts as a crucible for the cultural evolution of within-group cooperation. Once an exceptionally cooperative society evolves, often aided by new military technology, it expands to become an empire. Then competition within the empire favors factionalism, elitism, cronyism, nepotism and corruption in all its forms, causing the empire to fall apart, like a multicellular organism succumbing to cancer. New empires usually form at the edges of old empires, seldom at its center.

This sheds new light on the period of history known as the Axial Age, which gave rise to the current major world religions.[17] In each case, the religion functioned as a kind of glue, holding societies together at a larger scale than ever before—but always in the context of competition and warfare at a still larger scale. In this fashion, multilevel cultural evolution resulted in a modern world carved into nearly 200 nation states. These nations vary along an axis from highly extractive (governed for the benefit of a few elites) to highly inclusive (governed for the benefit of all citizens). Just like the empires of old, all nations are vulnerable to fear-based behavior and disruption from within, but the more extractive they get, the less they are able to function as cooperative units in economic or military competition among nations. It's the same old story of within- and between-group selection, differing only in the scale of the interactions.

The very idea of global cooperation had to await social interactions at a global scale. The Bahá'í faith is arguably the first to embrace all nations and creeds, originating in Persia (now Iran) in the mid-1800s. The first war to be called a World War started in 1914 and was followed by the first attempt to create a world-scale governing body, the League of Nations, in 1918.

We think that it is very important for a modern narrative of the Noosphere to follow along the lines that we have briefly described here. Not only is this narrative true to the best of our current scientific knowledge, but it is full of practical information on how to ascend to the final rung of cooperation at a global scale.

There is a growing sense that humanity is on the verge of entering a new octave, what scientists refer to as a major evolutionary transition and mystics sometimes refer to as a second Axial Age. An indication of a shift in consciousness includes signs of a growing interest in cooperation between groups, communities, networks and ecosystems. Fortunately, we are beginning to see a change in consciousness with the emergence of new sciences in fields such as physics and evolution, new technologies and new cultural movements such as the Holomovement. These are the positive signs that the foundational sub-structure of the Noosphere is healing in its movement toward wide-scale cooperation. It is to this practical objective that we now turn.

Consciously Evolving a World that Works for All

For cooperation and positive change to scale globally, it will require tools, practices and frameworks that foster change both locally and globally. Our own endeavors at Prosocial World (PW)[18] are our attempt to work toward a global Noosphere. Conscious evolution is possible scientifically and necessary existentially. However, for the Noosphere to become a conscious superorganism, it will require catalytic agents to give birth to this rapid, positive, multilevel and contemplative cultural change.

Positive cultural change can happen quickly when the right kind of agent is introduced. The critical nature of the environmental crisis can serve as such an agent. Cultural change occurs whether we want it to or not, but if undirected, can result in more problems than solutions. To quote the great New York Yankees baseball coach Yogi Berra; "If you don't know where you are going, you'll end up some place else." Conscious evolution of the Noosphere and the Holomovement aligns the positive forces of change with prosocial aims and behaviors. It is also important to understand the importance of a multilevel approach to this movement.

For the Noosphere to be truly conscious, the movement must be global and include the welfare of the whole Earth and all living beings. It must also be local and include the welfare of individuals working in groups, interconnecting with communities, organizations and governments, ultimately scaling up to networks working consciously with other networks globally. This means that the birth of humanity as a conscious superorganism includes the whole system AND the whole person, individually and collectively. We each meet the mystery of this inner or contemplative life in unique ways that correspond with and often influence our outer experience. If this is true for the individual, it is also true for humanity as a collective. Finally, for evolution to be conscious, it must be *culturally* conscious. This means becoming conscious of the stories that we are telling about ourselves. It means becoming deeply intentional and mindful of the cultural inheritance systems that we are passing on to future generations.

To consciously evolve a world that works for all might seem too ambitious for any individual or organization to play a meaningful role. On the contrary, there is a strong "bottom up" component that requires the participation of individuals and all organizations in their current forms. Thus, no matter what our current situation and capacity, we can play a meaningful role in the following ways. To make this point as strongly as possible, we will use the pronoun "you," as if we are engaging you, the reader, in a personal conversation.

Making the Whole Earth Your Primary Social Identity

If you were asked to introduce yourself, you might list a number of social identities: You are a male or female or have a non-binary sexual identity. You might be a husband, wife, partner or parent. You have an ethnicity and might belong to a religion. You will have a national identity and perhaps affiliate with a given political party. Each identity establishes expectations—for both yourself and others—about how you are likely to behave. The whole point of introducing ourselves to each other is so that we can start behaving appropriately toward each other.

Imagine asking someone to introduce themselves and receiving this reply: "I am first and foremost a human being and citizen of the Earth. All my other identities are in the service of my primary identity." This is what Multilevel Selection theory calls us to say. Why? Because every lower-level identity is likely to be disruptive at higher levels unless coordinated with the higher-level common good in mind. As we have learned from our shadow sides of our early beginnings as a cooperative species, self-preservation easily becomes self-dealing. Helping family and friends easily becomes nepotism and cronyism. Growing strong economies easily becomes social inequality and over-heating the Earth.

The only solution to this problem is to organize all lower-level activities with the welfare of the highest-level unit—the whole Earth—into our entire being. This approach provides support and greater clarity on how your whole-Earth identity needs to be coordinated with your other identities.

Meaningful and Appropriately Structured Groups

Perhaps the most revolutionary import of Multilevel Selection theory is to identify, not the individual person, but the cooperative (and typically small) group as the fundamental unit of human social life. These were the only groups at the beginning of human evolution and remain the "cells" of modern large-scale societies.

The individualism that has dominated since the mid-20th century, and especially since the 1970s, has done great damage to the cellular fabric of modern life. The sociologist Robert Putnam identified this trend in his classic book *Bowling Alone: The Collapse and Revival of American Community*. You can help to reverse this trend by helping to restore cooperative group-level activities in all aspects of your life. However, what is critical in this community restoration is the creation of appropriately structured groups.

The Emu problem exists at all scales. Seen through the lens of this context of cooperative groups as foundational, we can return to Ostrom's 8 principles for cooperation ("Table 1: Generalizing Elinor Ostrom's core design principles for the efficacy of groups").

Ostrom's Principle	Generalized Version	Function
1. Clearly defined boundaries	1. Shared identity and purpose	Defines group
2. Proportional equivalence of benefits and costs	2. Equitable distribution of costs and benefits	Ensures effectiveness within groups by balancing individual and collective interests
3. Collective choice arrangements	3. Fair and inclusive decision-making	
4. Monitoring	4. Monitoring agreed-upon behaviors	
5. Graduated sanctions	5. Graduated responding to helpful and unhelpful behaviors	
6. Conflict resolution mechanisms	6. Fast and fair conflict resolution	
7. Minimal recognition of rights to organize	7. Authority to self-govern (according to principles 1-6)	Appropriate relations with other groups, reflecting the same CDPs
8. Polycentric governance	8. Collaborative relations with other groups	

Table 1: Generalizing Elinor Ostrom's core design principles (CDPs) for the efficacy of groups

These guidelines should apply to just about any group with a common purpose, not just groups attempting to manage common pool resources. This "design principles" approach provides a powerful tool for improving the efficacy of existing groups and creating new groups. You can begin implementing the generalized version of Ostrom's Eight Core Design Principles in the groups of your life right away. They are as follows:

1. Shared identity and purpose
2. Equitable distribution of contributions and benefits
3. Fair and inclusive decision-making
4. Monitoring of agreed behaviors; transparency
5. Graduated responding to helpful and unhelpful behavior
6. Fast and fair conflict resolution
7. Authority to self-govern (according to principles 1-6)
8. Collaborative relations with other groups (using principles 1-7)

Think about all the groups in your life: Your family, neighborhood, school, church, business, recreational groups and passion projects. Think about meaningful groups that do not yet exist. Strengthening your existing groups and bringing new groups into existence will produce a double benefit. First, you will thrive as an individual by living in an optimal social environment. Second, your groups will be far more efficacious at getting things done than you can be on your own.

From Mindfulness to Conscious Evolution

If you are like most people, you have lofty aspirations that you find difficult to achieve, such as getting more exercise, becoming a more loving and supportive partner or reducing your carbon footprint. Groups also have aspirations—mission and vision statements and strategic plans—that are easier said than achieved.

One reason for this difficulty is not because we lack flexibility, but because we are flexibly pulled in other directions. We want to get more exercise, but our bodies rebel against unnecessary effort. We want to become more loving and supportive, but we also want to get our way. We want to reduce our carbon footprint, but we also enjoy the comfort of our temperature-regulated homes and the convenience of our cars. We want our groups to succeed, but we also have our personal agendas. It follows that some sort of mental work is required to stop being pulled in so many different directions so that we can achieve our valued goals, either as individuals or as groups.

"Mindful" has become a key word for our own personal work in being able to hold this tension and exists in two varieties. The first is derived from spiritual traditions, such as Buddhism, and eloquently expressed by spiritual leaders such as the 14th Dalai Lama and Thich Nhat Hahn. The second is derived from psychotherapy, in which mindfulness is said to be a "third wave" that builds upon behavioral and cognitive therapy. We have seen that while Elinor Ostrom and her core design principles became well known, first in the field of political science and then in the field of economics, they had to be generalized to appreciate their relevance for all cooperative endeavors. The same is true for the spiritual and psychotherapeutic varieties of mindfulness.

Generalization is needed to appreciate their relevance to all positive change efforts, no matter what the specific context.

This generalization, which can even be called a "fourth wave," is to view mindfulness-based practices as a form of conscious evolution. This can be seen by breaking Darwinian evolution into its three basic components: selection, variation and replication. Conscious evolution requires mindfully choosing our targets of selection, orienting variation around the targets, identifying and replicating the better practices, and iterating the process—again and again and again. This can be done by individuals to a degree but even better by groups.

From Groups to Multigroup Ecosystems

We have just stressed that conscious evolution is a continuous process. The cycle of variation, selection and replication must be repeated, like the generations of biological organisms. For this reason, this work requires establishing ongoing training and practice to nurture our cooperative relationships.

In addition, the same principles needed to govern relationships within groups must also apply to relationships *among* groups. This requires working with groups-of-groups on a continuous basis. Our own work with Prosocial World is pioneering such a framework at four levels. Individuals (level 1) are members of small teams (level 2) representing organizations (level 3) that expect to work with each other (level 4). This scaling framework also would apply to networks. The more the principles become internalized, the less outside training is needed and the more the framework can expand to include other organizations. This is truly conscious, multilevel, cultural evolution in action. In one of our projects in Latin America,[19] the organizations have very different objectives. Some focus on childhood education, others on wildlife conservation, but because the basic principles have been generalized, they apply equally to all contexts, providing a common language. No matter what their specific objective, everyone is working to become more cooperative and more adaptable at multiple scales. Once this generality is appreciated, the differences among organizations become strengths as everyone seeks how to help the others.

This multilevel and multi-context framework highlights the importance of multiple social identities. Part of the genius of our species is the ability to function as members of many different groups simultaneously. For our hunter-gatherer ancestors, there were hunting groups, gathering groups, kinship groups, warfare groups and different scales of tribal associations. Today, we have our families, neighborhoods, schools, businesses, religions and multiple levels of government. Amazingly, most people are able to recognize the appropriate social context at any particular moment and behave according to the norms of that context. This ability is part of our genetic heritage as a species, elaborated in diverse ways by our cultural heritages.

It follows that when it comes to conscious evolution, all of these identities remain important. It is not a matter of being only a citizen of the Earth or only a member of a small group. All of your current identities are the starting point for future conscious cultural evolution. Many of them deserve to remain strong, as long as they are coordinated with the global good in mind.

The Technology Dimension

An organism cannot exist without a communication system. Electronic communication appeared very early in the history of life—even before the evolution of multicellular organisms. Single cells and bacterial slime molds make use of electronic signaling as well![20] Today, we can speak to someone on the other side of the world, and are now realizing the capacity our worldwide electronic communication has to either support the evolution of our global brain or lead to a global war of all against all.

A key insight is *online interactions are no different from offline interactions in their need for appropriate structure.* When we survey the best and the worst on the Internet, we discover the presence and absence of Ostrom's core design principles. On the positive side, we can confidently buy things, climb into the cars of, and stay in the homes of total strangers thanks to automated systems that reward good behavior and punish deviant behavior. On the negative side, when a tech giant is designed mostly to make money for itself through advertising, the results can be catastrophic for the world as a whole.[21] This means that everything we have already said in this chapter goes for the online world. If a digital platform is not designed for the common good, it will almost certainly undermine the common good.

Integrating Evolutionary Science and Spirituality as a Way Forward

In the minds of many people, the more scientific and technological something becomes, the less spiritual and artistic it appears to be—as if the heart and the head can never become fully integrated. However, we see Science, Technology, Spirituality and the Arts as mutually reinforcing each other.

Revered spiritual leader Brother Wayne Teasdale coined the word "Interspiritual" to capture the synergy of different religious and spiritual traditions coming together. He was especially interested in the contemplative dimension of world religions and the essence of what these diverse religious traditions share in common. Through his experience of time spent in diverse spiritual communities, collaborating with religious leaders, researching and teaching world religions, he discovered an underlying framework that spiritual traditions share in common. He called these the Nine Elements of Universal Spirituality. They include:

1. Actualizing full moral and ethical capacity
2. Living in solidarity with the cosmos and all living beings
3. Cultivating a life of deep nonviolence
4. Living in humility and gratitude
5. Embracing a regular spiritual practice
6. Cultivating mature self-knowledge
7. Living a life of simplicity

8. Being of selfless service and compassionate action

9. Empowering the prophetic voice for justice, compassion and world transformation

Teasdale's interspiritual framework can be seen as complementary to Ostrom's core design principles. The story of the Noosphere cannot be just a scientific story. Human cultures have always been organized and transmitted through storytelling, dance, music and visual enhancements. The Arts will serve as the catalyst for integrating evolutionary science with evolutionary spirituality, allowing this vision of our evolutionary potential to truly become part of the cultural DNA of our species.

We are at a critical crossroads in our shared story. What comes next will determine the future of humanity and the future of the Earth as we know it. When the Noosphere is understood as a human group that qualifies as a superorganism, then it can be seen to have arisen at the very beginning of humanity at a tiny scale, and for this scale to have expanded throughout human history. Against this background, worldwide cooperation can be seen as ascending the final rung. Not only is this an awe-inspiring cosmology, but it also leads to a practical toolkit for helping groups become more cooperative and adaptable across all contexts and scales. The stakes could not be higher; tending to the Noosphere is critical for the emergence of a conscious, compassionate superorganism.

CHAPTER 10
QUICKENING HOLISM:
THE ESSENTIAL ROLE OF EDUCATION

by Peter Blaze Corcoran, PhD

WHY DO YOU SAY
by Konai Thaman[22]

why do you say
that all good things
must come to an end
it cannot be

the wind whirls
making the palm trees sway
sometimes gracefully
sometimes painfully

the earth travels around
the sun
making it rise and fall
and rise again

the moon is the same
moving around

the earth

never stopping

the seasons form a circle

around us

and we always come back

to where we were

good things do not come

to an end

they only wait

for our return

Education and Holism

For those of you reading this book sequentially, this chapter can be a hinge—a connection between cosmic awareness and action. In Part I, authors explore the undivided wholeness of the cosmic order, the evolution of consciousness and the implications of these ideas for our spirituality and stories. Part II explores practical action and experience arising from awareness of that undivided wholeness. In the same way that the explicate and implicate order are entwined, awareness and action exist in constant interplay. By its very nature as a conspectus of life, education involves a similar interplay between awareness and action. Education, often overlooked, almost always marginalized, can and should play a central role in the conscious evolution movement linking cosmological awareness and concrete action—thereby quickening holism.

This chapter sets out elements of a philosophy and pedagogy of education as we seek "to understand reality in its wholeness" (Part I). Education would seem to be a *sine qua non* of "experience, practice and action toward wholeness" (Part II). The task of education is to bring a better world into being through interrelated elements that are lodestars for transformative learning: gratitude and reciprocity, meaningful engagement with Indigenous traditions, a sense of wonder and place, reverence for life and intergenerational solidarity. These can be applied to facing climate anxiety and despair and to the construction of hope through action. This task can create in the learner a personal dialectic between action and reflection and between the felt and known universe. Education can support an adaptability and resilience which draws energy from the life force of the world—a thriving that can lead not merely to coping with difficult circumstances, but to transformation. David Bohm's ideas illuminate such synergies which are the source of often-surprising metamorphoses, such as those brought about by transformative education based on holism.

Elements of a Philosophy of Education for the Holomovement
Gratitude, Indigeneity, Reciprocity

As far as we know, there is a universal belief among Indigenous cultures that the proper response to creation is gratitude. In spite of the devastating effects of global colonialism, many Indigenous people have successfully retained and cultivated their ancestral practices, cosmologies and philosophies such that a resurgence of them in renewed forms is possible. Through these ancient bases of wisdom—the oldest human heritage of Earth spirituality—we can continue to deeply engage with a diversity of other cultures' beliefs. These life-originating principles have great value as we seek harmony with Creation (Corcoran and Bastida-Muñoz, 2018).

As we explore the entwinement of holism and a philosophy of learning, we can look to the foundation of Indigenous spiritual ecologies to situate ourselves in the world and in the universe. As Mindahi Crescencio Bastida Muñoz has written, "More and more, it becomes evident that the recovery of harmony, peace, unity and dignity lies in our return to the sacred origins of the ancestral wisdom where human beings are an integral part of Creation and not the peak of Creation" (Bastida, 2018, par. 7). This knowledge and human reciprocity with creation can be a philosophical foundation for education for holism.

Sense of Wonder, Sense of Place

The power of wonder to evoke reverence for the mystery of our being is another grounding of education for holism. It infuses Indigenous spiritual ecologies and the lived experience of humans in other traditions throughout all time. One of the most influential works on wonder and its implications for education is Rachel Carson's classic *The Sense of Wonder* (1965). Carson asked, "Is the exploration of the natural world just a pleasant way to pass the golden hours of childhood or is there something deeper?" She answered, "I am sure there is something much deeper, something lasting and significant" (Carson, 1965, p. 88).

Louise Chawla, a researcher in significant life experiences, says, "We do not need to consciously preserve these memories; we know that we can never lose them. . . they emit energy across all the years of our life. . ." (Chawla, 1990, p.). Speaking to this relationship, education philosopher, Maxine Greene shared:

> "Landscapes… are the lived places, the perceived places that represent our ground, our origin. They evoked the sensed, invited and felt realities that enveloped us all when we were very young before we circumscribed things with our minds… things existed as presences for us, our perspectival views of what surrounded us blended, moment by moment, into unified wholeness" (Greene, personal communication, n.d.).

Now all these years later we have, in addition to our own deep knowing, considerable educational research on wonder and awe. This sense of wonder is a dynamic element of education for holism. It is an inspiration for learning and reflection.

Wonder energizes, informs and inspires us; it embeds us in the world. Hence, a closely-allied notion is a sense of place. It is attributed to poet Gary Snyder that, "Education takes place in a place." Simply put, place matters. Identity, belonging, community, meaning, stewardship and many other concepts evolve in a particular place. American essayist Wendell Berry is said to have written, "If you don't know where you are, you don't know who you are." As with wonder, there is much educational research on the importance of place.

A sense of wonder and sense of place encapsulate in tactile experience what Bohm speaks of as the comprehension of "cosmos and consciousness as a simple unbroken totality of movement" (Bohm, 1980, p. 219). This is pivotal to transformative learning in which one's worldview, abilities and aspirations realign in vibrant and effective new forms.

The Earth Charter, The Mystery of Being, Reverence for Life

In the project of developing a philosophy and pedagogy of education for the Holomovement, I valorize the deep ethical discourse underpinning the Earth Charter. Although not written explicitly for education but rather as an ethical framework for an interconnected, ecologically sustainable future, the Earth Charter (2000) reminds us that fundamental changes are needed in our values, institutions and ways of living. Pope Francis (2015) in *Laudato Si'* states, "The Earth Charter asks us to leave behind a period of self-destruction and make a new start. But we have not as yet developed a universal awareness needed to achieve this" (Paragraph 207, p.137).

The Earth Charter is a statement of ethical principles for a sustainable future. They result from a successful process of convergence on norms that are widely shared. These core values, so clearly articulated in the Earth Charter principles, give us substantive and specific guidance as we work toward universal awareness. They help us interpret our beliefs in light of the perilous and terrifying trends of our current civilizational path. They express these values as a global, civic ethic of specific rights and responsibilities. These ethics can have significant value for the kind and quality of education which will support the transition to a sustainable, just, humane and peaceful future.

In speaking of its value, Steven C. Rockefeller, Chair of the Earth Charter Drafting Committee, has written: "The Earth Charter sets forth a world-affirming spirituality rooted in reverence for the mystery of being and reverence for life that finds meaning and joy in caring relationships with all that is" (Rockefeller, 2003, p. 9). This reverence, these caring relationships are at the heart of the Earth Charter's vision of a sustainable future—and of a philosophy of education for the Holomovement. Our ideals of democracy, non-violence and peace; of social and economic justice; of ecological integrity are like stars by which we can navigate our journey. We need such a vision. I believe world-affirming spirituality is needed to live and learn as part of a larger vision, despite whatever challenges and chaos we now face.

I note a line from the Preamble, "We must realize that when basic needs have been met, human development is primarily about being more, not having more" (Earth Charter Commission, 2000). This is about being more ethically and being more spiritually. This creates an expanding sense of self. We belong to the larger universe. If we take this as a tenet of education, we can shift the learner's view from the individual to "the larger living world," as the Earth Charter calls it. In this way, we can teach universal responsibility; we can teach larger circles of identity and right relationship. Thus, in the words of this book's subtitle, we can participate in embracing our highest, collective purpose to unite humanity.

Critically, these Earth Charter concepts are rooted in Indigenous traditions, where reverence for life and the mystery of being is derived from the foundational wisdom of Indigenous ecological spiritualities. They are central to the Original Instructions. They are part of the Indigenous Life-originating Principles that can guide us as we seek harmony with creation.

We can integrate these Earth Charter principles and Indigenous Life-originating Principles as we conceptualize a holistic philosophy of education. We live within each other, not outside each other. "Everything is enfolded in everything," Bohm writes (Bohm, 1980, p. 225). Such awareness is a source of a sense of wonder and place, reverence and mystery, gratitude and reciprocity—and is at the very core of ethical action.

Transformative Construction of Hope through Action, Philosophy and Pedagogy for Climate Anxiety and Climate Collapse

We have the opportunity to be thoughtful about the kind and quality of education that can advance transformative social learning and transformative social change. First, we want to recognize that education is a necessary process in moving toward conscious evolution. Democratic, transformative education is a necessary aspect of creating a sustainable future. If we think of sustainability and resurgence as metanarratives of our time, we are called upon to reimagine our institutions to allow for transformative learning.

With Arjen Wals, I have written elsewhere with regard to higher education and its leadership roles in the shift to a sustainable future:

> … multiple ways of looking at the world can best be summarized by four transformative shifts or movements that characterize transformative learning towards a more sustainable world: *transdisciplinary shifts* (looking at sustainability issues from a range of disciplinary angles but also in ways not confined by any discipline), *transcultural shifts* (looking at issues from a range of cultural perspectives but also in ways not confined by any one culture in particular), *transgenerational shifts* (looking at issues from different time perspectives—i.e. past, present and future) and *transgeographical shifts* (looking at sustainability from a range of spatial perspectives—i.e. local, regional and

global). This shifting between perspectives along these four areas needs to be well-organized by our institutions of higher education and ultimately demands a whole system redesign of our educational system (Wals and Corcoran, 2006, p. 107).

An example of the urgency of the need for such shifts is found in the climate concern of young people. A maxim of effective education is to "go to where the learner is." Tragically, many students of all ages and many citizens of the world are in a state of extreme anxiety about climate collapse. This condition can lead to grief and disempowerment. This crisis among youth is, I believe, under-diagnosed and a serious barrier to learning and conscious evolution.

A recent unpublished 2021 study by Caroline Hickman, and others, titled "Young People's Voices on Climate Anxiety, Governmental Betrayal, and Moral Injury: A Global Phenomenon," shows how deep the crisis of climate concern among youth is. The authors wrote:

> Distress about climate change is associated with young people perceiving that they have no future, that humanity is doomed, that governments are failing to respond adequately, and with feelings of betrayal and abandonment by governments and adults. These are chronic stressors which will have significant long-lasting and incremental implications on the mental health of children and young people. The failure of government to adequately address climate change and the impact on younger generations, potentially constitutes moral injury.
>
> As educators and education policy-makers, we face a dual crisis with regard to both climate and climate anxiety. Authors of the study say, "failure of governments to prevent

harm from climate change could be argued to be a failure of ethical responsibility to care leading to moral injury."

The study, since published in *Lancet Planet Health*, includes methodology and statistical analysis of surveys of 10,000 children and young people in ten countries. Authors interpret the data to mean that "Climate anxiety and dissatisfaction with government response are widespread in children and young people in countries across the world and impact their daily functioning. A perceived failure by governments to respond to the climate crisis is associated with increased distress" (Hickman, et. al, 2021, p. 863).

I believe education can help us recognize and honor despair and unleash within us the energies that inspire sustained action. That type of action can generate hope. But how does a student find the energy and intention to act? This is something education has long been able to do by facilitating the discovery of something that one loves to do that meets the world's needs. That love of a task—be it art, or music, or community organizing or marine biology entrains the doer in a flow state synchronous with the vast "sea of energy" of which Bohm speaks. Mysterious and beautiful energies flow into us from the living world. We learn to operate in the sphere of reciprocity, a flow state similar to that facilitated by mindfulness practices and other spiritual traditions. Finding something we love to do makes us a conduit of the unbroken wholeness Bohm speaks of so eloquently. It unleashes the living energies of the world within us.

Intergenerational Solidarity, A Cosmic View—On to the Multiverse

David Orr has written that we must equip our students to do heroic things. What we also must do is equip ourselves alongside young people to do heroic things through intergenerational learning and intergenerational collaboration. Such heroism is not the heroism of an individual, but of a deep courageous coming together with others. We need to stand together in intergenerational solidarity—learning from each other, teaching each other.

Indeed, we must reach across generations to be evolutionary agents, or even cosmic agents, working to bring forth the positive future human existence that flows through us. Jean Houston says, "The future human exists in us. This new mind, new matter, is waiting to become a revelation to others" (Houston, 2021). If we believe that, then the task of education truly is to bring this future into being.

Our task is to develop a post-humanistic discourse where gratitude, indigeneity, and reciprocity; sense of wonder and sense of place; and Earth Charter ethics, the mystery of being, and reverence for life are elements of a philosophy of education. Houston reminds us that the universe is a work in progress. Who knows what possible worlds exist in a multiverse context? Even as our cosmological understanding continues to evolve, so too will our thinking in education, and it will play an essential role in the on-going quickening of holism. Indeed, as the poet Konai Thaman says, "Good things do not come to an end, they only wait for our return."

Author's Note:

I am indebted to Liz Cunningham for our discussions and her thoughtful advice on this essay. As teacher and student at College of the Atlantic, we explored a philosophy of education with human ecology as a unifying principle. Our studies included process theology and David Bohm. We reconvened after 40 years to consider the essential role of education. Bohm wrote, "People who know each other well may separate for a long time (as measured by the sequence of moments registered by a clock) and yet they are often able to 'take up where they left off' as if no time had passed. What we are proposing here is that sequences of moments that 'skip' intervening spaces are just as allowable forms of time as those that seem continuous" (Bohm,

1980, p. 268). Bohm is referring to how electrons can pass from one state in space to another while skipping intermediate states. His insights reveal possibilities that inspire us to engage every occasion with our best efforts, noting that life-affirming synergies may unfold that defy our imagination.

In this essay, I have drawn from a variety of my writings on education. I am fortunate that much of this was collaborative work with leading thinkers in the field, including Arjen Wals, Maxine Greene, Alison Sammel, Mindahi Crescencio Batista-Muñoz, Rick Clugston, Mirian Vilela, Kim Walker, David Orr and others. I have also co-authored with very talented students, including Brandon Hollingshead, Joseph Weakland, Margaret Pennock, Eric Horne, and Philip Osano. I am deeply grateful to all for their contributions.

References:

Bastida-Muñoz, Mindahi Crescencio. *Message at the African Union* [speech given regarding interfaith peace]. World Interfaith Harmony Week of United Nations, Addis Ababa, Ethiopia, 2018, Feb 2.

Bohm, D. *Wholeness and the Implicate Order*. New York: Routledge, 1980.

Carson, R. *The Sense of Wonder,* New York: Harper & Row, 1965.

Chawla, L. "Ecstatic Places (1990)." In Gieseking, J., Mangold, W., Low, S., and Saegert (Eds.) *The People, Place, and Space Reader*. pp. 279-282, New York: Routledge, 2014.

Corcoran, P. B. and Bastida-Muñoz, Mindahi Crescencio. "Indigeneity and Harmony." *The Convergence Magazine*, Issue 2, pp. 14-16, UNITY EARTH, 2018.

Corcoran, P. B. "Radical Hope, World-Affirming Spirituality, and Intergenerational Action: A Vision for 2030." In Vilela, M. and Jiménez, A.

(Eds.). *Earth Charter, Education and the Sustainable Development Goal 4.7: Research, Experiences and Reflections* (pp. 231-238). UPEACE Press, (2020).

Corcoran, P. B. "The Values of the Earth Charter in Education for Sustainable Development."*Australian Journal of Environmental Education, 18,* pp. 77-80, 2002.

Earth Charter Commission, *The Earth Charter.* 2000. http://www. earthcharterinaction.org/download/about_the_ Initiative_history_2t.pdf.

Hickman, C., Marks, E., Pihkala, P., Clayton, S., Lewandowshi, E., Mayall, E.E., Wray, B., Mellor, C. and van Susteren, L. "Climate anxiety in children and young people and their beliefs about government responses to climate change: a global survey." *Lancet Planet Health* 5(12), e863-e873. doi: 10.1016/ S2542-5196(21)00278-3. (2021).

Hickman, C., Marks, E., Pihkala, P., Clayton, S., Lewandowshi, E., Mayall, E.E., Wray, B., Mellor, C. and van Susteren, L. "Young People's Voices on Climate Anxiety, Governmental Betrayal and Moral Injury: A Global Phenomenon," Unpublished Manuscript, (2021).

Houston, J. "Jean Houston's Keynote Address: World UNITY Week 2021 Closing Celebration." [Video]. 2021, June 30. UNITY EARTH. https://www. youtube.com/watch?v=1XcN7VgaJ2s.

Pope Francis. *Laudato Si'.* 2015, May 24. Encyclical. https://www.vatican.va/ content/francesco/en/encyclicals/documents/papa-francesco_20150524_ enciclica-laudato-si.html.

Rockefeller, S. "Education, Ethics, and the Ecozoic Era." *Earth Ethics,* Fall, pp. 3-9, 2003.

Sammel, A. and Corcoran, P.B. "Challenging the Plague of Indifference: COVID-19 and Posthumanistic Education for Sustainability." In Filho, W. (Eds.). *COVID-19: Paving the Way for a More Sustainable World.* Pp. 283-291. Springer, 2021.

Thaman, K., *Songs of Love: new and selected poems.* p. 19. Mana Publications. 1999.

Wals, A. and Corcoran, P.B. "Sustainability as an Outcome of Transformative Learning," In Holmberg, J. and Samuelsson, B. (Eds.). "Drivers and Barriers for Implementing Sustainable Development in Higher Education." pp. 103-108. Program and meeting document. 2006.

HOLO-EDUCATION AND THE UNITIVE NARRATIVE

by Evolutionary Leaders Education Synergy Circle:
Wendy Ellyatt, Jude Currivan, Nina Meyerhof,
Brian Russo & Gordon Dveirin

From our moment of birth, each of us contributes our presence and voice to the grand symphony of life. The patterns that organize our mind, bodies and spirits reveal that we belong to an intelligent universe. Our natural curiosity as children and this experience of belonging makes our lives innately meaningful as we take the journey of learning who we are in relation to the whole. Retaining our curiosity about ourselves and the wider world and its essential life-long learning and growth are inherent aspects of our development and fundamental to human flourishing. We are natural learners from the time that we are born, and the evolutionary process we embody means that each one of us is intuitively drawn to those aspects of our surroundings that serve our individual development.

As humanity and our societies evolve culturally, our self-generating communication networks and feedback loops give rise to our shared systems of beliefs and values. These values are also derived from direct and non-intellectual experiences of reality, such as wonder, that are unbounded by cultural and historical context. Such experiences provide insight into the novelty of our reality and inspire our capacity to express our curiosity and creativity amidst ongoing and emergent complexity.

Scientific breakthroughs are now enabling an understanding of the unified nature of reality that converges with universal wisdom teachings into an integral understanding. It enables a new and unitive narrative to underpin and frame the holism of its emergent worldview and the need for education to recognize the learner as instrumental in evolving the next phase of culture reflective of our era.

As it says in the new unitive narrative drafted by members of the Sustainable Development Goals (SDG) Thought Leaders Synergy Circle of the Evolutionary Leaders:

> "The only narrative that will be worth thinking about in the immediate future will be the one talking about the planet and all beings on it. This new narrative will need to be grounded in widespread, unitive consciousness, which includes a felt sense of unity with all life, unity with source of being and unity with evolutionary flow."

It is important to point out that in this learning context of Holo-Education, we are using the term "narrative" in its meaning as the form, structure or pattern of an ongoing truthful story of living into the wholeness of the unified field of existence. Thus, it is not a story like any old story, but the story of humanity's return to wholeness—the enfolding or embracing of the Implicate Order. This narrative simultaneously lives within us and sets out the structure and guidelines of our way forward into ever increasing wholeness.

In these pivotal times of both existential threat and evolutionary potential, it is vital that our educational structures and the teaching and learning they imbue within us are re-imagined and transformed in alignment with this unitive perception and the experience and embodiment of the universal values and ethical principles it naturally invites and nurtures.

The Holomovement in its entirety is essentially the unitive narrative in action. As we write here, Holo-education is then its application to life-long learning, the nurturing and remembering of our deep yearning to belong, the sustenance of our natural attributes of curiosity and creativity and the empowerment of human and planetary resilience, regeneration and flourishing.

With learners as the most important participants in building the bridge into holism, the student of Holo-Education is able to apply all learning from self to the whole by understanding and experiencing the innate interconnection and interdependence of all life. Holo-education is literally for life, and through the beingness and doingness of inner and outer development, enables the discovery of personal purpose and connection with others as "I am You, and you are Me, and we are One." Thus, holo-educational structures become a scaffolding for building new models of understanding within the context of the whole.

The 'Holo' in Holo-Education, which pertains to the entire Holomovement, recognizes the fundamentally holarchic nature of reality. This recognition entails that every aspect of learning reflects the whole and that every teaching about a thing is multidimensional by nature. Holo-Education is a model for teaching and learning about how the overall aims of the Holomovement can be achieved. By educationally inspiring and empowering unity through diversity, Holo-Education focuses on supporting and synergizing all interdependent sectors of life such as inclusive co-creativity, social justice and ecological regeneration to bring about and attain a whole-systems paradigm shift.

Holo-Education based on this narrative as a central foundation for curricula, can inform and guide the way we organize teaching and learning throughout life and, therefore, plays a fundamental role in the shaping of human societies and cultures. Our habitual behaviors can therefore be altered by no longer imitating what comes before but by encouraging and nurturing young people to forge new thinking and experience the potentials of Holo-Education. This type of education connects us to our communities and tells us what is important to those around us, as we heed the call for collective intelligence as never before.

Ultimately, education is a foundational social contract that is not only a childhood preparation for an unknown and uncertain future but also sustains us throughout our lifetimes. The radical re-imagining of education is now urgently necessary to co-create a regenerative future and realign its core purpose on the organizational and nested patterns of Nature. This is our responsibility and evolutionary opportunity to heal our dis-ease of separation and be in right relation with Gaia.

Co-Creating A Holo-Education Future

The word education is derived from two Latin roots: *educare*, which means "to train or mold," and *educere*, which means "to draw or lead out." We can observe how the empirical education systems have been overly focused on the impositional training aspect of education to the detriment of a holistic approach, which draws out students' creativity and genius. As educators prepare their students to solve the greatest challenges of the 21st century and achieve their great evolutionary potential, it will be through the resurgence of holistic education interwoven with technical and skills training. This must include 'learning how to learn' that nurtures curiosity and creativity and gives the innovative edge to succeed. This head, heart and hands teaching approach is the all-encompassing ethos of Holo-Education.

In this way, people of all ages can leverage the wisdom of our ancestors with our modern innovations to initiate the next phase of conscious evolution. Our young people are the architects and navigators of the coming phases that include such transformational development on a global scale. With their potential to move us beyond the future that is currently predictable, we can educate the next generations to fully honor humanity's role as a planetary steward to regenerate our world. This is a tall task from our current paradigm. Our youth will need to be supported not only in understanding the cultural patterns of the past, but also in fully developing their inner and outer capacities and potentials as powerful agents of change and continuing their education as life-long students.

To draw out these capacities in our students, Holo-Education goes beyond the conventional goal-oriented approach currently dominant in education systems. Holo-Education can achieve its goals without having such a goal-oriented approach dominate its instructional framework, whose existing over-reliance is detrimental to cultivating curiosity and authentic learning. Extrinsic rewards, such as grades, can inhibit intrinsic motivation, limit learning and diminish creative problem-solving. This drive toward extrinsic rewards doesn't simply reduce our intellectual curiosity and our creative problem-solving skills, it also shifts the focus away from our social brain and engagement to our economical brain, causing us to act differently in everything we do.

Therefore, it is vital that our Holo-Education model assists the transition from the transactional market mode norms of the current education system driven by the "What's in it for me?" mentality. Instead, we embrace an education model based in reciprocity, driven by the "social norm mode" of "How can we help each other succeed for the good of the whole?" It is the intrinsic motivation of this model that rekindles our curiosity for knowledge and social connection to care about what we learn so that we support each other's life pursuits. This is the solution space that imbues authentic hope and empowerment in the next generation and for many generations to come.

The need for ethical and values-based education impels us to develop a more unitive and universal framework that resonates with the rise of the empowered voices of individuals and communities who are driving our rapid evolution. Thus, we move beyond an education which still maintains the individual as the centerpiece, to Holo-Education which furthers an experiential holism to include an evolved consciousness to move from the *me* to include the *we* and the *all*.

To take this deeper is to know that the next relevant educational model educates on how to tap into the unitive consciousness experience and translate it into societal actions for external global harmony, equity, justice and peace. To achieve our potential to find balance, belonging and wholeness, we must lead with our hearts, use our minds to further our understandings of how our Universe works, and then learn how to behave ethically as one family of humankind and kin with all life.

Doing so is to reimagine education in life-long, and both personal and societal, contexts underpinned and framed by the unitive narrative, nurturing ongoing open-mindedness, inclusive-heartedness and intercultural empathy. This includes definitions of success that are not confined to personal boundaries, but that encourage the optimized functioning of the system as a whole.

Such competencies may be developed in Holo-Education curricula that seek to nurture a range of skills and qualities as articulated by the Inner Development Goals (IDGs), created by the open-source initiative of the same name, which are now being explored by initiatives around the world. The core IDG elements encompass:

Being - relationship to self
Thinking – cognitive skills
Relating – caring for others and the world
Collaborating – social skills
Acting – driving change

These emphasize creativity, collaboration, flexibility and resilience, as well as recognizing the informational and technological expertise requisite as 21st century skills. Curricula can then be designed holistically, putting the health of living systems and Gaia at their center. The learner can study the emergent understanding of our sentient universe, that in its entirety, meaningfully exists and purposefully evolves as a unified entity.

The development of Holo-Education is necessarily a progressive and generational process, as extensive un-learning of the status quo of the established worldview is a precursor for the holistic perspective and whole-systems transformation necessary. Through the provision of tools and resources that support public understanding of the core principles underpinning the unitive narrative, Holo-Education guides us in the crucial transition toward a future where life-long learning is recognized as our evolutionary birthright and where education systems actively foster the understanding and experiential realization that we are biologically, emotionally and spiritually interconnected and interdependent. It shows us that progress is recognized not only as what we invent and achieve, but is, instead, a dynamic state of inner and outer being-doing that allows every one of us to optimize our understanding and abilities within the relational contexts of families, communities, nations and global societies. This includes the balanced development of self-awareness and the prosocial moral and ethical capacities that we will need for a regenerative future.

Holo-Education endorses the importance of letting go of past structures and honors the fact that each successive generation embodies new and emergent potentialities that cannot be fully predicted, as they are part of a beautiful universal mystery that is constantly unfolding. This appreciation calls for new forms of experiential learning environments and relationships that nurture human development in all its co-creative forms and promote universal peace and harmony as its most fundamental of educational aspirations. It includes the development of new forms of technology that enhance, rather than undermine, the process. Holo-Education, as the unitive narrative text states:

> "Invites us to inwardly hear the wisdom of our hearts and
> respect the complementarity of feminine and masculine

attributes. And thus, its unity expressed in diversity guides us to a wholeness of both the inner being and outer doing in our lives. It supports us in integrating our innate health and wholeness, both individually and communally and as a planetary species."

We are at a collective moment of choice, and this time has enabled initiatives such as the Holomovement and the articulation of a unitive narrative to emerge. In also inspiring and empowering the necessarily vital transformation of education, conscious educators and lifelong learners alike are invited to champion Holo-Education. This is our opportunity to further develop and synergize tools and best practices so that all of us know, experience and embody our connection to the Whole and exercise our choice to act for its greatest good.

Resources:

Craft, M. "Education for Diversity." *Education and Cultural Pluralism.* London and Philadelphia: Falmer Press, 1984.

Meyerhof, N. "Authentic Education—Inner and Outer Peace." Children of the Earth, 2016. https://www.coeworld.org/news/authentic-education-inner-and-outer-peace

Source of Synergy Foundation / Evolutionary Leaders, *Unitive Narrative,* 2022. https://www.evolutionaryleaders.net/unitivenarrative; https://sdgthoughtleaderscircle.org/unitive-new-narrative/

Johnson, K., Ulfik, R. and Winters, S.M. (Eds.). *Universal Principles and Action Steps.* New York, NY: Light on Light Publications, 2021. https://issuu.com/lightonlight.

UNESCO. *Reimagining our futures together: a new social contract for education.* 2021. https://unesdoc.unesco.org/ark:/48223/pf0000379707.

Capra, F. *The Hidden Connections: A Science for Sustainable Living.* New York: Anchor Books, 2004.

https://www.innerdevelopmentgoals.org/.

https://www.aeseducation.com/blog/what-are-21st-century-skills.

Duraiappah, A. K., Van Atteveldt, N., Buil, J. M., Singh, K., and Wu, R. *Reimaging Education: The International Science and Evidence Based Education Assessment,* UNESCO; Mahatma Gandhi Institute of Education for Peace and Sustainable Development, New Delhi, 2022. https://unesdoc.unesco.org/ark:/48223/pf0000380985?locale=en.

CHAPTER 11
THE ART OF ALTRUISM: REDEFINING OUR TRUE NATURE

by Rhiannon Catalyst & Jill Robinson

In the preceding chapters, we have explored our profound interconnected-ness as a species within our local, global and cosmic ecosystem. Now, let's dive into the science, heart and art of how and why we nurture these relationships in our everyday lives.

How these acts of generosity and reciprocity manifest will vary depending on situations and people. Like our diverse and dynamic planet, altruistic behavior is not a one-size-fits-all activity. Nor should it be. Being conscious of how we can continually evolve our understanding of altruism, we are better equipped to embody the many ways we can support, help, nourish and be present to each other and our living environment. This is a story in which we all participate, and when acting from the heart with art and intention, we have the opportunity to embody loving connection as a heroic agent of change.

The Science and History of Altruism

Scientists, philosophers, economists and theologians have hotly debated the existence of true or "pure" altruism for centuries. Darwin saw altruistic behavior as a grand paradoxical problem, a threat to the theory of evolution and survival of the fittest. If we are all in competition to pass down our genetic material, how does altruism add up in the animal kingdom, where it is clearly found among species from bees to ants and vampire bats? Evolutionary biologists like W.D. Hamilton and E.O. Wilson tried to reconcile this by observing animals acting altruistically mainly toward others in their own family tree, creating an evolutionary benefit and the probability of altruistic behavior to be passed down to future generations. The ideas of kin selection and inclusive fitness were born. In this framework, kin selection assumes we only see our immediate biological relatives as family and that the fitness of a human being is not directly connected to the fitness of "unrelated" individuals.

The wisdom of our Indigenous relatives and global consciousness communities know this to be false and the definition of "kin" tragically limited. When Western scientists defined kin selection, an idea we see reflected in the Miriam-Webster definition of "altruism," we weren't yet squarely in the Anthropocene. Our needs as a species have changed dramatically, our fate and wellness inexorably interwoven, as COVID-19 and climate change continue to teach us at a global scale. The challenges of our times have made it clearer than ever that the "hurt of one is the hurt of all." As so many others in this book have already shared, we are all the "kin" and children of Gaia, and our wellbeing is entangled in this web of life.

How our planetary family evolves depends on our extraordinary capacity to connect and care for each other and the planet, as well as how we define these relationships. E.O. Wilson later denounced kin selection as the basis of altruism and created an alternative theory stating:

"The origins of altruism and teamwork have nothing to do with kinship or the degree of relatedness between individuals. The key, is the group: Under certain circumstances, groups of cooperators can out-compete groups of non-cooperators, thereby ensuring that their genes—including the ones that predispose them to cooperation—are handed down to future generations. This so-called group selection ... is what forms the evolutionary basis for a variety of advanced social behaviors linked to altruism [and] teamwork."[23]

Wilson's conclusion offers a boost for the Holomovement's vision of unity, radical collaboration and a need for each of us to support and be supported in following a sense of purpose. It's a grand vision. In its sweeping scope, however, it's also easy to pass off as a naive dream when discussed from the perspective of our present-day resources and spectrums of privilege, inequality and intersectionality.

One of the most persistent counter arguments for instinctive, altruistic behavior is the declaration that all acts of altruism are driven by the expectation of personal gain, even if that gain is simply feeling good about the act. We know our brain's reward centers light up like fireworks when we give of ourselves. However, we propose several problems with this limiting and materialistic perspective of altruistic behavior and shared story of human behavior. It's time for a new definition and art of altruism to be championed— one that allows for conscious evolution, symbiosis and collective surviving and thriving of the species to emerge.

Toward a Truth of Human Nature and Behavior

In these changing times, we are being asked to confront deeply ingrained notions of human nature and dismissive attitudes toward instinctual acts of compassion and cooperation. Generations of scientists, philosophers and economists have tried explaining altruism through a lens of egoism.

In *Prosocial: Using Evolutionary Science to Build Productive, Equitable, and Collaborative Groups*, authors Paul Atkins and David Sloan Wilson elucidate how the story of self-interested herders bringing ruin to all came to dominate economic theory. In the famous "Tragedy of the Commons" parable, "Each man is locked into a system that compels him to increase his herd without limit—in a world that is limited."[24]—therefore concluding that people cannot be allowed to self-govern or expected to cooperate.

What if, as so many are discovering, the whole premise is flawed? What if we are not inherently competitive, and teaching competition and egoism doesn't ultimately lead to a more successful species? New economic models are reflecting this heart-opening revelation. Alternatives such as Doughnut economics champion sustainability and regenerative development over unchecked economic growth. Testing on the ground in cities such as Amsterdam has yielded powerfully encouraging data, and important new questions and ideas. We know our models, and narratives, need to change.

In 2009, Elinor Ostrom was awarded a Nobel Prize for laying out a set of core design principles enabling groups to avoid the "Tragedy of the Commons" and successfully cooperate and manage common-pool resources. Her work highlights the point that, when exploring our human nature and behavior, it's not simply a question of "Are we or are we not altruistic by nature?" In the complexity of our evolution and environments, we find altruism, much like cooperation, is a muscle that must be used.

Our true, cooperative nature is uplifted by scientific evidence of our biological beginnings and sustained by our intuitive understanding through personal experiences, spiritual practices and Indigenous wisdom. Previous chapters already have highlighted examples of our ability to collectively evolve and thrive through meaningful relationships and collaborative group interaction. However, we still have much work ahead to overturn the narrative of innate selfishness. Stories like the "Tragedy of the Commons" are deeply embedded in the psyches of many leading political, economic and social institutions (Prosocial).

Robert Frank, an economist at Cornell University, compared economics students with anthropology students and found that "after just two terms of training in the economic view of life, economics students were more likely to believe that others act selfishly and, most importantly, they were less likely to help others in situations where they had the opportunity to do so" (Prosocial). Another study of one thousand people from Britain by Common Cause revealed some extraordinary implications of the way we think about ourselves[25]. While 74 percent of participants valued "compassionate values" over "selfish values," 77 percent underestimated the degree to which others held compassionate values and overestimated the degree to which others held selfish values. The story has become a self-fulfilling prophecy.

How do we align ourselves with the altruistic nature we know within ourselves and extend this understanding outward in our relationships and communities? The cultivation and activation of empathy is arguably one of the most important avenues toward awakening a visceral sense of our interconnectedness to the whole, which in turn can serve to inspire stewardship, a sense of our responsibility and care for the planet as well as our fellow humans. Fortunately, studies have shown that empathy and compassion can also be taught, and that honing these skills (that are both innate and learned) can dramatically improve communication, connection, overall emotional intelligence and our ability to cooperate.

Understanding our true nature, innate and learned power to cooperate and collaborate toward a common good, is profoundly important to the success and survival of our species. As astronomer Carl Sagan reminds us in his book *Pale Blue Dot*: "The visions we offer our children shape the future. It matters what those visions are. Often they become self-fulfilling prophecies. Dreams are maps."

Not "Mere" Semantics

Here's the rub: the core definition of the word "altruism" stems from the Latin root "*Alteri huic*," meaning "to this other," and tells a tale reinforcing the story of separation. Altruism is defined by Merriam-Webster as an "unselfish regard for or devotion to the welfare of others" and a "behavior by an animal that is not beneficial to or may be harmful to itself but that benefits others of its species." In both of these explanations, the word "other" plays a key role, as does the inclusion of self-harm and a lack of personal benefit as necessary expressions of altruistic behavior.

What we have learned so far about our cosmic beginnings, unitive narrative, ecological blueprint and potential for supercoherence seems to contradict the very word so many of us use to bridge the material/spiritual divide. It is time to evolve our language to encompass our full potential for collaboration, connection and compassion.

Common descriptions of altruistic behavior give synonyms of self-sacrifice and self-denial. We suggest shifting this perspective to align with our understanding of our unitive nature. Positive and progressive models of altruism understand the healing power of reciprocal, symbiotic and regenerative behavior. As Ram Dass said, "True compassionate action comes out of the awareness that we are all inseparable...We are all part of the same thing, and therefore your suffering is my suffering."

By upholding these values in our collective narrative, how might we visualize our personal and planetary potential, lifted up by a shared story of collaboration and reciprocity? Learning the art of altruism within the context of "Me AND We" is critically important to create a regenerative cycle of giving. What would we experience if our service to ourselves, others and the whole also was allowed to include personal nourishment? While holding space and deep reverence for bold, inspiring acts of altruistic self-sacrifice, we humbly suggest a shift in the way we view everyday practices of altruism as imperative to the sustainability of our species.

In shifting this perspective of altruism, we can reconnect and re-unite with ourselves, one another, and the natural and cosmic world in everyday life while celebrating our birthright as unique and purposeful beings with diverse gifts. Professor of Environmental Biology and enrolled member of the Citizen Potawatomi Nation, Robin Wall Kimmerer, writes in her book *Braiding Sweetgrass: Indigenous Wisdom, Scientific Knowledge and the Teachings of Plants*: "Many indigenous peoples share the understanding that we are each endowed with a particular gift, a unique ability. Birds to sing and stars to glitter, for instance. It is understood that these gifts have a dual nature, though: a gift is also a responsibility." (Kimmerer, 2013, p. 347)

George Leonard, president emeritus of Esalen Institute and one of the leaders of the Human Potential Movement put it another way in his teachings of Integral Transformative Practice: "Don't hoard yourself." Ultimately, our individual gifts and purpose are necessary for the well-being and flourishing of self and society. Our being is interwoven within the cosmic life process, AND collective flourishing requires a soul-based nurturing of self if we are to evolve collectively as people and planet.

This is not just wishful thinking. Extensive research links our well-being and health with collaborative participation in supporting the health of our communities. The findings are vast and resounding. Increases in self-esteem, social relationships and lower mortality rates,[26] as well as reduced blood pressure and longer life span are just some of the positive indicators associated with volunteering and civic engagement. A 2013 study at Carnegie Mellon University found that older adults who volunteered for 200 or more hours per year had a 40 percent decreased risk of high blood pressure.[27] Overall improvements to mental health connected to generously giving one's time to a cause is naturally connected with finding an increased sense of purpose.

By cultivating the *art* of altruism, we embody what it means to give compassionately and generously. In Stephen Cope's *The Great Work of Your Life: A Guide for the Journey to Your True Calling*, he writes:

> "It is precisely Arjuna's offering of himself to the urgent call of the moment that will turn his gifts into world-transforming dharma. If you bring forth what is within you

it will save you. Yes. But this saving is not just for you. It is for the common good. If you bring forth what is within you, it will save the world. It will rescue the times. It will save the whole people." (Cope, 2015, p. 53)

Cope goes on to write the consequence of ignoring what is our personal calling and transformation—the result being destruction of the self and the whole people.

Howard Gruber, a psychologist, activist and historian of science wrote in "Creative Altruism, Cooperation, and World Peace"[28] that "creative altruism… expresses the highest development of the individual and at the same time depends on cooperation and understanding…[It] probably depends above all on a sense of the self expanding—expanding in our era toward world-consciousness." In his reflections of guiding principles for creative altruism, he suggests: "fulfilling our highest moral obligations requires creative work and cooperation."[29] In this artful approach to altruism, we reconnect with our birthright (and responsibility) as profoundly unique and vital cells within a divinely interwoven body of living systems.

In our proposal for evolving the definition, it is equally important to understand what is NOT altruism in this context. Like so many of our human traits, there is a razor's edge between the light and shadow side of our behavior.

Artful altruism is not an act of pity for the materially or spiritually impoverished, a "savior complex" incognito, a sense of moral superiority or "fixing" the ailments of others. Nor is it an act requiring self-denial or a loss of personal agency. These outmoded expressions of egoism masquerading as altruism can be an illusory escape hatch from deep self-reflection and self-care, often serving to reinforce the schism of separation. Entire movements and past narratives of charitable giving have unconsciously wrestled with these shadows. Many have been founded on toxic notions of altruistic behavior, often stemming from roots of settler colonialism and evangelistic religious practices that require acknowledgement, restorative justice and healing.

It's critical to acknowledge privilege and the vast economic imbalances we seek to heal when speaking of altruism, some having far more freedom to give (financially and energetically) and to focus on cultivating higher purpose while seeking core basic needs of survival. That said, giving of our purpose and heart can also BE one of our core needs for survival. The challenge is not limiting our altruistic perspective to a materialistic exchange of giving and receiving. It will be an ongoing practice in reciprocity and purpose—allowing for the values Joni Carley speaks to in her earlier chapter to guide and support our cultural evolution. In our evolving story of our collective humanity, organic participation in the sharing and receiving mirrors the finely-balanced eco-systems of our natural world.

This shift is not at all far-fetched. Today we see more grassroots organizations, like Purpose Earth, empowering grassroots change-makers with creative solutions to our global problems and supporting generationally and culturally diverse leaders transforming local communities. Our growing recognition of the richness of creative capital and wisdom present when we bring together diverse cultures, generations and disciplines further empowers the unfolding of our collective purpose and potential.

In the beautiful and healthy expression of love, altruistic behavior, however, does not mean an expectation of working for free, especially in our artistic, spiritual and non-profit communities. We still have to pay the bills and earn a living wage. Together, we must continue to financially support that which we want to see survive and thrive. By valuing creative, mission- and spirit-driven work, we create a sustainable system supporting creative expression and generosity, critical to our ongoing transformation. Sites like "Buy me a Coffee" and "Patreon" are a few examples of platforms encouraging this support via small personal donations. Just as you might buy a cup of coffee for a street performer or local poet, you could pay that same amount into a donation fund.

Artists are often the first to give in times of need, supporting our mental health and well-being, yet many times their funding is the first to be questioned. The sustainability of arts and culture, and those providing creative expression, are vital to our planet.

Finally, in redefining altruism, we must recognize the importance of self-care in supporting our larger communities. As we've increasingly come to understand, we must take into account "burnout" experienced and reported by healthcare workers, social workers, and those working as professional altruists. Taking care of ourselves is taking care of the whole, giving stamina to the important work ahead. Three recent studies independently connected lack of sleep with reduced willingness to help others. "Sleep loss leads to the withdrawal of human helping across individuals, groups, and large-scale societies."[30] Fascinating scientific data connecting self-care with increased generosity reinforces the interconnectedness of personal and planetary health.

In summary: altruism does not mean martyrdom. Sustainable and artful altruism of today can, and must, become consciously symbiotic. In all cases, our ongoing understanding of altruistic behavior within the Holomovement reflects a deeply-seeded impulse toward unitive experiences that are life-affirming, inspired by love.

Altruism as an Expression of Activism

The Holomovement is our rallying cry for cooperation and collaboration, despite the stories of scarcity and separation driving us toward competition and isolation. We can feel it when we choose to practice our transformative power of compassion (one of the most valuable altruistic gifts we have to give, and it's certainly not always easy) toward a fellow human being driven by fear at the root of those same illusory stories. It's there when we choose to give support to aid those facing the very real material limitations of a world grossly out of balance. We can recognize these moments in our daily experiences. These divine acts are rooted in how we say, "Good morning!"

and our energetic presence in a challenging meeting or while sharing lanes on a freeway.

Throughout history, there are prolific stories documenting our altruistic impulse in action. In the aftermath of Hurricane Katrina in 2005, New Orleans became a living example of the collective altruistic spirit to rebuild and regenerate. Similar accounts are shared from the aftermath of the San Francisco earthquakes of 1906 and 1989. In so many instances, it is not the predicted tribal-like division and hoarding of resources that forms a critical mass of action. What we experience instead is the natural outpouring of community spirit and compassion to cooperate and rebuild.

Embodying our place within a conscious and purposeful universe requires more than mental resonance for the vision. The challenge is embodying and trusting in our shared humanity and planetary/cosmic connection in body, heart and soul as well. For this trust to permeate within our collective psyche, it's vital to recognize our innate ability to practice and participate in the art of altruism. This is not a passive behavior. This expression of activism requires deep spiritual work and presence. We can begin again and again each moment. Anonymous financial donations and heroic acts of volunteerism are altruistic, and so too are loving fully, deep listening, and acts of compassion. Being present to our purpose and sense of belonging within an altruistic eco-system is to embody a "me AND we" vision for change.

The polarizing climate of our challenging times also begs the questions, "How are we extending our love and connection to those driven by fear and separation, those with opposing viewpoints? For those of us also privileged with financial means, how can we aid those searching for basic necessities of survival? How can we give of ourselves beyond these categories?"

Research supports the power of these daily exchanges to boost the health of people and community. Lynne McTaggart's fascinating study on altruism in healing offers insight into the power of intentional connection and altruistic presence. She writes in the prologue to her book, *The Power of*

Eight: Harnessing the Miraculous Energies of a Small Group to Heal Others, Your Life, and the World: "This story is about the miraculous power you hold inside of you to heal your own life, which gets unleashed, ironically, the moment you stop thinking about yourself."

McTaggart's message throughout her book is that "the most powerful transformational state of all is altruism." It is exciting to consider the potential power of small groups of people to heal and transform the lives of others, as well as their own, through short, focused sessions of intentional meditation.

Our daily altruistic behavior offers us a tangible glimpse of the Holomovement in motion. When we have the language to articulate these experiences, we can better attune ourselves to the miracle of our connection and context within a conscious universe. As His Holiness the 14th Dalai Lama expressed, "If we are to protect this home of ours, each of us needs to experience a vivid sense of universal altruism." We are far from answering all our questions about how altruism can be practiced most artfully—this is a collective exercise in redefining and acting on very direct, grounded levels that also speak to our highest nature.

It's time to redefine what altruism means and how we practice this ancient, intercultural, interspecies, biologically and spiritually pragmatic art form. By working together to create a new reciprocally balanced way of being, we are strengthened to give what we can from a place of joy and abundance.

Shifting our narratives, our beliefs and value systems is not only a matter of evolving forward—it's remembering what we've lost along the way. Indigenous leaders have long understood this to be true. Mindahi Bastida, of the Center for Earth Ethics, has been teaching the importance of reciprocity and gratitude for the gifts given to us from nature, with wisdom passed down through generations of his ancestors of the Otomí-Toltec nation. International Educator Patricia Anne Davis, an Indigenous elder of Choctaw-Navajo/Chahta-Dineh lineage, teaches in the Love Currency Embassy reframing win-lose models into win-win models, and "remembering and awakening to use our whole-brain thinking, our conscience, intuition and co-creative imagination for living the loving way, as a way of life."

Activating the full potential of the Holomovement is a practice and teaching of empathy, compassion and collaborative evolution in the art of altruism. In an emerging unity consciousness that touches all realms of human experience, it's necessary to let go of core negative beliefs while healing intergenerational trauma, giving hope to so many across the planet. This healing comes hand-in-hand with rising calls for justice, equity and addressing the material and climate realities created by ages of imbalanced distribution of wealth, power, and abusive use of nature's gifts.

Healing the illusion of separation, giving ourselves permission to feel good for doing good and teaching cooperation and compassion are all radical acts in our human evolution. As we embark on this new exploration of our altruistic expression, Dr. Martin Luther King, Jr. reminds us "...all life is interrelated. We are all caught in an inescapable network of mutuality, tied into a single garment of destiny. Whatever affects one directly, affects all indirectly. We are made to live together because of the interrelated structure of reality."

As in so many cases, when facing our world's greatest problems, we can look to nature for inspiration and answers. Trees share nutrients and information through vast mycorrhizal networks connected to the trees' root systems. These intertwined tree and fungal networks serve to share resources not only between trees of the same species, but with other tree species as well. The health of the forest, just like us, relies upon a dance of generosity and distribution of the abundance of resources. Luckily, we are wired for generosity and cooperation, like our tree relatives.

We have the power to catalyze positive change on levels never before experienced in the history of our species. If we practice altruism artfully, and redefine the word to allow for models of mutual aid and benefit, we can support the co-creation of a culture of symbiosis that values and reflects our true nature. Let's make the most of the fact our brains light up when we help each other! Perhaps one could argue that we have evolved to feel good for doing good because our very survival depends on it.

CHAPTER 12
BUILDING BRIDGES TOWARD UNITIVE HEALING: THREE PERSONAL PATHS OF COMMUNICATION TO UNITE AND UPHOLD JUSTICE

by Elena Mustakova, EdD, Dr. Marty K. Casey
& Amikaeyla Gaston

In this coming together across our different worlds, we are called to restore the fullness of communication—that powerful, mysterious, and pervasive force that connects all living things and is foundational to life. As we hear this call, we begin to notice how shrunk our living spaces have become in our separate worlds, how withered, lonely, hurt, threatened, insecure, aggressive we often feel, and when communication breaks down, and living things disconnect from each other, they wither and die.

A tide is rising—a tide of awakening, of re-membering, and re-connecting to the fullness of communication which sustains life and connects all with the source of the Divine. We are starting to actively reshape the space we currently occupy as a divided species. We are shifting with swift determination toward a healthy, whole ecosystem in a way that fosters diversity, innovation and radical imagination, all while being in alignment with universal consciousness.

In this chapter, we describe three different and deeply convergent paths of healing the communication gap by uniting hearts and minds and building communities to transform our divisive social reality into unitive justice. Sharing these personal stories of healing are co-authors: Dr. Elena Mustakova, Dr. Marty K. Casey and Amikaeyla Gaston. In this offering of deeply personal encounters, we can be inspired to reflect on our own paths of healing and realize a collective vision of unitive justice and peace.

Dr. Elena Mustakova is a spiritual philosopher, psychologist, and award-winning writer and social scientist, whose work is inspired by Bahá'í ontological understanding of reality as a spiritual phenomenon of the evolution of consciousness. Drawing from a language of universal, spiritual principles, Elena describes a globally-emergent systematic approach to healing intergenerational wounds across cultures and continents. Her account describes endeavors to help unite people in diverse communities through a dedication to rational spirituality, unitive justice and society-building.

Dr. Marty K. Casey is an actress, singer, writer, and producer. She is the Founder and President of Show Me Arts Foundation, the first arts organization formed immediately following the unrest of Ferguson, Missouri, as well as the Founder of the UnGun program. In the section below, Dr. Marty shares her journey in creating the UnGUN Institute, which creates a safe space for traumatized lives to heal and transform. Inspired by the transformation of lives marred by crime and hopelessness into lives of conscious choice and mental freedom, she has expanded her program into a national institute in the United States that seeks to "ungun" the collective psyche.

Amikaeyla Gaston is an international, award-winning singer, activist and Founder and Executive Director of ICAHSI (International Cultural Arts & Healing Sciences Institute) and World Trust Educational Services. In her story, she recounts surviving a hate crime and near-death experience setting her on a trajectory to understand the human psyche and how to access restorative justice through peace and forgiveness. She explores what it takes to broaden our field of scope, remove our myopic blinders, and see ourselves in others as All One.

Communication Between Worlds to Unite, Heal and Build Justice
Elena Mustakova, EdD

I am Bulgarian-American, and by age thirty-three, I had already seen a wide range of divisions and rifts in Europe, Africa, and the United States: ideological ones, deliberately crafted by a totalitarian communist regime; class ones, upheld by old Europe; and religious, racial, and political ones in both Northern and Southern Africa, and in the United States. As a result, I spent the next 30 years becoming a part of a worldwide spiritual and social transformation movement.

The Bahá'í faith, which first upheld the oneness of religion and race in the mid-19th century, has been spreading the understanding of the interdependence of nations and cultures in a unitary evolutionary process since the early part of the 20th century.[31] This worldwide movement takes a systematic approach to developing spiritual capacities that allow people to transcend limited loyalties and identities, and to join their different stories of race, class and ethnic background into a shared sense of emergent unitive justice—of evolving together beyond our wounds and divisions, toward a more united world. Into this laboratory for social change, I infused my clinical and social science experience through mentoring, workshops, talks, publications and media work. It became a steep learning curve in the deep processes of integral transformation involved in building unitive justice—justice that both honors the integrity of each individual and perspective, while preserving the integrity of very diverse communities and broadening the sense of interdependent belonging.

This endeavor toward spiritual empowerment and social transformation has unique variations across multiple countries and local communities with which I have worked. But it always challenges people to heal deeply hidden mindsets of prejudice, to attune to all that stands in the way of genuine bonds of intimate fellowship and collaboration across significant differences.

It is important work guided by a worldview of oneness, of universal spiritual laws and values that underlie all wisdom traditions, and by a transformative spiritual language that reflects these universal laws and values.

In it, every person is a leader as we engage together in building unity and more just collective processes. The emphasis is on balancing feminine and masculine, and on leading through a spirit of love, humility, and fellowship that uplifts, elevates and inspires. In my years of work as a social scientist, I've found that this healing requires meaningful communication.

Healing begins with recognizing and acknowledging our hidden sense of vulnerability across social contexts. Whatever our particular circumstances and beliefs, we each experience the fragility of the human body and psyche, and know viscerally that we have to build defenses, because society divides us into groups, identities and competing interests, pitting us against each other, and we feel unsafe. We learn early to compensate by telling ourselves stories in order to live. We then often turn these stories into unexamined positions that we defend.

By listening deeply and holding a safe space for hurt, rage, and, ultimately, deep vulnerability, we can begin to re-construct our sense of self and our relationships to trauma and explore what it means to be an authentic expression of our true self within society. In these experiences, we can begin to recognize the commonalities we share in our personal stories and realize that something unites our infinitely different faces of suffering—*a shared spiritual horizon*. Genuine healing always involves evolution to a higher order of consciousness.

Part of healing is learning and practicing communication that unites. Despite our diverse environments and cultures, we collectively long for truth, for more goodness and beauty in life, for more wholeness. That is the horizon we all reach for, in one way or another, often very privately. Ideologies, religious and secular, often highjack that longing. In my experience with

Bahá'í communities, people become united in the recognition that our efforts are only partially just and quite imperfect; yet as we collaborate, greater truth and goodness emerge. With this understanding, we can appreciate, filter out and apply the best of our heritage in the process of coming together.

This work in healing and unity-building ultimately supports unitive justice. It acknowledges the painful past, while also lifting people above the mindset of scarcity and competition for resources and allows them to discover that prosperity on the individual level only works when there is prosperity of the whole. This way of understanding justice channels the divine into the social realm. It upholds that *only in our movement toward greater unity do we find greater justice*. It protects the dignity of each person as a soul which becomes increasingly more conscious and evolves toward unity consciousness.

Communication that bridges worlds is one that seeks to apply universal spiritual principles to personal and social issues. By creating an interpersonal space of safety, and consulting from a source of spiritual principles, we can form collaborative relationships. In the context of this radical spiritual understanding and expansion of community, we can find our voice within and as a collective.

This movement is a world-wide laboratory for building bonds of the heart, developing spiritual eyes and conscience and redefining what is socially possible. Such a regenerative, planetary process continually challenges participants to examine their own mindsets, to be more attuned to how they use language, to find and grow within a higher love that fosters wholeness. It is also a steep learning curve to create genuinely consultative governing bodies representative of human diversity.

The evolutionary horizon motivates people in local communities to study and deepen their understanding. Conscious communication allows us to reach out to different groups and expand through deep listening with open minds and hearts and embracing diversity of perspectives, to cultivate partnerships, and to grow out of limited identities into a world-embracing sense of global citizenship. While individual and cultural uniqueness is valued and protected, the ethic of "we," of the one human family, grows stronger. People from every walk of life and every background learn to serve together the practical advancement of unity in diversity in our world.

Healing the Soul Through Art and Heart

Dr. Marty K. Casey

I'm so proud to be born and raised in the city of St. Louis, Missouri. I have watched my city rise and fall many times. However, I have only seen it shatter to silence once, and this was one time too many.

After the unrest of Ferguson on August 9, 2014, two things became evident. One, a lot of hurt people needed to heal from one senseless act of violence that shook the city to its core, and two, Ferguson could, at any time, be anywhere in the world.

Hurt people, hurt people. Healed people, heal people. In an instant, Ferguson became divided. Some believed a police officer was a cold-blooded killer. They saw the cause of the tragedy in the fact the officer served in a community of people whom he was unable to relate to, based on cultural and racial differences. The other half of people believed the officer was just doing his job when he encountered what they labeled as an "out-of-control teenage thug" with a long history of blemishes. Both sides were describing the other horribly to build a case against each other. No matter where the truth crossed paths, it was clear that the unnecessary act of violence resulting in death could have been avoided with better communication, laws, and justice in the face of adversity.

For me, the fine details mattered less than the end result. A child was dead in the streets for hours, as the whole world witnessed through live social media outlets in real time. This appalling event left us with the feeling of no respect for human life or dignity. The anguish that the parents and loved ones must have been experiencing haunted me for weeks. I felt moved to help heal and find solutions, and I started the first artistic non-profit after the unrest. Show Me Arts Academy was formed and started serving children on February 28th, 2015. My goal was to create a pathway to help as many children as we could by using the arts to take their focus off the news headlines and away from social media—to expose them to a new and safe world where they could escape through the arts. This became a personal quest.

Along with a team of volunteers, we collectively served over 3,000 children in the city of St. Louis, providing them with endless opportunities to be seen, supported and heard. Show Me Arts Foundation rolled out a program called Spreading The Love (STL). This was a group of talented children from 17 different zip codes from around the metropolitan St. Louis area. We wanted to use the arts to close in the division from the impact of Ferguson by taking these singing sensational children on tour to Washington, D.C., New Jersey and New York. They used the power of their voices to convey the message that every child across America deserves to be protected against excessive policing. Everywhere we went, we stopped to do a "Pop Up Concert" to shift the energy and atmosphere. The impact was so powerful that it caught the attention of some very popular people, including Beyonce![32]

Although working with the singers in Spreading The Love was very special, I desired a bigger challenge. I wanted to see whether we could put this effort into curriculum that could shift the trajectory of children with a past stained by crime. The eight-week program called UnGUN was created and rolled out from the St. Louis Juvenile Detention Center in May of 2016.

We went behind the walls to work specifically with seven boys whose past offences ranged from car theft and robbery to first degree murder. After these children entered our program, they transformed right before our eyes. The tools and techniques introduced to them weekly, coupled with hip hop dance and DJ engineering, allowed us to focus on the children and not their rap sheets. Discussions, writing assignments and the arts helped them to express their pain. Our consistent showing up helped build a strong bond with each of them week after week.

There was one young man that we referred to as the leader of the pack. He effortlessly kept everyone in line. He demanded respect from each of them and extended that same respect to me and the program. He also set the bar high for each of them to pay attention, participate, and learn the routine that they would be performing at the end of the eight-week program. He expressed himself emotionally in his writing assignments and gained better knowledge of himself with each exercise and expression. He challenged himself to dance; he learned how to DJ; and he didn't hold back from sharing his back story of what led him down a path of destruction prior to his conviction. I watched him work through deep hurt and pain that caused him to react every time he encountered conflict. We worked weekly on techniques like breathing, stretching, journaling and music with messages that helped to feed his soul.

This expression created through dance strengthened their core and forced all of them to work as a team no matter "what side of the tracks" they were from. Different gang affiliations and beliefs could not stop their desire to keep going as they practiced to succeed. The last week before the program was over, as they prepared for the culminating performance, the young man was pulled from the program. We were devastated. He was the leader, the nucleus of the group, and the example of possible change with encouragement. I knew he had been UnGUNned.

I was told that he stopped talking and eating, and that he refused to see anyone but me. I agreed to see him to try to get him to eat. I entered his room, with the guard standing nearby, sat next to him, and stared at him and his plate of uneaten food. Without words, I started our breathing exercise, hoping that he would join, and he did. His breaths were weak. I told him that in order to free up his body from pain and the lump in his throat, he first had to free up his mind. I reminded him of how far he had grown in the program, that he instantly was a leader and that, now, he needed to lead himself by practicing the dance steps and hearing the music in his head. I told him that no matter what happened in court, since he had aged-out and was now being charged as an adult, they could only take possession of his body. I then told him to try to eat something so that his body could assist his mind in thinking positive thoughts. I asked him to never forget me as I would not forget him.

Because of this young man, I extended UnGUN to grow beyond a program. Because of him, it's now UnGUN Institute, LLC. Our national team is dedicated to counting *lives* through this work, not deaths. We are determined to bridge the divide through healing and love.

Being Beyond—The Power of Believing and Belonging in Uncertain Times
Amikaeyla Gaston

"It is not light that we need, but fire. It is not the gentle shower, but thunder. We need the storm, the whirlwind, and the earthquake."

— Frederick Douglass, Abolitionist, Scholar

We are in an extraordinary time. A time of being actively called into action through a vast vortex of individual realities all colliding with one another, and to prevent continual conflict, we are called into our truest truth—the truth that we all must serve as 'ministers of healing' for ourselves and one another as we shepherd in the dawning of this new day and way of beingness as All One.

In this extraordinary moment in time, we need to muster all our strength, corral all our community and creative teammates, and call on our deepest superpowers. Be the fire, thunder, storm, whirlwind and earthquake. This is what it will take to be more than just a cerebral theorist, but an active participant in the Holomovement. To be a generator, as well as a reflector, and energize the flow between source and self, all while being a potent and effectual contributor to the evolution of humankind.

We, as multidimensional humans and as variegated as the plants, can actively reshape the space we currently occupy as a divided species, shift with swift determination toward a healthy and whole ecosystem. And we can do it in a way that fosters diversity, innovation, and radical imagination, all while being in alignment with universal consciousness when we move into the state I call 'Being Beyond.'

Our voice is our primal power, and rhythm is the heartbeat of the universe. Through the language and medicine of being seen, being heard, and making a rousing loud and lasting difference, we can invite the curative effects of authentic, creative expression into our lives. In this experience, we heal our spirits, unleash our purpose and create new stories that bring forth a just and flourishing world.

We are in a time where we not only can make a difference, we MUST. I love languages and etymology, and I looked up the origin of the word 'must.' It's Urdu, from Persia, and means "to be compelled as if by intoxication." So that's what we are talking about here—conjuring an innate drive that defies logic and calls you to go and Be Beyond.

Beyond the "ists" and "isms" of our body wrappers, beyond our individual comfort levels, beyond doubts and fears resulting in binary thought and competitive lifestyles, we enter into the beauty of our communal, molecular connections and continue to believe that the impossible is possible. We must continue to dare to hope; dare to be dauntless; dare to be fearless, brave, courageous, and bold, even when we are tired, weary, and feeling lost and alone. We are all one, even when we are alone, for we are all connected and are all our relations. You are a relative to me, and me to you, and all of us to each other—so when I get down, frustrated, and petrified by these challenging times, I have to remind myself that we are all a part of each other. To love myself fully, I need to love...all...of...us.

So, what would it take to broaden our field of scope, remove our myopic blinders and see more of the world through the eyes and stories of others? We are here because we are being called to see and find the immeasurable value in sharing and hearing our own voices, as well as others. This is an invitation to heal ourselves on a deep, molecular level and embrace a broader perspective. This is our chance to break free from old thought patterns, habits and assumptions and expand our minds and authentically express ourselves boldly and bravely around things that might be hard to share and say.

When I'm afraid and feeling alone, I sing this old spiritual that my grandmother used to sing to me while she rocked me...

> *'by and by*
> *when the morning comes*
> *my sweet mama will carry*
> *me home*
> *she will tell me the story of how we overcome*
> *and we'll understand it better*
> *by and by'*

It soothes me—such hope even in despair—and when I sing it, I think of American abolitionist Harriet Tubman and try to imagine what she had to do to muster the resilience and grit to do what she did! I went home recently to Washington, D.C., to commemorate the opening of the beautiful National Museum of African American History and Culture, and to be a part of all the festivities with family and friends that had congregated to remember...

(by and by when the morning comes)

Remember not only my ancestors and what they went through when brought chained in boats across the Atlantic, and were bought and sold like chattel to others who viewed them as animals, as product and disposable...

(my sweet mama will carry me home)

Or how this country that we call home came to be...

(she will tell me the story of how we overcome)

But to remember how we survived and thrived and continue to live and give and share and care and be parents, grandparents, and children of the earth, salt, sea, dusk and dawn...

(and we'll understand it better by and by)

As I stood in front of Harriet Tubman's prayer shawl and hymnal, I wept and remembered her words of courage, her intrepid spirit, the fact that she ran by moonlight through the trees, felt the moss and lichen to determine the right direction, ate plants from the earth to keep her strength, drank from the streams and swam across rivers to make it to freedom. I wept and remembered that I am her, and she is me. She is all of us. She is our story and our now. So, whenever I spiral into sadness and despair, when I watch the news and lament the state of affairs of our country and the world, I remember...

I remember that my ancestors had to face all of this every day and then some, but they stood strong and powerful and carried on, and I am their legacy. You are the legacy of your ancestors—their hard work, their knowledge, their survival spirit. You not only owe it to yourself to live a long and healthy, whole life and to share your vision and message with others—you owe it to them as well!

Being Beyond and moving into a state of "All One with All Relations" is going to feel challenging, and although growth happens slowly, it happens. We are starting on the micro-granular level to look at what needs to be done to shift the infrastructure of our minds, our culture, and our world to create a community of belonging. We are drawn, on an ancient cellular level, to dig deeper into our psyches and muster the courage to make changes in ourselves and our communities. We are called to claim our bigger selves, live our fullest lives, and contribute with joy, openness, and all our senses.

And I say this as someone who survived a near-fatal hate crime.

I was purposefully run over by five, white men in a truck and was dragged 86 feet on a gravel road. I suffered near-fatal lacerations to my organs, third-degree burns on over 70% of my body, and smashed ribs which punctured my lungs. Yes, I died under that truck. I left my body, soared over the murder site, flew into the clouds, felt the air course through the molecules of my soul, heard the music and words of my ancestors and came back with the stories and sounds which healed my wounds as I spent over a year immobilized in a burn unit.

I detail my NDE (near death experience) in my Tedx talk entitled "Dare to be Dauntless."[33] I called it that because that incident, born out of hatred and racism, not only made me a survivor, but also a thriver.

After the incident, I began studying the powerful healing effects of music, as well as sacred ethnomusicology, and sang for His Holiness the 14th Dalai Lama, who encouraged me to create the International Cultural Arts and Healing Sciences Institute (ICAHSI). ICAHSI partners with organizations such as United Nations High Commissioner for Refugees, the U.S. State Department and embassies around the world, alongside local artists, educators and healers, to bring our "Music as Medicine" programming to those whose lives have been jeopardized and frozen by the ravages of harm and war.

I've been all throughout the United States, Europe, Asia and Africa, but for the past 12 years, I've been primarily traveling specifically to places such as: Lebanon, Jordan, Syria, Palestine, Azerbaijan, Kazakhstan, Tajikistan, Turkmenistan, Sierra Leone and Nigeria. I've met the most incredible people in these countries, whose beauty stems from their strength, courage, resilience and transformative power of spirit in the face of social unrest and grave tragedy. In that near-death experience, I had the honor of connecting directly to the source of the Divine and now know that this lifetime is our opportunity to learn what it means to love and care for ourselves and each other.

I truly believe that the wealth of our harmonious health lies in how we access our authentic expression and creative voice, which is our Primal Power. When we find the courage to rise up, share our lives and stories and speak our truth into the powerful beauty of All One, we make a loud and lasting change in ourselves and the world. For we are in an extraordinary moment in time—a time when we CAN make a difference. We MUST.

These stories of healing offer personal insight into our own potential for bridging worlds and bringing about unitive justice. Through a language of the spirit, music, art, and movement, we can shift the story of scarcity to one where we collectively thrive.

SPOTLIGHT FEATURE
DECLARATION FOR UNITIVE JUSTICE

by Evolutionary Leaders Unitive Justice and
Global Security Synergy Circle:
Elena Mustakova, Scott Alan Carlin, Robert Atkinson,
Jonathan Granoff, Joni Carley, Jude Currivan, Audrey
Kitagawa, David Lorimer, Chief Phil Lane Jr. & Earl Possardt

Justice is the cornerstone of an ever-advancing civilization; it maintains the inherent balance of life, protects human rights and helps ensure global harmony. Justice is a unifying force that expands with the evolution of civilization and its moral code.

Our civilization faces its next great evolutionary leap—interdependent planetary cooperation toward building the ethical, cultural, governmental and legal structures that protect global human security. This leap is propelled by emergent scientific knowledge of unity as our existential reality, and it requires a new understanding of justice *based on a unitive narrative*.[34]

Unitive justice is a system of balance and inclusion, acknowledging a living web of interconnectedness of all life and offering meaningful support to all involved in instances of injustice by simultaneously restoring and maintaining community harmony. As practiced by Indigenous communities, this system of justice served to bring the community together as a whole and can now be a model for the emerging global community. Unitive justice transcends and replaces punitive justice. A fully functioning global system of unitive justice can reshape and prepare communities worldwide for effective human security, conscious interdependence, and equitable relationships on all levels.

In the Anthropocene Epoch, when humanity has become the dominant force in shaping planet Earth, we have reached a tipping point where we recognize that our current structures, which over emphasize the pursuit of security through military nationalism, must change to a human security model based on the necessity of protecting our one planet home. We are reminded by Indigenous peoples of the truth that we must live in harmony with the regenerative processes of nature.

Eight billion people living in a world with profound social, economic and political inequalities, and without recognizing the limits of nature, are pushing the Earth's living systems toward collapse. Gender inequity, colonialism, slavery, racism, religious prejudice and bigotry, and other forms of oppression, along with current debt- and military-based norms, have led to a system of disequilibrium and injustice that no longer serves humanity and that endangers the entire planet.

At the same time, we have reached a point where our technological innovations governed by market forces are exacerbating environmental degradation, and the advanced modern weapons we produce diminish security the more they are perfected. The pursuit of war to achieve political ends presently puts humanity at risk of extinction.

Climate change, the biodiversity crisis, new global pandemics, and other planetary boundaries demonstrate the need for a *new context for re-defining justice*. These threats cannot be met at the governance level of cities, states or nations, and require new levels of global cooperation through governance structures that can achieve sustainable human security.

We the Peoples, must now choose to either disregard our current destructive systems or to forge a new unitive path of truth, justice and human security. Now is the time for *a unitive understanding of justice* that transcends our many limited loyalties, that both honors and unites our cultural identities, celebrates diversity, and transforms the scarcity economic mindset, which promotes outdated, dysfunctional and destructive systems.

Unitive justice acknowledges the harm caused by exclusionary hierarchies of power and responds to the prophetic words of Dr. Martin Luther King, Jr., "a threat to justice anywhere is a threat to justice everywhere." Unitive justice is a call to acknowledge the wounds of injustice in our painful past. Unitive justice is a new horizon where all of us can rise together, collaboratively, toward greater wholeness, universal security, and deeper, more systemic justice.

Unity as the Purpose of Justice

Unitive justice provides a new framework wherein the interdependent nature of our global crises becomes the crucible for cultivating loving kindness and for strengthening our communal responsibility to the greater whole.

Emergent scientific knowledge of our biological evolution and of the Cosmos is revealing that unity is not merely an aspiration to be hoped for beyond all odds, but rather that unity is our existential reality. Our quest to grasp this fundamental truth propels an emergent evolutionary leap toward unitive consciousness, wholeness and interdependent planetary cooperation, enabling effective governance of human conduct that protects rather than endangers the living systems of the planet. Unitive justice provides *a practical link* between the emergent understanding of our existential unity and our individual lives.

It recognizes that there can be no justice for children without just relationships among genders, no economic justice without environmental justice and no justice for one cultural group through oppressing another. Unitive justice transcends our understandings of retributive justice and helps to transform our current emergency into the emergence of a just and flourishing future for All.

Unitive justice provides *new ground* for protecting the integrity and wellbeing of individuals and communities, for harmonizing and celebrating our cultural differences, and for creating effective political engagement to address global challenges. It offers *a common platform* for the vast number of global movements that are working toward a unified and peaceful world.

Unitive justice recognizes that the human family is one, and that the rights of the individual to have their inherent dignity and safety protected, as upheld by the Universal Declaration of Human Rights (1949), are dependent on the safety and prosperity for the whole. Unitive justice provides a critical pillar for *establishing human security*, grounded in the science of our interdependent relationship with the natural world and with each other. Unitive justice calls for the establishment of institutions and the rule of law that protect human security and free us from dysfunctional, violent and unjust practices and systems. It promotes ethical, cultural, governmental and legal structures that best accommodate the reality of our unity.

Unitive justice simultaneously advances human freedom while also embracing a renewed ecological consciousness. Unitive justice requires a regenerative relationship with Nature wherein we no longer regard it as an object, a thing we possess, but as "a unique, indivisible, self-regulating community of interrelated beings."[35] Unitive justice is a call to join hands in honoring the Earth Charter: "To move forward we must recognize that in the midst of a magnificent diversity of cultures and life forms we are one human family and one Earth community with a common destiny."

While this effort specifically addresses Sustainability Development Goal (SDG) 16, Peace, Justice and Strong Institutions, unitive justice is a call for collectively working together as truth tellers and ambassadors of love to acknowledge the interlinkages between all 17 Sustainable Development Goals and the interdependencies among all beings.

CHAPTER 13
A MYCELIUM NETWORK IN ACTION: WEAVING UNITY AND DIFFERENCE INTO A MOVEMENT OF MOVEMENTS

by Masen Ewald
Dedicated to Terry Patten

"Here and there, and in increasingly more and more places, deep friendships, powerful alliances, fuller cooperation, and new levels of community will break new ground, building know-how and new capacities. These pilot projects and cultural experiments might at first seem like exceptional fringe phenomena on the edges of culture. But when the capacities they cultivate become crucial to collective well-being, they will be understood as having been far more central than they appeared."

— Terry Patten

Maybe we all know the moment. Our favorite political candidate is attempting to land their final remarks at the debate, or an artist we admire is in the final stretch of a moving acceptance speech, or a team leader is reaching the height of a motivational talk. We listen intently, anticipating a moment of clarity and inspiration to move our hearts and minds forward in a fresh way, and then we hear it again: "We need to come together!"

In extremely divisive times, "we need to come together" might provide some relief. To some extent, it's almost always true and, therefore, a safe call to action. However, it can also feel like a missed opportunity—it falls flat. Why? One reason is we've all simply heard it so many times. Another reason may be that it lacks specificity about *how* we come together, and the social imagination and actionable ideas for uniting our many disparate factions. Or, what if it falls flat because we sense something deeper?

The story that "we need to come together" genuinely intends to unite us, but it *begins* by separating us first. It validates our very real challenges, but it also neglects that unity is our primary nature. If we presume that we are separate from each other, it seems to confirm the inherent brokenness of our society and the inevitable challenges of our differences. If we already presume our inherent unity, the story can feel empty and disappointing— lacking the insight of wisdom and the power of deeper truth. Is there a more effective call to action for our moment? Can a new invitation carry the simultaneous truths of our inherent unity and the ongoing need to enact it? Can we sense that we are already together and endeavor to *stay* together, *collaborate* together and *move* together?

"We need to come together" may also sound like we're being asked to sacrifice our differences for sameness, when, in fact, we sense that our best ways forward would honor our differences as sacred strengths. True unity will never look like uniformity. Honoring our differences as sacred is not just an act of tolerance for the sake of social harmony. Difference is how reality naturally expresses itself, and it's essential to how we evolve.

In fact, one of the primary functions of unity is to protect difference and reassert it when it is suppressed. For instance, our social movements can often be viewed as parts of society reasserting their crucial importance to the whole in the wake of being rejected, neglected or oppressed. Whether such movements focus on cultural values, race, gender, sexuality, war, land, healthcare, ecology, poverty or numerous other issues, we may be served by interpreting movements as expressions of unity itself sending us a message. Many of us are familiar with Dr. Martin Luther King, Jr.'s comment, "A riot is the language of the unheard;" however, his next words are just as essential—

"What is it that America has failed to hear?" Do movements of all kinds arise because an important truth (even if a partial or subjective truth) is not being heard?

If we practice this perspective of unity, we might more easily see the primary purposes of societal movements that emerge. A message of "Black Lives Matter" is not interpreted as "Black lives matter more," but instead "Black lives *inherently* matter, and our society is violating this truth." Likewise, the commonly heard phrase of "Proud to be American" is not interpreted as "America is superior to all and has no flaws," but instead, "We are grateful to live in a country with certain liberties, and we are committed to preserving them." Of course, some movements adhere to their core truths better than others—our movements are messy, complex and naturally express many of our separative habits, so their core truths can become distorted by their missteps.

Sometimes, our differences that seem in utter contradiction to each other are actually simultaneously working to advance society in important ways. For example, a movement of rationality and atheism might help to expose the falsehoods of literally-interpreted theism, reduce the extremism of religious movements and encourage the adoption of science within a sector of society. While, simultaneously, a movement of wisdom, spirituality and consciousness studies might help to expose the inherent limitations of our modern scientific worldview and revive practices and insights from our religious traditions. Both movements might be benefiting the evolution of society, even while they can appear to be at odds. However, it's also critical to remember that some movements are not healthy expressions of unity but rather intensified separation—resisting unity and clinging to dominant societal patterns. As we actively listen for the truths of our movements, we can be curious and open-minded *and* fiercely protective of unity and difference as they arise together.

Inspiration Found at the Forest Floor

Earth's natural systems may best reflect the complex and invisible nature of societal change. Given our current collection of crises, we might especially learn from an unsung hero of our forests—fungi. A kingdom to themselves, neither plant nor animal and comprising over a million species, fungi go about their role in the forest nearly invisible, benefiting from darkness and operating mostly underground. One of their specializations is to break down and decompose the decaying organisms of the forest in order to regenerate soil, feed other organisms and nurture new life. If fungi thrive, the ecosystem can thrive in diversity and balance.

Societal movements are also most active at the "forest floor." They support all that we love about human civilization in countless ways we cannot see. They are new, strange and unknown. They alert us to unhealthy forces in society, and they make space for new possibilities. Like fungi, many movements are not always immediately attractive to us because they deal with the dying, transforming and rebirthing of our values and systems. They change *us*.

Our movements often express themselves through one of three dimensions: *movements within us* (changing ourselves), *movements between us* (changing our relationships) or *movements around us* (changing our systems and environments). Does change start with any of those dimensions or are they constantly interacting and interdependent?

Personal views about how our world changes are reflected in our collective movements, and we tend to under appreciate the dimensions of change that are less aligned with our perspectives. Going forward, in order to address the hyper-complexity of our challenges, we may need all the dimensions of societal change to experience major successes—not only because of the number of crises we're facing but because addressing any one crisis requires advancing on other fronts simultaneously.

From major sectors like environment, culture, economics and technology, to fringe movements that don't quite fit our models of activism, it would be impossible to properly acknowledge the millions of courageous projects in motion. However, our collective moment is calling us to find inspiration and wisdom at the forest floor.

The Movements Within Us

When we look at human society, we look into a mirror. Its amazing beauty, uniqueness, organization and creativity all reflect the goodness of which we are already capable as human beings. Likewise, our own insecurities, dysfunctions and tendencies toward separation are also on display in pervasive conflicts, failures to coordinate and systems that too often incentivize personal advantage over elevating others. When multiplied by eight billion people and magnified by media, technology and system dynamics, some of our individual tendencies create collective madness. How do we see a new society when we look into the mirror?

Once we live from our inherent unity, the stubbornly static image of society comes to life as a moving process. The dynamic relationship between our lives and society at large becomes obvious, even auspicious, and it presents an opportunity to evolve our world by evolving ourselves. Our social movements have long pointed the finger back at ourselves. Today, many movements are inspiring us to look further into the mirror than ever— to restore our sense of *meaning*, to cultivate our *wisdom*, to broaden our *perspectives*, to *heal* our harmful patterns and to catalyze our *agency*.

While many of us grow up conditioned to relate to citizenship passively— assuming our politicians, CEOs, religious figures, celebrities and journalists wield the only real power—today's movements urge that it's no longer enough for us to simply vote, recycle, donate and stay well informed. When we truly shift from *spectator* to *participant*, opportunities to engage appear all around us, from skill-specific volunteer commitments to social entrepreneurism to crowdfunding for local projects. While our collective moment absolutely requires unprecedented action by our leaders and institutions, it may also require a culture of mass volunteerism and engaged citizenship unlike anything we've previously attempted.

Citizens expressing agency may feel called to lead. Effective leaders in the years ahead may need to demonstrate different capacities than leaders of the past, and would be greatly resourced by today's *movements of perspective and awareness*. While critical thinking and global perspectives are essential, such leaders would be fluent in several *ways of thinking*. They would be capable of imagining the systemic effects of their decisions, as well as how systems interact with other systems. Yet, all the perspectives in the world won't get us where we're going if we don't cultivate the wisdom to guide us.

As science and academia continue to validate ancient spiritual insights, values and esoteric practices, we are seeing exciting new *movements of wisdom*. Self-awareness, emotional intelligence and empathy are not only being championed for mental health, but as ways to benefit the world through personal growth. As these *movements within us* free our attention, open our hearts and deepen our capacities, new opportunities begin to emerge when we encounter each other.

The Movements Between Us

When we sense our unity, we are sensing relationship. We are in relationship with our world, including our opponents, whether we like it or not. The extent to which we allow or resist relationship determines our ability to enact unity.

Could a number of our crises be addressed by solutions that already exist if we were capable of communicating, compromising and coordinating more effectively? While there are crises that still require breakthrough solutions, it is easy to imagine the massive impacts we might have by healing cultural tensions, befriending other ways of life and coordinating more effectively. It's not as easy to imagine *how* that can happen, but many inspiring movements are working to weave our social fabric in unconventional ways—from movements of healing to interpersonal practice to alternative models of community and collaboration. Movements of interpersonal practice are also developing our relational capacities of empathy, compassion, attentive listening, authentic communication and conflict resolution in group settings.

Other movements aim to address polarization by connecting groups across political and cultural lines, suggesting that heightened tensions are less about misaligned values and more about our communication failures. Some innovative interpersonal practices add elements of meditation and somatic awareness to empower participants to relate beyond their social personalities and experience greater intimacy, spontaneity and intuition. Such practices are increasingly adopted by meditation practitioners and are already common in many wisdom communities.

We are seeing unconventional communities of all kinds on the rise. Perhaps some of the most important expressions of community are those uplifting oppressed or marginalized members of society, offering safe spaces of shared culture, belonging, healing and empowerment. We see communities restoring dignity to our core individual identities—from race and cultural history to female empowerment and feminine wisdom to healthier expressions of masculinity and respect for all gender, sexual and nonbinary identities. We see communities elevating the voices and wisdom of Indigenous cultures. We see spiritual practice communities dedicated to both personal and cultural transformation. We even see some communities convening to explore the potentials of community itself—experimenting with new ways of communicating, collaborating and governing.

The emergence of such communities is no accident. Our collective crises are our failure to coordinate on behalf of the whole planet, and this has given rise to *movements of collaboration*.

Just as we tend to prioritize ourselves, our families and our companies over the whole, our world leaders and corporations are also incentivized to prioritize their supporters and stakeholders. Many of us sense that these incentives are central to so many of our challenges, however, they're especially problematic now as we face existential, planet-wide emergencies. The whole of life needs to be prioritized on several fronts as soon as possible. With no global entity wielding the authority to act for the whole, our movements of collaboration are working to design new governance models, demonstrate their efficacy and promote their adoption within companies, governments and social institutions.

The movements *within us* and *between us* are laying essential foundations for how unity could be expressed in society. However, to enact unity at scale—perhaps not perfectly but enough to create long-term well-being for the whole — it is critical that we also learn from the inspiring *movements around us*. With limited time and resources, which movements would be the most effective at transforming our companies, economies, technologies, governments, natural ecosystems and beyond, to help us live in greater alignment with the whole of life?

The Movements Around Us

In our modern era of amazing scientific and technological breakthroughs, we are perhaps most accustomed to thinking of societal change as the movements *around us*—innovations, policies, resources and other systems. However, it has also become commonplace for us to shrug our shoulders at our systems' dysfunctions. While the movements *within us* and *between us* are imperative, we are misled and naive if we think we can address our crises without unprecedented updates to these many interdependent processes and structures. So, where do we begin?

When we look more deeply, we see movements everywhere already working *in the system* (improving processes), *against the system* (stopping harmful processes) and *around the system* (creating new systems and processes). While some of us believe that our systems simply need updates and regulations, others insist that our systems are already experiencing stages of collapse, and that fundamental redesigns are required.

Historically, the collapse of systems has sometimes led to momentous advancements for societies that would have seemed impossible just years earlier. Could this be a possible silver lining to our current situation? After all, our systems are not naturally occurring phenomena but social tools that we've built. We can, hypothetically, rebuild them or build new ones. Fortunately, many of today's *movements around us* are advancing fields of study, new system models and prototypes for how humanity might transition to systems of unity. Movements of energy and ecology attempt to address our environmental emergencies, while movements of regenerative living emphasize self-reliance and hyper-local resilience. Movements of alternative governance and economics prioritize greater transparency, agency and trust, while movements of ethical technology wisely steward the responsible use of powerful innovations.

Given the magnitude of the possibilities and the risks we are facing, how might enough of us—including those who wield power in our current systems—loosen our attachments to the systems we prefer and become open-minded to new designs? There are incredible, vitally important, large-scale potentials in the *movements around us*. May we be wise to not build too fast without ensuring movement advances *within us* and *between us*.

A Movement of Movements

When we journey down further beneath the forest floor, we discover that fungi are even stranger than they seemed. Their mushroom caps and stems are anchored deep underground by a mycelium—a vast root-like network that spreads through the soil in all directions, connecting to the roots of trees and plants. Mycelia are not just bumping up against plant roots to compete for space. By remaining connected to many root systems simultaneously, a mycelium helps distribute water, nutrients and even electrical currents to other organisms. Through this network, the forest enacts its unity—taller plants share nutrients with young saplings that cannot reach enough sunlight, stress signals are sent and received triggering symbiotic responses between species, and trees are even able to sense their physical distance from one another, enabling optimal room for both growth and resource distribution. When a mycelium thrives, its neighbors thrive, and the forest thrives.

Our natural ecosystems have evolved to literally communicate with each other in their own ways, but not always above the surface and certainly not without a sophisticated infrastructure, mutual benefit and continuous attunement. It also seems that some of the healthiest sectors of our societies behave similarly. Is there a mycelium growing between the roots of our societal movements?

Our millions of movements are *implicitly* part of such an ecosystem, but we tend to stay in our own areas and trust that our allies are advancing in theirs. What becomes possible if more of us *explicitly* participate in this ecosystem as a unified, networked whole, as we see in the forest? What if thousands of movements become more intentionally and tangibly connected to the whole? Could millions of participants and thousands of organizations make such a shift in orientation? Could it clarify our collective purpose in a way that makes us more effective?

When we begin to orient to our own work grounded and guided by our inherent unity, we see the potential for a *movement of movements*. We recognize that it's already happening in many ways *and* that so much more coordination is possible. When we zoom out to view the whole forest, we become heartened by the courageous work of so many initiatives, and we discover new paths forward.

Shifting our perspective to see a movement of movements is not necessarily easy. For some, it could mean a whole new worldview and new life priorities. It may be even more difficult to enact. As we begin to radically collaborate to save humanity from itself, we would inevitably encounter the same human challenges from which we're trying to save it! The pervasive incentives to prioritize *our* movement, biases and tribal tendencies, legal and financial obstacles, coordination failures and more would all resurface.

But then, an even bigger opportunity emerges. We remember that the obstacles in our path are the same obstacles that our very movements emerged to address! Our friends are the experts of new practices, processes and technologies that can guide us on the way. Who among us would be open to help enact a movement of movements? Would they be capable of committing to the wellbeing of the whole, even while they represent their own interests or goals?

Clearly, the most essential quality to ignite such a process would be an authentic commitment to the whole. In a movement of movements, we would not necessarily see eye-to-eye and align on a single vision, but we would need to truly befriend each other amidst our differences. People who see technology as the primary lever of change would become friends with people who see ecological awareness as most essential. Those who assume policy is our strongest tool for social justice would become friends with those who believe depolarization is a prerequisite to good policy. As our friendships deepen, so would our trust. Our attachments to our own movements would loosen, and we would open to new ways of seeing. We would appreciate our friends' expertise, and we would realize that our successes require one another.

Potentials and Features of Collaboration

Our moment calls us to prioritize unity over competition. A movement of movements may accelerate our impacts through the discovery of: new strategic alliances and joint initiatives; more effective coordination with existing allies; amplified reach of communications; wiser decisions through distributed power; the elimination of redundancies and closer alignment across projects, information and platforms.

Our commitment to collaboration also presents an opportunity to *elevate public understanding* of the interdependent nature of our crises. Perhaps our collective work as a movement of movements would begin to be perceived as a more defined sector of society, similar to an industry or a field of study. Organizing thousands of previously siloed initiatives into global, collaborative networks would be an extraordinary event that could legitimize our field, command credibility, influence leaders, empower journalists to communicate more effectively, educate funders about the interdependence of initiatives and attract many skilled participants into our movements.

One significant collaborative opportunity is to *advise project development*. Involving leaders from various domains who can share their expertise about the systemic effects of a proposed initiative could help us more effectively and responsibly launch our projects.

However, launching new initiatives is often a challenge for movements with limited financial, informational and technological access. A connected network of collaborative partners reveals new relationships and tools to help all of us *access new resources*. We could design our collaboration to incentivize resource sharing in order to enable efficiencies, cost savings and mutual benefit—from knowledge and data, to strategic relationships, to physical and digital tools.

Collaboration between movements is not a new idea. While it does happen, it is rare, difficult and often prevented by a lack of alignment on *how* to collaborate. If we clarified the features of our work together, would we be more likely to engage? Would more funders trust the efficacy of collaboration?

It may serve us to imagine some key operational features of a movement of movements. *Movement maps and dynamic tracking* of our initiatives would help us see one another, our relationships, our progress and our next steps. Mapping our organizations, communities, participants and data with user-friendly, collaborative tools could reveal unexpected patterns that connect us, enable interoperability, synchronize related projects and provide a sense of coherence. However, our maps will only realize their potential if we also build the human relationships that bring them to life.

Two essential features of a movement of movements are *weaving* and *facilitating*. While traditional career networking prioritizes individual advancement and is typically reserved for the most ambitious, weaving prioritizes the well-being of the whole network. Weavers might help identify complementary missions, compatible skill sets, missing connections, neglected communities, mentoring opportunities, redundancies and potential resource exchanges. Most importantly, however, weaving is initiating and fostering the relationships that are vital to the system and empowering a web of weavers who can enable positive flows of participation and resources.

They may also work closely with facilitators, who would skillfully cohere us in gatherings to ensure that our connections become meaningful, trustworthy friendships. With our maps, tools and relationships in harmony, new approaches to coordination become possible.

For a movement of movements to be worthwhile, it needs to operate at a high level of coordination. If our collaboration is too confusing or tiring, or if it resembles the failures we see in society, we won't embrace it, and we won't remain committed to it during its challenges. Fortunately, some of our movements are offering new *alternative coordination processes* that could re-pattern our ways of working together and replace dysfunctional processes in society. We could experiment with collective decision-making methods that account for both global and movement-specific needs. We might implement fewer hierarchies and different incentives for leaders, while also avoiding the dysfunctions of flat organizational structures. To coordinate well within new processes, we would strive toward a degree of agency, integrity, tolerance and generosity that is uncommon in modern work culture. If we're successful, we will demonstrate collective power and attract support.

While some of our movements are sufficiently funded or operate outside of the philanthropic sector, many others are often pitted against one another for funding. How do we finance our movements so that we feel secure enough to collaborate and ensure that parts of the whole are not significantly underfunded? Could we catalyze a new era of *collaborative fundraising* that prioritizes joint initiatives, movement-wide investments and collectively managed pools of resources? Could we support one another through alternative business models, crowdfunding or digital currencies? How might such models coexist with traditional funding? In any case, the gravity of our crises is calling for both bold financial risks and careful investments.

A movement of movements is not an idea but a nascent phenomenon already arising from several recognitions: we are attracted to each other's work, we feel energized when our work connects, we need each other to succeed and the whole of life needs us to succeed. It is another expression of unity reasserting itself. A movement of movements may not grow quickly at first or demonstrate operational maturity in the beginning, but it is immediately strengthened by our commitment.

Do we feel called to come together beneath the forest floor? Would we express the resolve, the relationships and the ingenuity needed to connect our roots? Which roles might each of us play?

A Radical Commitment in Practicing Unity

Like any undertaking that could challenge us for decades or a lifetime, enacting unity in the years ahead requires a radical commitment. Our choice is not such a simple one— are we living at a time of amazing potential or impossible challenges?

If we assume that a positive future awaits us because "humanity has always found a way," we run the risk of living in denial. If we assume there will be an irreversible collapse of civilization, we run the risk of our despair becoming a self-fulfilling prophecy. In *both* cases, we run the risk of inaction.

Perhaps, we don't need to assume one future or another as much as decide *how we will be* with the fact that we don't know all the answers. Will we be spectators and see what happens or will we be participants who enact what happens? If we decide that our most sane response is participation, it doesn't necessarily mean we need to turn our lives upside down, but it may require that rare, life-long commitment that we reserve for our most sacred endeavors.

Radically committing to our moment can carry profound momentum. Where will it take us? How can we best contribute? Which practical actions can guide us?

If we truly commit to *enact unity*, we commit to do so within us, between us and around us—like the dimensions of our movements. However, seeing through our tendencies of separation and learning to enact unity is an ongoing challenge, with successes and missteps, and so we can embrace our commitment as *practice*. We are always learning.

Perhaps one of the most influential practices available to us is how we direct our attention. Becoming aware of our attention and using it consciously can be a powerful move that benefits us, our friends and our culture. We might dedicate more of our attention to participating in movements we admire or realigning our careers, so our skills and work can more directly benefit the whole. As we do so, it may serve us to first imagine how we can join and collaborate with existing efforts, instead of immediately creating something new.

As we've seen, there is so much already happening on the forest floor that invites our contributions. Whether we are called to heal the roots of an old oak, nourish a new bloom of wildflowers or weave mycelia connections between them, we will find many others who are excited to see us. This unity we discover when we "come together" is the same unity that has been guiding us all along.

Our very sense that everything is connected shines more brightly the more we remember and trust it. It's the *first* light we know—our inherent unity that exists before separation, before darkness, before our judgements, conflicts and crises ever arise. In the first light of unity, there is no widespread anxiety or lack of meaning, no culture wars or political polarization and no fear of existential doom—there is only our open, free-feeling, loving attention and relationship to all of life. Here, we are free, curious, grateful and generous. We see difference without seeing separation. We restore wholeness where it's forgotten. We realize that coming together is a matter of *remembering* again and again that we *are*.

None of us know what the most beautiful human future might be. Instead of beginning with grand visions to *change* the world, could it be enough to *more radically love it,* trusting that love also changes what needs to be changed?

Humanity is a movement—shaped by every one of our thoughts, conversations, decisions and collective actions. If the human movement is truly meant to make us greater and more unified than we now are, then we will more than imagine it—we will take joy in making it *real.*

How deep is the joy of serving the wholeness of life? The extreme nature of our moment guarantees us amazing breakthroughs along the way, yet these turbulent times could also bring tragic reversals as well. But if we engage it wholeheartedly, it will also lead us toward some of the most meaningful human lives that have ever been lived.

One of those most meaningful lives ever lived was the case of my dear friend and mentor, Terry Patten. Terry and I worked for many hours over the last year of his life to contribute our perspective at *A New Republic of the Heart* to the development of the concepts around a possible movement of movements, perhaps called the Holomovement, that we have explored in this chapter. It thus seems most appropriate to end with these thoughts from Terry:

> "The grassroots movements working to transform our world and save the planet are both autonomous in their endeavors and deeply connected to a larger vision. Following our unique sense of purpose and collaborating with like-minded communities and beyond is a founding principle of the Holomovement, an example of Unity in Action. Our social and cultural mycelium networks are ways to amplify the pull of collaborative coherence awakening individual purpose to best serve the good of the whole. The "Holomovement" is an

apt name representing the diverse sociocultural movement toward a just, fulfilling and sustainable human presence on Earth in accordance with the cosmological parameters of the physical universe.

To do this, we must first understand two aspects of existence—our dynamic but fractured and threatened world, and our underlying wholeness and unity. Only by honoring both of these realities simultaneously can we make sustainable changes in ourselves, our communities, our body politic and our planetary life-support system.

Let's not underestimate the potentials of the great underground reservoir of all that is good and healthy in our connectedness to one another. Our inherent desire to serve wholeness and health in part expresses something deep and transpersonal, our social mycelium ... Thus, although we certainly continue to be citizens of communities, cities and nations, we also become citizens of something broader and deeper. This is already occurring.

It will be increasingly important for us to recognize ourselves as "citizens" of that deeper connectedness, wholeness and goodness. When we arrive in a commitment to act in accordance with all in us that is healthy and connected, practicing wholeness as a way of life, we become trustable citizens of what I call a "new republic of the heart."

CHAPTER 14
EARTH VOICE AS HOLOMOVEMENT: SERVING THE WELL-BEING OF ALL LIFE

by Duane Elgin

Communication is the lifeblood of human evolution. It is our ability to communicate that enabled us to evolve from hunter-gatherers to the threshold of a workable planetary civilization. Now we are being pushed by hard necessity to mobilize our capacity for communication and connect with ourselves as an overall, human community. A growing climate crisis is not a singular challenge, it is part of a whole-systems crisis impacting the entire Earth. In addition, the human community faces growing shortages of fresh water, enormous inequities of wealth and well-being, unsustainable population growth, the mass die-off of animals and plants, and much more. *These and other forces will, within a few decades, produce the devastation and collapse of the entire world system—economically, socially, politically, and more.*

Communicate or perish seems to be the fundamental choice of our times. With robust, collective communication, we could move through the unraveling and collapse of the current world system to a new future on the other side of a great transition. Yet, is it realistic to imagine the people of the

Earth waking up and communicating with ourselves at a planetary scale and choosing a different pathway ahead?

A few years ago, I had the opportunity to raise this possibility with a Google executive. I asked him, "Could we create a global network of communication that connects the people of the Earth in a single forum to tackle our common challenge of living sustainably on the Earth?" He stared at me with some puzzlement for a few moments and then said, "You don't understand. That network has already been built. As soon as you open a browser on your computer—like Chrome or Safari—you are connecting into a global network—the internet. You may need tools to convert communications into different languages, but we have those technologies as well."

What good fortune! The technology for lighting up the world with meaningful communication already exists. At the very time we urgently need the ability to communicate among ourselves as a species, we find the world deep into a communications revolution. What is lacking is a global movement to use these technologies for constructive change. We need an Earth scale, citizen's movement to connect the whole world in collective conversation about our common future. We need an "*Earth Voice.*"

Mobilizing our voices as citizens on behalf of the well-being of the whole Earth is a movement of the highest order. A key stumbling block is that the internet is not being used to foster the well-being of life on Earth. Instead, the internet is being used primarily for commercial purposes—promoting mass consumption and mass entertainment. If citizens were to choose, the internet could also be used to support discourse among the people of Earth regarding our common future.

When I explored how practical it might be for humanity to come together in simple dialogues about our common future, the results were astonishing. In 2022, roughly two-thirds of the people on Earth have access to the internet through their cell phones. By 2030, the percentage of people with internet access is estimated to jump from two-thirds to three-quarters. This means that a majority of Earth citizens have cell phones and hold the Earth's future in their hands.

The next great superpower will not be a nation or even a collection of nations. Rather, it will be the billions of ordinary citizens who encircle Earth and can use the internet to call, with a collective voice, for unprecedented cooperation and creative action to care for our endangered planet, and for we humans to grow ourselves into a mature, planetary civilization. The new superpower of an *Earth Voice* could emerge swiftly from the combined voice and conscience of the world's citizens mobilized through the Internet that already encircles Earth.

How could we have a simple conversation among the people of Earth regarding, for example, climate change? I imagine a short video that focuses attention on the issues being considered which is then followed by a series of votes that appear on cell phone screens with a diversity of languages. As votes come in, they are uploaded in real time on a simple website where they can be seen by people around the planet. Illustrative questions could be:

1. Do you see significant changes to the Earth's climate impacting animals and plants? From "low" (hardly) to "high" (ruinous changes are evident).

2. How important is it to tackle the challenge of climate change? From "low" (not important) to "high" (extremely urgent).

3. Are you willing to make major changes in how you live in order to get climate change under control? From "low" (unwilling) to "high" (very willing IF others will join me).

These are not technical questions. Instead, they focus on the more subjective feelings of people and their willingness to listen and respond to urgent challenges facing our future. An important companion to outreach is the ability to receive and process this simple feedback from billions of people. We now have supercomputers with such extraordinary capacities that they can easily receive and count the votes of billions of people and show them results on their screens in real time. By combining blockchain technologies for privacy with the reach of the internet, super-computers can enable confidential voting by billions of citizens in secure networks. The bottom line: A simple and secure *Earth Voice* for global communication could emerge within this decade.

The work of *Earth Voice* is not to micromanage government through direct democracy; instead, it is for citizens to discover their widely shared views and priorities that can *guide* their representatives in government. It is not the role of the *Earth Voice* organization to become directly involved in complex policy decisions; instead, it is to enable citizens to express their overall views that can guide policymaking. Involving citizens in choosing our path into the future will not guarantee that the "right" choices will always be made, but it will guarantee that citizens will be involved and invested in those choices. Rather than feeling cynical and powerless, citizens will feel engaged and responsible for our collective future.

The legitimacy and empowerment of an *Earth Voice* organization within the Holomovement depends on honoring a few, key principles:

1. No advocacy by the independent and non-partisan *Earth Voice* organization.

2. Trans-partisan presentation of diverse views in the Electronic Earth Meeting

3. One person, one vote with accurate representation assured by using block-chain technologies (and validated with scientific sampling)

4. No attachment to outcome by the *Earth Voice* organization. Electronic Earth Meetings are advisory and respect the role of government representatives to make complex policy decisions that respect the role of citizens in making their sentiments known to policy makers.

Democracy has often been called "the art of the possible." If we don't know how our fellow citizens think and feel about collective efforts to create a sustainable and purposeful future, then we float powerlessly in a sea of ambiguity—unable to mobilize ourselves in constructive action. However, once we develop the simple capacity for sustained citizen communication, we will have the means to achieve a basic, shared understanding and working consensus regarding appropriate actions for a positive future. Once citizens know what other citizens around the world are willing to do, and once they are settled in their own hearts and minds as to what constitutes appropriate action, then they —and their representatives in government—can act swiftly and with authority. Actions can then come quickly and voluntarily.

We can mobilize ourselves purposefully, and each person can contribute his or her unique talents to building a life-affirming future. Because we can do this, we have a responsibility to try. Because global communication and understanding are vital if we are to work together, we citizens have the responsibility and obligation to mobilize the powerful tools of collective communication now available to us. The future is calling us to develop our collective voice—an *Earth Voice* that serves the well-being of all life. Because the hard work of building the technological system has already been done, with an Earth-scale citizen's movement, we can move swiftly to transform possibility into reality.

Beyond simple votes on key issues to build a global consensus (for example, the priority we give to responding to climate change, or sharing access to fresh water), we are engaged in something even deeper and more significant: *We are building a new sense of identity and collective empowerment as a species.* Pushed by adversity and pulled by the promise of a healing journey, the global nervous system could awaken a new capacity for collective self-awareness. A new "species mindedness" or Earth-scale reflective consciousness could powerfully emerge. We could learn to observe ourselves—to know ourselves and guide ourselves to higher levels of collective organization and action.

When the people of Earth are not simply on the receiving end of media as a collective witness to our endangered future, but also empowered by the tools of global communication that we hold in our hands for two-way dialogues, then a new and powerful force for creative change is unleashed in the world. If we can claim our wholeness as a human family, a remarkable transformation is open to us. Recognizing ourselves as Earth-citizens brings with it an expanded sense of:

1. *Identity*: Recognizing we now live in an intensely interdependent world means we see ourselves as an inescapable part of the Earth system. An Earth-scale identity does not diminish other identities such as nationality, community and ethnicity; instead, it places them in a larger context that calls forth our mature participation as Earth citizens.

2. *Empowerment*: With the power to vote on key concerns literally in our hands, *Earth Voice* forums could have a powerful guiding influence on public policies. As noted earlier, the next great superpower will emerge when the individual citizens of Earth come together in dialogue and consensus-building.

3. *Esteem*: When we recognize securing the future is a team effort and we are all in this together, then we are rising to a new level of maturity and consciousness as a species. We are rising above historic differences of wealth, privilege and power and participating in a system where each person's voice and vote counts equally in speaking and voting for humanity's future.

A transformational path requires far more than renewable energy, shifting diets and electric cars. We require an evolutionary uplift if we are to transform a planetary catastrophe into a path that serves the wellbeing of all life. The most critical uplifts are widely recognized and available to us—but they require us to accomplish this together. The path ahead means:

1. Choosing communication over conflict
2. Choosing to go through this rite of passage and into our adulthood as a species
3. Choosing reconciliation as a path that heals the wounds of history
4. Choosing to live in right relationship with a world brimming with aliveness
5. Choosing to grow our personal and collective consciousness
6. Choosing to come together in regenerative and supportive communities
7. Choosing to live more ecologically by embracing an ethic of simplicity

There is no fantasy here. Each one of these uplifting choices is already widely recognized and familiar. The challenge for we humans is to embrace these uplifts together! *Our collective participation and effort are essential if we are to turn away from planetary tragedy.* A critical challenge is to break free from extreme absorption in our personal lives and to connect with other humans in a collective conversation to participate in a common effort of healing, restoration and regeneration.

To move forward on our journey, we humans must expand and deepen our collective communication at a scale that matches the scale of the challenges we confront—and that is the entire Earth. It is vital that we collectively recognize how vulnerable our future is at this singular moment of time. We have entered an extraordinarily rare interval in history—a choice-point in our collective journey where the future of humanity and the rest of life on Earth will be altered irrevocably by choices we make now. We can either descend into ruin or rise in an uplifting transformation. We cannot predict where humanity will go from here, for a simple reason: Our future depends on our conscious choices—or failure to choose—both individually and collectively.

A crisis pushing us to take urgent action did not have to be our destiny. Nearly half a century ago, in the 1970s, most of humankind recognized we faced immense challenges. It was then that we could have chosen to mobilize ourselves and adapt more gradually to a radically changing future. Since then, we have consumed, at enormous cost to our future evolution, any extra margin of time in order to keep the status quo alive for just a few more decades. Now it is too late to choose a path of gradual change. Having used up our breathing room for gradual adaptation, humanity now confronts severe consequences if we don't respond swiftly and make sweeping changes in how we live on Earth.

We are an endangered species. Technological changes alone will not save us from a ruinous future. We must now come together as Earth citizens and work, shoulder-to-shoulder, with shared action and purpose. To illustrate: the "climate crisis" is just one part of a complex, whole-systems crisis involving nearly every aspect of how we live on Earth. Although technology is vital for responding to this crisis, it is more fundamentally a communications crisis, and we have the technology and tools required to respond at a global scale. What is missing is agreement among ourselves that we want to make transformational changes in how we live and work as a whole human family. Communication is the force that animates an Earth-scale society.

If we are to come together in common effort and bend the evolutionary curve upwards in favor of the well-being of all life, then we must rise to the urgent challenge of mobilizing our tools of collective communication—the internet, television, film, and radio—come together to build understanding, and develop working agreements for collective actions.

For the first time in human history, we have a way to listen to and talk with one another as members of one family. By awakening to ourselves as a planetary species and seeing ourselves whole, we have the potential for an evolutionary leap forward. We are now blessed with cell phone technology we can hold in our hands which enables us to awaken the Holomovement into action. Let's step forward, find our collective voice and begin the long journey of healing our wounded world.

Author's note:

The ideas and inspiration for an "Earth Voice" movement have deep roots in my life. I invested the decade of the 1980s in community organizing in the San Francisco Bay Area to create a "community voice" movement. I co-founded a non-profit organization called "Bay Voice" with the trans-partisan objective of creating a means for the entire region to come into conversation regarding important choices for our collective future.

We began by doing extensive research on the legal rights of citizens to request that the airwaves be used to serve the needs of citizens in addition to selling to the wants of consumers. What we found was that, in the U.S., citizens literally and legally own the airwaves at the regional level which is the scope of the media footprint of television broadcasters; specifically, ABC, CBS, NBC and Fox. Because they use airwaves owned by the community, they have a strict legal responsibility to serve "the public interest, convenience, and necessity" before they serve their own profit-making interests! With this key understanding, the Bay Voice organization: 1) objected to the renewal of their broadcast licenses (worth about a half-billion dollars each); and 2) called for the development of "Electronic Town Meetings" patterned after the success of the New England town meetings.

The results were powerful. First, broadcast TV station licenses were held up for nearly two years pending renewal, and this was a powerful demonstration of the seriousness of our effort. Second, in 1987, we demonstrated the ability of the citizens of the San Francisco Bay Area to express their collective voice with a pilot, "Electronic Town Meeting," that was aired in prime time on the ABC-TV station. This "community voice" gathering was seen by over 300,000 people in the Bay Area. Importantly, a pre-selected, scientific sample of citizens offered their live feedback in response to key questions and six "votes" were offered by the random sample during the hour-long Electronic Town Meeting. A brief overview of this "community voice meeting" can be seen in the first 3 and a half minutes in this video clip: https://youtu.be/a53 hL5Z1WHE.

The bottom line is that, in 1987, we saw how an Electronic Town Meeting in a regional setting could be very successful in reaching very large numbers of citizens and receiving their feedback. The question 35 years later is whether we can co-create some form of electronic gathering to bring the human family together in conversation and consensus building for our common future. Just as we mobilized television and telephones to create an Electronic Town Meeting for the San Francisco Bay Area in 1987, we now have the opportunity to mobilize the internet and cell phones to create global electronic meetings that give a voice to the people of Earth on behalf of the well-being of all life.

SPOTLIGHT FEATURE
GIVING A NAME TO A NEW STORY

by Lynnaea Lumbard, PhD

The purpose of this book is to give a name to something that is already happening, that many of us have intuitively known for years. We have been called to work for the benefit of Humanity and the planet, dedicating our lives to healing and wholeness. We've understood that we, as humans, need to work together to be in right relationship with our home, Earth. Naming our multidimensional efforts as a movement, a Holomovement, brings us together in a unitive pattern, giving us much more collective intelligence while letting us know that we're not alone. Like learning that we're a "Boomer" or a "Millennial" or a "Gen Xer," we recognize that we are a part of a larger field of shared challenges and common experiences. But no matter how old we are now, we are the generation of humans trying to navigate our own transformation into species maturity.

When we connect with each other and exchange our knowledge and findings, like mycelium under the trees that exchange their nutrients, the forest and the field grow stronger. The Holomovement gives us and our work a name, a form, a direction and the kind of relief and safety we feel when we know others have our back and are working alongside of us. We don't have to be doing the same thing, any more than the heart and lungs and brain have to be doing the same thing to support a thriving body. Our calling is to co-create a thriving body for Humanity, which can only exist in a relationship of care and partnership with a thriving Earth. It will take all of us integrating our own initiations, honing our own gifts, and working together to regenerate human communities in patterns of collaboration and compassion.

This coming together in harmony is what creates the possibilities of an Earth Voice, a unified humanity giving voice to the wholeness of interconnected life. This will not be an easy process. It's not lost on any of us that we are in a Great Transition, whether we call it the "Great Turning" or the "Great Unraveling." How we navigate the currents and tides of change will make a difference for our future. Navigation takes skill, knowledge, accurate data, a purpose, a direction and intention. We need to know where we're going and learn how we might get there.

Story can help. Stories show us pathways through difficulties and can tell us what to look out for and what decisions to make. They guide us and give shape and meaning for our experience. Ten years ago, Duane Elgin and I got together to create a wiki that would gather the stories and storytellers that might help us through this Great Transition. He was already starting to speak about Growing Up, the Hero's Journey, the Transformation of the Caterpillar and Planetary Birth. Together, we brainstormed more patterns of change and transformation that had wholesome outcomes—a new baby, a butterfly, an adult—as these are processes we know and trust.

Over the years, the wiki has morphed into the Great Transition Stories website,[36] which today names not only a dozen successful patterns of change but also highlights the growing number of emerging stories that are embodying the values of the Holomovement from the soil to the soul. Biomimicry, Regenerative Communities, Gender Reconciliation, Conscious

Evolution, Clean Money, Interspirituality, Healing Trauma and Centering Indigeneity name but a few.

The purpose of a larger, archetypal story is to give an image, a form, a pattern for how something happens collectively. Most of us have had experiences of feeling we are falling apart, our old beliefs dissolving into chaos and confusion like the green gooey stuff inside a cocoon. In such times, we often find ourselves retreating until enough imaginal cells start rising to form a new perspective that brings us out in another dimension, like the butterfly. If we look around, belief systems everywhere are now dissolving and changing. Where might Humanity be in the process of coming into a whole new consciousness, an awareness of a larger dimension, or an expanded vision of ourselves? What would "WE" be called? Homo Universalis? Holo Sapien?

Further, what about the times we feel like we're being squeezed, as if we're in the birth canal? When I recognize that something is being born, like a baby or a project or a book, then I can relax and trust the process, as birth is an intrinsic path of how life evolves on our planet. Taking this to the idea of Humanity going through a Planetary Birth, what kind of new human is trying to be born, and how will we midwife it or bear the birthing process?

Initiation is another Great Transition Story, perhaps one of the most relevant for now. The Hero's Journey is the story of how the individual soul gains strength, clarity and consciousness on the path into maturity. It chronicles the challenges of adolescence: finding our calling, facing our shadow, honing our vision and taking responsibility for our role in serving the greater whole. A feminine version of Initiation is told in the story of Inanna's descent to the underworld, where she is stripped of seven layers of raiment until she is hung like a piece of meat on a hook. I experienced this early in my own journey, feeling like I was losing everything, falling apart, descending into depression. Coming upon this most ancient of myths, the first ever recorded, had me learn the lesson of just 'being with' and staying present with compassion. It's what taught me the power of story and that I was in a sacred process and how to make it through.

If we understand that Humanity itself is in an initiatory process as a species, these stories give us names and patterns for understanding what's happening and how to be with this experience. We can even witness the stages of our own journey, like now when it feels like we—our country, our world—are having to face our collective shadow in order to come into a new level of integration.

How do we build communities centered in well-being? That's our task. It's actually what we're in the middle of now, taking the step into a second-tier evolution, where the innate pattern of evolution is altruism, working for the good of the whole. When we move from just the individual's struggle, to re-entering the community bringing our visions and gifts, we discover that collaboration and cooperation with our fellow initiates is what creates thriving communities and ecosystems.

Then arises the step of bringing all of these communities and movements together and connecting them into a larger whole. Like evolutionary biology lays out, evolution always has proceeded with fragments coming together to first form a cell, then cells coming together to form a multicellular organism. These then come together to form a larger body. Bodies come together to form an even greater whole that has been called a superorganism. That's happening. Now. We're in the process, and we are also consciously co-creating it. We are in the Holomovement. Consciously coming together in the Holomovement is what will create Earth's Voice.

CHAPTER 15
THE HOLOMOVEMENT AS A RETURN TO WHOLENESS

by Julie Krull, PhD, Shamini Jain, PhD & Teresa Collins

"The nature of reality and of consciousness is a coherent whole, which is never static or complete, but which is an unending process of movement and unfoldment... Particles are not individual entities but are actually extensions of the same fundamental something."

— David Bohm

Scientific and spiritual traditions alike have understood the nature of our collective reality to be inextricably intertwined—and as a result, ever-evolving. Bohm describes our universe as an undivided wholeness where everything is in an "unending state of process or becoming." Therefore, wholeness cannot be seen as the achievement of a static oneness or an ideal state to be realized. Wholeness is dynamic, a "wholeness-in-motion" where everything works together in an interconnected, interdependent process. This is the holomovement.

It could be argued that our return to wholeness isn't really a return at all. It's simply a remembering or recognition of the true nature of reality where we embrace ourselves as "extensions of the same fundamental something" in our interbeing and becoming. The Holomovement invites us to embody our inherent wholeness, demystify the mysteries of the implicate order and nurture our innate capacity to live for the good of the whole.

We have built our world around the false belief that we are separate—separate from each other, separate from Earth and all its inhabitants, separate from the very foundations of life. The illusion of being separate from the creative, dynamic life force of wholeness-in-motion has led to whole-systems breakdown, wide-spread destruction and escalating global crises. Yet, separation is merely an illusion, a faulty, outdated scientific model, and a developmental stage of consciousness that we are rapidly outgrowing.

To understand unity is to understand the holomovement. To experience unity is to experience wholeness-in-motion. Both science and direct experience are invaluable pathways as we wake to the Holomovement that is moving us.

The Holomovement as a Return to Wholeness

Science is now advancing Bohm's model of wholeness and demonstrating his premise that all things found in the explicate order emerge from the unitive holomovement and ultimately fall back into it. Bohm's pioneering exploration into physics, philosophy and consciousness fueled his search for unity and wholeness at the crossroads of science and spirituality. He theorized there is an omnipresent consciousness that in-forms all creation. In her book, *The Cosmic Hologram: In-formation at the Center of Creation*, Dr. Jude Currivan says, "Mind and consciousness aren't something that we have, but rather what we and the whole world are." Currivan describes the recent scientific discoveries across multiple disciplines and all scales of existence, that support this revolutionary leap in our understanding of ourselves and the unified nature of reality. The science, based on thousands of leading-edge researchers, reconciles our understanding of unity and wholeness with spiritual experiences and universal wisdom teachings, to affirm Bohm's omnipresent consciousness.

Evolutionary biologist, Elisabet Sahtouris, describes our evolutionary transition from "feisty competitive hostilities" to "mature, friendly cooperation." As a species, we're waking to our unified nature and moving from late adolescence to early adulthood. This shift in consciousness is moving us to consciously participate within the holomovement and create cooperative communities that care for all life. This evolution of consciousness is at the core of what we're seeing emerge on the planet, inspiring this larger movement of movements.

There's no one concise model or theory within the science of consciousness. Significant progress has been made with promising theories that are being developed and a wealth of experimental data is being generated. However, the notion of "stages" or "levels" of consciousness is helpful as we understand what is occurring with the radical transformation, global crises and breakdowns (and breakthroughs) on the planet.

We're witnessing how the illusion of separation has been a distinct stage of development in the collective human psyche. Most models move from tribal to unitive or non-dual wholeness, with many levels in between, and identify the specific value systems within each. These models recognize the shift in two, main tiers of the continuum, from separation to unitive consciousness—or a consciousness of wholeness.

So, whether you call it a leap of consciousness or a spiritual awakening, we do know that people who operate from separation consciousness show distinctly different characteristics and values than people who are centered in unitive consciousness. The shift toward wholeness is often induced or influenced by differing (or altered) states of consciousness. As science continues to reconcile with universal wisdom teachings, so does the swelling phenomena of mystical experiences.

The direct experience of unity and wholeness-in-motion is considered a mystical or spiritual experience, sometimes thought of as an altered state of consciousness. It's often dismissed as "woo-woo" by the rational mind. Yet in 2009, according to Pew Research, 49% of Americans have had a mystical experience. Experts estimate it is much higher now. Abraham Maslow believed everyone has mystical experiences; we just safely label them as peak experiences or dismiss them all together.

A revolutionary shift is now underway as we better understand wholeness, unity and the nature of reality. Increasing accounts of near-death experiences, the popularization of mindfulness practice and meditation and the expanded study of plant medicines are but a few topics that have helped to pave the way for further exploration into mysticism. Our direct experience of unity is undeniable. That ephemeral glimpse of eternity can come in a split second, and seeing the ineffable underpinnings of a vast, interconnected, interdependent web of life shifts our worldview. Unitive consciousness weaves the seen and unseen into Bohm's undivided wholeness-in-motion in a profound experience of peace and belonging.

From the scientific underpinnings to the direct experience of unity, our return to wholeness offers a roadmap through our existential crisis. Einstein said, "We cannot solve our problems with the same thinking we used when we created them." All the solutions we need already exist for rapid social and ecological regeneration. We simply need to shift our perspective from the illusion of separation to the understanding of wholeness-in-motion as we redesign a world that works for everyone.

The good news is the whole is beginning to see itself as whole. Individuals and organizations around the world are stepping up to restore our sense of undivided wholeness. Projects and programs are popping up around the world. From social activism to peace initiatives, a growing movement of movements is evolving into a coherent whole.

We are waking to the understanding that we are part of a whole living universe and coming into right relationship with the wholeness-in-motion of Life. Recognizing this impulse as the holomovement gives us a unified, coherent, shared purpose and vision. The holomovement is our journey to wholeness, and we are participating as conscious members and co-evolutionary partners.

In our dynamic wholeness, no one is separate from it, and nothing is outside of it. A return to wholeness begs us to live into the emergence—the unfoldment—where we not only embody and express unity, but also shift our worldview and consciously participate in the Holomovement as a single, undivided whole, consciously partnering with the impulse of evolution to heal on a global scale.

Bohm suggests, "Wholeness is a kind of attitude or approach to the whole of life. If we can have a coherent approach to reality, then reality will respond coherently to us." Universal wisdom teachings, direct spiritual experience and the scientific understanding of unity support this approach to the whole of life—a return to or remembering of—wholeness. Wholeness is the medicine of our times. At the heart of this impulse is whole-system health and healing. As we work together toward greater coherence and cooperation, let us remember we are the holomovement expressing and recognizing itself in form.

Biofield Science and Healing the Collective

A key area of science that points to the nature of our interconnection is biofield science. The term "biofield" was a term coined by Western scientists in the 1990s at a National Institutes of Health meeting in the United States—in part to help understand the effects of healing through energy and consciousness. They described biofield as "a massless field, not necessarily electromagnetic, that guides the homeodynamic functioning of a living organism." Biofields can be examined at multiple levels of scale—from cells to communities.

When we look at the rigorous, published data in biofield science, whether from clinical trials examining the effects of biofield healing on pain, mental health, and even immune and hormonal function—or even how biofield healing can reduce tumor spread, down to cell signaling in the body—it becomes clear that our consciousness not only matters, it also has powerful effects on our abilities to manifest change on both the subtle and physical levels.

We are at a pivotal point in humanity's evolution. Given where we are in human history, it might behoove us to implement what we've learned about the groundbreaking research in biofield science. Yet, these are more than just fascinating studies to talk about at a dinner party. These findings are begging us to awaken to our human healing power and shift the way we experience each other and the world as a result.

When we look at all the data behind biofield healing, alongside the ancient wisdom that explained the practices, purposes and spiritual cores from which these healing methods came, it reminds us of two, fundamental truths crucial to remember and enact. One, we are fundamentally interconnected down to our consciousness affecting another's healing. Two, we are far more powerful as agents of healing than we can ever imagine.

The biofield, and the science behind it, beseeches us to come to a full realization that we don't end here—we don't end at our skin. We are interconnected beings, both within and between our body-minds. As we explore the biofield through the study of healing, we realize how buying into this fallacy of separateness is greatly hurting us. When we don't see ourselves connected with each other and the Earth, we feel powerless, alone and left believing our suffering is because of bad genes, bad environments or other factors beyond our control. We might feel that the only action we can take is to mask our symptoms with material things or substances. In the illusion of separateness, we also numb ourselves to each other's suffering instead of realizing we have the power to instantaneously alleviate someone else's pain—and even prevent that pain from occurring.

Biofield science and healing reminds us that the key to our thriving as human beings is first to understand and affirm our power to realign our world into one commensurate with our highest human potential. Believing in healing possibilities is a start, and to help scale up the future of biofield healing as a collective will require key ongoing steps including: deepening our scientific inquiry through collaborative, interdisciplinary biofield science research at top-tier universities; communicating results of studies to the public, as well as stakeholders in policy and health care; and developing biofield-based technology for preventative medicine diagnoses and treatment. Another critical component includes providing evidence-based education on biofield-based self-care—how to sense and work with biofields to enhance health and prevent disease.

Our next, immediate step in scaling up healing includes sharing perspectives of both scientists and healers with the broader global community. In general, healers need to have a greater voice at the table as we advance biofield research and technology as well as, of course, education and practice. This includes fully incorporating Indigenous perspectives and Indigenous wisdom holders in healing and medicine. Indigenous healing systems have always taught principles of holism, critical for the healing of ourselves, each other and the planet. Understanding the fundamental interconnection between our bodies, minds, spirits, climate change and the biofield as a connective medium for healing is an example of Indigenous wisdom ignored because of the colonization of medicine across the globe.

In many ways, we need to mend the fractures in understanding that have kept us from believing in our personal power to heal ourselves and each other. It is time for us to listen deeply to the wisdom of the elders, who understand on a deep, embodied level how we can shift our entire way of being to one of harmony and interconnectedness instead of the fallacy of separateness.

For us to truly understand the mysteries and realities of healing, we must embark on the healing journey ourselves. The path of healing and the path of spiritual liberation are one and the same. It is fundamentally about recognizing the divine Shakti at play within us, and between us, and understanding that even those who appear to think and act very differently from us, are fundamentally of the same source and substance of Creation. Healing isn't about just bringing us comfort, making a wound close faster or taking away our pain (all of which might happen). Healing is fundamentally about realigning with our soul's force and power to live a life of harmony within ourselves, with each other and with the planet.

The good news is that the healing path is accessible to all of us. Although there are diverse languages and practices of healing in every culture, healing itself requires no specific religious belief. Through the path of healing, we learn to stop identifying with things not truly connected with our spirit. We can delight in the interconnections of our own being and being with others, and we can spread joy as well as feel others' pain. The best way we can foster healing for others is to ensure that we are also making ourselves whole.

We can marvel at how nature heals herself and explore how those fundamental laws of healing can be applied to ourselves and our society. We can feel the full vital life force within us and become fully alive because we have ignited healing power within us and between us. Understanding our interconnected reality and the role of coherence can propel us into collective healing—a return to wholeness.

The Unified Field of Consciousness and Global Coherence

> "*Imagine a world of oneness. Where every part of life is doing everything to make sure your life is optimized, and you are doing the same on behalf of every part of life ... what would the world be like with this? Imagine ... this is oneness. Every possibility comes from oneness.*"
>
> — Rich Shealey

Life knows oneness, and is doing everything to ensure our lives, and all life, are optimized—in coherence—and moving toward wholeness. Unfortunately, we have not been doing our part on behalf of the whole, and our manifest reality reflects this. Yet, it seems the increasing chaos and incoherence of our times is fueling the awakening of our unified nature. In the article "Coherence: Bridging Personal, Social and Global Health," HeartMath Director of Research, Rollin McCraty, PhD, writes:

"Of the many new, scientific perspectives that emerged from the 20th century, one of the most profound is that the universe is wholly and enduringly interconnected and coherent. Complex living systems, including human beings, are composed of numerous dynamic interconnected networks of biological structures and processes. Coherence implies order, structure, harmony and alignment within and amongst systems—whether in atoms, organisms, social groups, planets or galaxies. Thus, every whole has a relationship with and is a part of a greater whole, which is again part of something greater. In this context, nothing can be considered as separate, alone or lacking relationships."

With this awakening, an awareness of our unique presence within the interconnected whole—the unified field—deepens, and we begin to experience our natural state of coherence. This harmonious state is where our hearts, minds and bodies are united in cooperation and flow, inspiring us from the inside out to be all we already are, for the good of the whole.

The holomovement as Bohm sites, weaves the implicate and explicate order together—an event horizon between the field of consciousness and the material universe; a vibratory sea of coherence and potential from which everything is arising and returning. You and I are included. Imagine the holomovement as the "cosmic fascia or connective tissue" holding this unbroken wholeness as it materializes into a multiplicity of expressions.

Wholeness is not a destination to be reached, it is an ever-evolving, constantly emerging manifestation of the holomovement—responding and innovating, composting and building, stretching and contracting, exploring, pausing, reaching, shifting, leaping and always moving toward greater coherence and wholeness. This process is happening at all scales from the smallest particle to the infinite vastness of space. We are discovering through science and direct experience that we are an intrinsic part of this extraordinary dance of consciousness and form and that our unique part matters.

As we awaken to our unified nature, we begin to feel the holomovement drawing us inward to our own center—into coherence. This point of stillness connects the implicate and explicate order inside each of us, and from this unified wholeness, the holomovement materializes uniquely as YOU and ME, all for the good of the whole. Each of us is a unique and vital expression of wholeness-in-motion!

It's time to make a fundamental shift from thinking we are "making it happen," to relaxing into "being" wholeness-in-motion happening. We are not creating the holomovement, the holomovement is gathering us into a multiplicity of diverse clusters and functions—islands of coherence. This is needed to fuel a leap to a higher order. Nobel laureate, Ilya Prigogine, said, "When a complex system is far from equilibrium, small islands of coherence in a sea of chaos have the capacity to shift the entire system to a higher order." When we place our trust in oneness and allow our contributions to be inspired from the inside out—from our inherent state of coherence—we naturally begin to move *with* and *as* the holomovement. We move to a higher order. The only way through our current crises is to consciously enter this unified dance with life from a state of heart-centered coherence.

Our incoherence—a vibrational state arising from the illusion of separation—is distorting the signal we are receiving from the holomovement that informs our unique role and function within the whole. The more our awareness is in a state of separation, the fainter or more distorted the signal is. David Bohm also reminds us:

> "[If we have coherence] we will produce the results we intend rather than the results we don't intend. That's the first big change. Then we will be more orderly, harmonious, we will be happier... the major source of unhappiness [on our planet] is that we are incoherent and therefore are producing

results that we don't really want, and then trying to overcome them while we keep on producing them."

Our commitment to cultivating greater coherence—personally, socially and globally—is an essential key to manifesting a future equal to our potential, for the joy and fulfillment of the self and the good of the whole. So how do we cultivate our capacity for sustained coherence at this critical juncture in our evolutionary journey? The answer is simple, yet a lifelong practice—attend to your own awakening awareness of oneness above all else and join with others doing the same.

Consciously choose to align your thoughts, words and deeds with a unified worldview. It is a moment-to-moment choice to emerge from the deeply rooted illusion of separation gripping humanity into our natural state of coherence. Coherence cultivation practices can help calm our nervous system, neutralize stress reactions, help us discern better choices and increase our clarity and responsiveness to life. The more attention we give to the cultivation of coherence, the more we will begin to feel the holomovement flowing in, around, and as us—guiding and informing us to be our best selves.

HeartMath Institute, a leader in personal and global coherence research and application, offers this simple and quick-coherence practice that naturally evokes this state of heart-centered presence and can be done anytime, anywhere. Let's do it together right now.

1. *Heart-Centered Focus*: Place your attention on your heart center.

2. *Heart-Centered Breathing*: Imagine you are breathing in and out of your heart center.

3. *Heart-Centered Feeling*: As you are breathing, bring into your awareness a life-enhancing feeling or emotion such as gratitude, love, joy, compassion, care, hope.

4. Circulate this feeling throughout your body with your breath and radiate this feeling outward into your local environment, into your interactions, and into the world.

Coherence cultivation practices like this one bring us right into our bodies where we can instantly impact our own health and wellbeing, and naturally impact the health and wellbeing of the whole. Imagine what is possible when we consciously choose to bring coherence cultivation practices into the heart of our daily lives, relationships, schools, teams, projects and board rooms. Imagine what is possible when we put this purpose first. At HeartMath Institute, they believe when "individuals and groups practice increasing their heart coherence, it paves the way for a collective momentum that has the potential to transform and uplift consciousness at a global scale."

As we come into coherence, individually and collectively, we will be drawn into resonant clusters—omni-centered, diverse, islands of coherence— all working together within the wholeness-in-motion. In coherence, we instinctively trust the emergent process and are inspired from the inside out to be the part of the whole we were uniquely born to be. From our natural state of coherence, we collectively activate, accelerate and nourish our innate capacity to live for the good of the whole.

Nurturing Our Innate Capacity to Live for the Good of the Whole

"Indeed, the attempt to live according to the notion that the fragments are really separate is, in essence, what has led to the growing series of extremely urgent crises that is confronting us today."

— David Bohm

Bohm's insight into the "extremely urgent crises" is spot on, and he shared this insight back in 1980. Forty years later, we have escalating economic, social, climate and health crises that many refer to as a runaway train. Are our current crises an unstoppable or uncontrollable situation? When we recognize the holomovement as a return to wholeness, further explore biofield science and the future of collective healing, and consciously practice personal, social and global coherence, we discover hope. We can literally sense the new pattern—our innate capacity to live for the good of the whole.

Bohm said we are internally related to everything, and consciousness is an internal relationship to the whole. As humans collectively expand into unitive consciousness and evolve, we begin to consciously embody and awaken to our inseparable participation within wholeness-in-motion. This responsibility reaches beyond our individual selves and our species to the very foundations of life and future generations. We realize our shared needs for a healthy planet support the core needs for all life—living soil, healthy water, vitalizing food, fresh clean air, physical and emotional safety, comfortable shelter and manifesting potential.[37] Our personal, collective and planetary health are all interconnected and interdependent.

Throughout this vast and diverse global movement, we also recognize that diversity is essential. Biodiversity extends beyond different ecosystems to all life, including humans. Therefore, unity and harmony in diversity becomes the goal, where we assure all parts of the living system are supported to realize our unique potential and serve the greater health and wellbeing of the whole.

As we recognize this pattern, we begin to see it everywhere—from the personal, to local and global. It is a blueprint for a world that works for all. Our fundamental interbeing and belonging with the whole community of our planetary home, Gaia, breaks through the illusion of separation and quickens the wisdom of our hearts. It's life affirming and fills us with purpose.

This impulse of evolution is waking the human family to its co-evolutionary partnership and responsibility. We take our place in the evolutionary flow and understand we exist to evolve within the dynamic, never-ending wholeness-in-motion, toward greater levels of individual and collective expression. It reveals an innate patterning that fosters a new frontier of collaborative, synergistic, and cooperative relationships.

Finding our place in the ever-evolving unfoldment of wholeness-in-motion is our individual and collective experience. We can trust that the impulse of evolution, itself, is guiding the journey. Our task is to embody and express unitive consciousness with a discipline of coherence. It's an unimaginably beautiful and peaceful way of living—being informed by and informing the whole of Creation. Abiding in this wholeness, we nurture our innate capacity to serve the good of the whole.

CHAPTER 16
PURPOSE: THE SOUL OF THE HOLOMOVEMENT

by Rev. Deborah Moldow
featuring Justin Faerman, Jean Houston, PhD
& Constance Buffalo

All life has purpose. It is purpose that gets us up in the morning and drives our actions throughout the day. Most life forms are consumed with surviving—finding nourishment and avoiding peril—and proliferating. Human beings, in spite of being relative latecomers to the Earth's population, have flourished across the globe in diverse environments. Our survival success, coupled with our cognitive abilities and our unique shaping of the world around us to meet our desires, has resulted in what psychologist Abraham Maslow dubbed a hierarchy of needs. In this useful model, we can see that our purpose evolves over time, both individually and collectively.

Once our basic needs are met, we begin to move into higher levels of purpose and evolving through the stages of: 1. Physiological needs; 2. Safety needs; 3. Love and belonging needs; 4. Esteem needs; to 5. Self-actualization needs.[38] We become progressively more at choice about the direction we take, be it choosing a career or a mate or finding a purpose that is greater than serving ourselves, our family, our community, our faith or our nation.

These higher levels of purpose become increasingly collective, and collective human purpose is one of the most powerful forces on the planet, both for good and for evil. Collective purpose built Stonehenge and the Pyramids, the Roman empire and the Crusades. It colonized foreign lands for profit and for faith. It waged world wars and developed the worldwide web. Western civilization's inexorable march toward progress constructed the modern world with all its marvels of education, opportunity and communications—and its disastrous separation from the natural world that gives us life. Collective purpose on the part of the privileged has brought us to a critical threshold whose current course has the potential to lead the human race, and perhaps many other life forms with us, to the brink of extinction.

What can help us to change course? We are being called to an unprecedented level of shared purpose that represents a whole new phase of human evolution. People across the planet are feeling this call and responding by seeing past the limitations of earlier ways of thinking to possibilities beyond what our present systems can provide. These creative souls are reimagining what it means to rise up together in common cause to radically transform our concepts and our behavior, to become responsible stewards of our creative powers so that we may learn to live in harmony as an integral population within the web of life. This is no less than a Holomovement, where every part is essential to the success of the whole.

Futurist Barbara Marx Hubbard said, "In the next 30 years we can destroy our world. With the very same powers—spiritual, social, scientific— we can evolve our world. Our mission is to serve as catalysts for a planetary awakening in our lifetime, to take a non-violent path to the next stage of our evolution."[39] But what will it take to help midwife this path to conscious evolution?

The Source of Synergy Foundation,[40] founded by Diane Marie Williams in 2006, began bringing together in retreat individuals whose life work pointed to a new paradigm for human consciousness taking us beyond our assumptions: what life could be if we were to design a future based not on survival of the fittest but respect for all life, with abundance and opportunity for all. A community of like-minded, open-hearted visionaries came together as the Evolutionary Leaders Circle.[41] The Circle is comprised of authors, educators, scientists, faith leaders, artists and activists, each thinking outside the box and leading us to new ways of envisioning our relationships with one another and the Earth.

One quality shared by all members of the Evolutionary Leaders Circle is a heightened sense of purpose. They have each followed what Jean Houston calls "the lure of becoming," a powerful impulse pulling them to forge new paths of thinking, creating, imagining and communicating their vision to others. As they gather in the community of Evolutionary Leaders, they join together in partnerships and Synergy Circles around various areas of common interest that inspire their personal sense of soul mission and empower them toward greater impact in the world. They recognize one another through their shared sense of collective purpose. It is the diversity of their approaches that strengthens the interweaving of their contributions into a powerful force for good.

Three Evolutionary Leaders

As examples of Evolutionary Leaders inviting all of us to join them in shared purpose, we will explore the contributions of three members of this community: Justin Faerman, Jean Houston and Constance Buffalo. Each of these leaders shares a passion for helping humanity to find its way through the current challenges to an entirely new way of living that enhances and expands our own personal gifts in service to the next stage of human evolution, growing a Holomovement in action. The three pieces included below speak to the importance of purpose in personal, yet universally understood, ways.

Justin Faerman expresses how each person's individual purpose impacts the destiny of humanity as a whole, co-creating the Holomovement that we can only manifest with our collective intention. Jean Houston urges us to answer the call of the Future Humans we are destined to be, reminding us that we have within us the tools of our creative imaginations to go beyond the limitations of the past, activating our sense of purpose to step into a whole new version of the human species. Constance Buffalo reminds us that our individual purpose is deeply embedded in the evolution of all who share our planetary home.

So, perhaps our first purpose is to remember that we are part of the web of life, honoring all that came before us as we strive for a future where all can flourish. This truly is our moment of choice for our souls' highest purpose. Will we make the right choices on the road ahead?

Your Role in the Destiny of Humanity

Justin Faerman

> *Nothing exists without purpose, therefore purpose exists within everything.*

No matter which level of reality you examine, from the microcosm of a cell to the macrocosm of a galaxy, the same essential patterns of organization are found playing out over and over again at different scales of being. What seems to be a whole at one level is simply a smaller part of a larger organism or ecosystem on another.

This repeating property of reality is often described as a "fractal" or "holon" and is perhaps most obvious in the human body, where a single cell is part of an organ and an organ is simply a part of our body as a whole. In the same way, an individual human can be considered to be a cell of our species, and our species can be considered an organ of our planet, and on and on ad infinitum, as far as you can take it out to the edges of the universe as a whole.

What this pattern reveals is that in nature all things serve a specific and complex purpose that is essential to and intricately interwoven within a larger whole. Therefore, by extension, you are no exception and rather, quite the opposite: you are an integral part of both the human species, the ecosystem of planet Earth and, taken to its maximum extreme, the destiny of the cosmos as a whole.

Because you exist, you have a purpose—but, just like a cell can be cancerous or life-giving, you have a choice as to how to use the life you have been given. You can contribute to the health of the organism of humanity, the wellbeing of the organism of the planet and ultimately the harmony of the cosmos, or you can contribute to its destruction, stagnation and decay. To choose purpose—by its very nature—is to choose life; to choose health; to choose the wellbeing of the whole.

Humans continually make the mistake of assuming that their impact could only be minuscule in the grand scheme of things, but the butterfly effect of cause and effect magnified over time shows us the exact opposite is true. Even the smallest gestures and decisions can echo out to alter the course of history in unimaginable ways. An ounce of love offsets a pound of pain. A few words of inspiration and hope can stop armies, and a revolutionary idea can topple empires. A single act of kindness can save untold lives. Determined action can overcome even the most seemingly insurmountable challenges we might face. History is filled with examples of all of these being true, and there is no point of greater contribution that you can have to the unfolding of a positive future than in living your purpose fully. It is how you play your greatest role on the stage of the universe. Thus, it is worth all of your effort and time to discover it and live it to the fullest extent possible, because in the final analysis, the destiny and fate of humanity lies in your hands as much as anyone else's.

This ultimately is the basis for the Holomovement—that by both playing our individual, purpose-driven and therefore inherently positive role in the grand scheme of things and uniting with others under these same auspices, we can unlock the next phase of our collective evolution that can only come about when the proper conditions are in place. Like a puzzle of incredible intricacy and scale, each one of us holds an essential piece that is necessary for the health and wellbeing of the whole.

This is the way of nature, and it is to the supremely sophisticated forces of nature that we owe our very sustenance. When an intelligence that vast endows every living and inanimate thing with purpose, in my view, we would be wise to discover and surrender to our own, for our very existence must then depend on this fact.

When viewed through this lens, life becomes much simpler. Discover your purpose, live it to its fullest extent possible and help others to do the same. On some level, all the existential crises and problems we face in this world are simply due to our deviation from this fact; therefore, one of the greatest contributions you can make to the destiny of humanity is to play your role in the unfolding of this larger plan. As you live your purpose, it enables and creates the conditions needed for others to do the same. It is only together in a unified Holomovement that we will be able to rise to the occasion and overcome the evolutionary challenges we face.

The Role of Purpose in Becoming the Future Human

Jean Houston, PhD

Human beings "thrive" on meaning and purpose. Bringing meaning and purpose together is so important because world-wide societies are crying out for assistance in the transformations of their cultures, their people, their business, their institutions and to bring a new vision of the possible Earth into reality.

We, of course, have to begin with ourselves so that we can be operating with the fullness of our being. I think the global need is to achieve a new humanity and a new way to nurture the human species while we work to heal our home. The need is to develop what I have called the "possible human" in the "possible society" in a more "possible world." So, this whole issue of purpose has to do with the art of world making, spirit catching, "mind growing," in a time of soul-quaking transformation. Thus, the complexity of our time requires both a greater and a wiser use of our imaginal capacity—a rich playing of the mental and emotional instrument that we've been given. I believe that the world really requires skilled facilitators, coaches, entrepreneurs, evacuators and teachers to guide and lead the shift to a set of new global values and local practices. That is what I am so, so deeply involved in now.

There is a term that has come in my mind that doesn't go away, and it's the old geo-biological term "speciation." There is the fossil wall with lots of fossils because the wall's been there for thousands of years, and things look the same for ten years, twenty years, a hundred years, and then suddenly BOOM JUMP: something new has been added to the species that makes it continue on a more practical, creative and life-giving form. I believe we're in "jump-time," a time of speciation, and part of the speciation is the call to purpose.

I can't tell you how often my students say, "I want to find out what my purpose is." I have them go through imaginational exercises of their purpose, and you know what? It's not good enough. There is something deeper, richer, more potent that is trying to come through. They have been born into a time of whole-system breakdown, which ALWAYS is a time that precedes a renaissance, and it precedes the time when something new is being added to the human instrument, as it is when you look at the fossil record—it happened with the fossils—there's a jump! It may be subtle; it may be large. In our time, I believe it is both subtle and large, and something else so extraordinary there is almost no name for it, because we are in a time of evolutionary speciation. A new human species is ready to emerge.

So, I ask people, "What is buzzing in you? What is developing?" Since we live in what I call "jump-time," the maps no longer fit the territories; the expected is the unexpected. Everything that was, isn't anymore. Everything that isn't, is coming into being, because we are in an era of quantum change—

the most radical deconstruction and re-construction that the world has ever seen. More and more history is happening faster and faster—faster than we can make sense of it. Life paths that have contained us, that have sustained us across literally millennia, are vanishing as we speak, like Gaia's species that are hourly becoming extinct. We are guests at the wake of a way of being that has been ours for thousands of years.

That's why I believe all the people reading this are among the most important people who have ever lived. Other times in history thought that they were it, but this is it! What you do makes a difference as to whether we grow or whether we die—whether we evolve or whether we perish. We know, or we have at least a kind of vibratory sense, that we have the power to direct the process of life itself along lines very different from those that the prophets of gloom proclaim as inevitable. In our time, we have entered into the crossroads between worlds, between species, between ourselves and forever.

So, the people who are reading this right now, I think you all know yourself to be the pilgrims and the parents of this emerging era. No old formulas or stopgap solutions will suit for this new world to be born. We have to bring new mind into time. That's why we all go around asking the great questions: "How do we make a better world? What must we do to serve the larger story, the larger narrative that we are all caught up in?" Because we're living in the changing of the guard on every level—in which every "given" is quite literally "up for grabs."

I think this is the momentum behind the drama of our world: the breakdown, the break-through of every old way of being, knowing, relating, governing, believing… I mean, it shakes the foundations of all and everything, and it is allowing for another order of reality to come into town.

What does it take to be an agent of a time of whole system transition? Whole system transition is a condition of interactive change that affects every aspect of your life as you know it. It includes what I call the "re-patterning" of human nature in this jump-time, this time of growth. This is no less than the re-genesis of society, and these factors are further energized by the dual impetus from the larger ecology, the pulsing from the Earth, the universe, the cosmos. I think we're cosmic agents, and we are coded for these times. There's the impetus that comes from the larger ecology, and these kinds of forces determine the direction of our "jump" into the future.

Purpose and change are optimistic because they focus on the emergence of patterns of possibility never before known or available, and so, we are able to integrate inner and outer dimensions of life in ways which infuse new depth into psychological and spiritual growth, and new purpose and responsibility into social transformation. I think people today know this and are carriers of these dynamic patterns. Spiritual growth really is key to activating the emergent stages of our human evolution.

This is the momentum behind the movement of consciousness into a whole new understanding of purpose. We are purposed beings, and our lives are always looking for the purpose that is just behind the curtain. And the curtain opens to not just a funny little man working the machines. It is the great universal Source—itself, herself, ourselves—that says it is time to wake up now. It is time to do and be what you were born to do and be.

Choosing the Red Road

Constance Buffalo, Red Cliff Band of Chippewa

> *Our prophecies say that a time will come when*
> *you will choose what becomes of the Earth.*
> *That time is now.*

These are the days of the great choices that our prophecies have foretold. The prophecy for this time was written for you, our non-native friends. It says that you will be given a choice between two roads that will decide our future. These roads have been interpreted in many ways. The Black Road is one of separation and good for yourself, at the expense of others and the world around you. The Red Road is one of a return to caring for the well-being of the whole of life.

If the Black Road is chosen, then the destruction which was brought when the Europeans came to this country will come back and cause much suffering and death to the people of Earth. If the Red Road is chosen, the final prophecy, called a Fire, will be ignited—a fire of peace, love, collaboration and regeneration. But in order to make the choices that will lead us on the right path, we need to first establish a sense of kinship with all life, from which our shared purpose can arise.

"Kinship" can mean many things to many people. In our Anishinaabeg communities, perhaps better known as Chippewa or Ojibwa, it means that you "belong" in the most expansive sense of the word.

When I meet someone new on our Red Cliff reservation in the deep woods of Northern Wisconsin, I will be asked, "Who are your people?" I introduce myself by my lineage so the listener understands where I fit into our tribal family, the clan I was born into and the nesting of families through which we may be connected. This is a microcosm of our larger humanity where each person brings their unique purpose into the world to interlace with our collective tribe of life.

For me, it also means that I belong not only to our people, but also to you and to the land and to all the life of our forests and waters. I am a daughter of our tribe and of the great stands of birch, hemlock and cedars. I feel the saltless ocean of Lake Superior's waters move through my blood and am humbled by the colorful, undulating Northern Lights, said to be the dancing of our ancestors. You too, are a child of the earth, sacred as the waters and arriving now to offer your own spirit to this time of great decisions.

In my case, to be a member of our tribe is to live as different expressions of a complex culture with an unspoken covenant. We live as the Fourth World through our respect, relationship, reciprocity, responsibility and humility.

It is said that *Gitchie Manitou*, The Great Mystery, had a vision. It showed the stars and Earth, its creatures and beauty, the beginnings, growth and endings of things. Also present were all the fears, love, hate and joy of this world. Then the vision slowly took form.

The *First World* was made up of the rock, water, fire and wind, each receiving its own power and spirit.

The *Second World* emerged from these four substances, and the sun, moon, stars and earth came to be. From them came the life-giving waters, the mountains, rivers, forests and oceans that filled our Earth, each with its own reasons for being and gifts to share. These were intermingled with the flowers, grasses, trees and vegetables with their own life-giving beauty.

The *Third World* was filled with all the animals, the flyers, walkers, crawlers and swimmers. They too, had their own spirits and their own roles in the emerging flow of life.

The *Fourth World* was the last, and humankind was born. We are the youngest of creation; we are the ones who depend on the previous Three Worlds, the "more-than-humans," for our lives. While they can survive very well without us, we cannot live without them. They are our elders.

When we pray, we invite our ancestors from the Three Worlds into our prayers and decisions. As they show up for us, we have a responsibility to them. When we sit in council, representatives attend from the clans of the warriors, peacemakers, dreamers, medicine people, the spiritual voices and leaders. Their purpose is to each bring a different perspective on the situation under discussion. We have chosen well when our decisions benefit the Three Worlds, the well-being of the people and the children who will come in future generations.

It may be difficult to comprehend that Indigenous people, who have faced near extinction and loss of lands and violations of every kind, continue to hold such faith and sense of purpose. It's actually quite simple: we see all the worlds as sacred and our spirits intimately connected *not to every "thing," but to the animate spirit in all forms of life*. This is more than respecting creation;

it is a reverence for all our relations. It is the absence of separation that we call love, and the difference between a homocentric reality and a holocentric one.

As we find our way through events that have no precedent, our relationship to the other Three Worlds teaches us to love and care for all our relations. We do this first by praying that as we work together, our words and actions come from a clean mind, heart and spirit. Sometimes, our most important purpose is just to grow together.

The path of the Red Road is especially important now. That these choices exist means that options remain for peace and hope and that you have a mighty purpose and responsibility.

It is said that a New People will arise who will fulfill the prophecies. If you are one of those, have courage and join with others to heal our foolish disregard of each other, the abuse of our fragile planet and the "more-than-humans" who are also endangered.

We, those of our tribes, will be praying for your success and helping in any way we can. The children of tomorrow are now in your hands.

———————————◆———————————

We are in the liminal time between eras, stepping boldly into the new territory of the emerging consciousness where there is no map to follow. The path forward starts to appear, forged by every step we take into the new consciousness, each Evolutionary Leader—and so many more across the globe—supporting the journey. We are called to find that sweet spot where our individual purpose and passion align with our collective purpose to be of service to the greater good. Everyone is needed for this grand adventure: poets and pundits, artists and architects, farmers and financiers, dreamers and doers at every level of community from families to towns to cities to nations united. As we leave behind the glory of the one, we will find even greater joy in the One. We join in network upon network, co-creating the Holomovement and building the matrix to support a thriving future the only way we can: together.

EPILOGUE

by Emanuel Kuntzelman
including Jonathan Granoff, Olivia Hansen & David Gershon

We bring this anthology to a close in contemplation of the soul's purpose and how it synergizes with the Holomovement. Clearly, many souls hear the call, but will a critical mass of society choose the "Red Road" and steer humanity toward a resolution to the challenges we face? It will require a commitment to unity and wholeness such as humanity has never experienced before.

We believe it can be done. Whether we think our life is a one-shot deal, as the Abrahamic traditions have advised, or a many lifetimes opportunity to find the soul's purpose as close to half the world population believes, the urgency of the times screams out at us to make a difference. However, it's not necessary to believe in any sort of Divine Being to see the cliff's edge before us. Fires, floods, fear, famine and so many other calamities are becoming ever more a part of our lives. No matter our spiritual beliefs, or how seemingly far apart our value systems seem to be, no one can deny that we have a collective problem to overcome.

It is up to every individual to find our purpose and put it to work if we're to correct course. In this singular moment, we each have a profound role to play. There has been no other time in human history when we will have had such an immense impact on the karmic field of humanity. We have learned a lot as a species, but it seems we may have forgotten even more.

Jonathon Granoff, revered leader and president of Global Security Institute, shares his personal reflection on what is at stake in remembering our soul's purpose in these urgent times, and urges us to remember the forgotten "why" to lead us back to wholeness:

> "Too often, we forget why we are here, who we are and how to pose and answer these most important questions. I believe we are here to learn and know through essential love. This process can guide our actions and reveal the birthright of being human.
>
> We are deeply inquisitive creatures sent into this creation to discover something which may not look like anything we can see. We are to learn of something which we cannot control, measure or own.
>
> How are we to judge the success of institutions if we do not know how to judge the success of our individual lives? Without a standard of being human, without a human purpose, how can we determine what direction our institutions should go? What cannot be measured is marginalized.
>
> The self, love, compassion, consciousness and the soul are not part of "truth discovery" since they are not amenable to measurement and control—criteria for scientific knowledge. If original purposes are lost, the important questions cannot be answered. If what it is to be human is not first understood, all the efforts expended lack purpose.

Procedure overcomes purpose. The "how" overshadows the
"why."

We are able to know through love, and that knowing
helps make us human. To know the mystery of that
which sent us into the world, we must know the self, the
consciousness within the body; that is knowing. We must
inquire into who we are. If we do not gain this knowledge,
then what have we gained?"

The Holomovement invites us to re-discover our sense of awe and
wonder in our evolutionary unfolding. In doing so, we realize the magnitude
of finding and embracing our true purpose and the impact our actions have
on the greater good of the whole. It is time to put the tiny yet powerful
stamp of our contribution into the flow of the cosmos. Somewhere, deep
within the depths of our soul, there is a call to contribute to the "art of
altruism." In knowing our wholeness, we can embody what it means to give
compassionately and generously in a way that nourishes and supports "me
AND we" and, ultimately, the cosmic ALL. As the poet Rumi reminds us,
"Even when tied in a thousand knots, the string is still but one."

After nearly 14 billion years of evolutionary process, we are humbled
to realize how much work the universe went to in creating our souls within
this divine wholeness. Yes, we have fallen into the depths of materialistic
temptation and a profound sense of separation, but we also still hold a hope
and an inherent knowing that we are One.

Olivia Hansen, founder and president of the Synthesis Foundation and
the Spiritual Life TV Channel, offers her deeply spiritual reflection on our
interconnection:

"The One Life expresses Love, Light, Higher Purpose and
Compassion that radiates out continuously and is available
to us all—core to all that is. These energies encourage the

evolution of consciousness in all forms and express the inherent oneness and connectedness of life.

We may appear separate outwardly, but our soul is part of the One Soul. Can we identify with others as souls? Can we look past their outer forms and differences and see them as expressions of the One, just as we are those expressions too? Because in reality, there is no other. There is just ONE, the One Divine Life manifesting in a great, vast diversity and multiplicity beyond our full understanding. This One Life with its essential unity in its diversity.

The ancient and ageless wisdom teachings have long taught us this narrative. These shining ideas have been embedded in religious, philosophical and cultural forms and expressions over the ages and now, science is able to theorize and prove many of these expanding understandings.

The vision of what can be, and the potential of humanity's higher destiny and potential resonates in our souls. But we must choose it; we must work toward it and create it outwardly together.

We know the many problems that exist in our world today. But we can give energy to the Good, the Beautiful and the True—allowing them to manifest. In helping our brothers and sisters along the way, there is equity and opportunity for all to live into the beautiful possible life that awaits. The energy we hold in our hearts and minds will grow and thrive.

So let us give energy to the Good, and to the Divinity that is immanent within us, and to the Divinity that is transcendent in the world. Together, let us bring in the transformations so many traditions speak of—the Call has gone out to each of us. Let us step up and together embrace and activate change for humanity and all the kingdoms of our beautiful world and beyond. Now. Together. ONE."

Even in this beautiful vision of unity, travelling upon the Red Road back to our beginning will be a challenge. We are being asked to practice in every moment what it means to embody our evolutionary potential. As Ken Wilber expresses in his Interval piece, it is never too late to "wake up, grow up, open up, clean up, show up," and when our octave comes full circle, ultimately "link up and lift up" in loving Wholeness. In answering Ken Wilber's question as to whether this book is fully-baked in its vision, we must humbly say that this is only the first, small step in making the great turning of the Evolutionary Pilot Wave.

We are aware that the expression of the Holomovement is heavy on philosophy and theory, and still in its early stages of practice in action. It is our full intention, however, to proceed rapidly with developing the integration of the Holomovement into society at large.

David Gershon, social change expert and co-founder and CEO of Empowerment Institute, points out that it is time to stop talking and start doing whatever we can to navigate the turn and get us on the ascent toward wholeness. Below, David provides the following context and questions to consider as we evaluate and design effective social change strategies:

> Here are framing questions to evaluate the effectiveness and potential scalability of social change ideas or social innovations. This set of inquiries explicitly requires people to shift their attention to positive social change, versus an analysis of its disfunction or rant about one of our broken social systems. Given the sense of urgency, we must evolve into change agents with a vision for the future, all the more so given we only have a decade to right the ship.

The following questions below will help you get started:

1. Whom do you wish to empower to do what?
2. What behaviors do you wish these people to adopt?
3. What does behavior change at scale look like?
4. What is your strategy to achieve this?
5. How will you implement this strategy?

Here are framing questions around social change effectiveness:

1. What is your theory of change?
2. Why do you think it works or can work?
3. What is its track record or how will you test it?
4. What strategic issue(s) will it be applied to and why?
5. What is your definition of success and why?

For anyone creating large-scale social change initiatives, answering the 10 questions above will help you better evaluate the potential strategic effectiveness and scalability. Taking time to reflect and answer these questions with care will also help to articulate financial needs and attract funders. In addition to answering the questions above, listed below is a set of criteria for working with time and social impact. The operative idea here is accelerating social change.

1. How can your strategy accelerate the magnitude of social change?
2. How can your strategy accelerate the speed of social change?
3. How can your strategy accelerate the quality of social change?

The pages in this book have endeavored to answer most of these questions, but let us summarize. We aspire to empower everyone on the planet who wishes to join in this transformative movement, engaged as if our lives depend on this participation, and act in conjunction with the deepest spirit of compassion in the human heart. Our strategy is to encourage and guide small groups, synergy circles and holons of Right Action to emerge, grow and collaborate with the like-minded groups they find, thus turning this movement into a ripple, then a trickle, and then a veritable tsunami of human consciousness uniting every sector of society.

That is our theory of change. It will work, because we believe as did anthropologist Margaret Mead, who said: "Never doubt that a small group of thoughtful, committed citizens can change the world. Indeed, it is the only thing that ever has." Further, it will work on a grand scale because of the urgency of the situation and the new tools of communication we have at our disposal.

This book has been launched in conjunction with a gathering in Sedona, Arizona, with the title of "Igniting the Holomovement," where we have discussed and honed our strategies to have the most impact in embracing our collective purpose to unite humanity. Will these early endeavors accelerate the magnitude, speed and quality of social change? That remains to be seen, but there is no lack of will or energy in realizing this vision. Together, we are igniting the Holomovement that has gone dormant in the human spirit, giving power to a fire of love and goodwill, and spreading its light to every corner of the planet.

May we all find the courage to seek our quantum potential and thereby find our highest collective purpose—that unique, one in eight billion chance to figure out what we were born to be. It is there, in that sweet spot, where our talents combine with our will to serve the whole and give us the strength and vision to make this world a home for future generations. There is, after all, an infinite capacity in the Source of consciousness, and therefore in the heart and soul of ourselves. We can find inspiration in William Blake:

To see a world in a grain of sand
And a heaven in a wild flower.

Hold infinity in the palm of your hand

And eternity in an hour.[42]

That hour has come. The time is now. As we make the great turn toward home, let us imagine how a swarm of bees working in harmony, seeks a new hive. When it is time for the bee colony to find a new home, they all set out to together. When one or more find the perfect place, they don't just dive in quickly to occupy the best part of the real estate. Instead, they stop on the spot and emit a message encoded in pheromones, sending it out to the field. Then, finally, when the bee farthest afield receives the message, it heeds the call, moving toward its source, meeting up with the next group of bees, and then the next, continuing onward until the swarm of bees hovers in front of their new home. Like Bodhisattvas on the threshold of Nirvana, they wait for everyone to join the whole and only then enter together, almost as if all were one.

It is this moment, here and now, when we too are finding our way home, embracing our highest purpose within the flow of the Holomovement. In this rallying cry, we hope to offer clarity and a unified way forward on this trajectory of human history. There is a new human on the horizon. Barbara Marx Hubbard called it *Homo universalis*. Call it what you will, or don't name it all, but please don't ignore it.

May we all embrace our collective purpose, meet up in the ascent to the implicate order and unite humanity in the flow of the process.

ENDNOTES

Introduction

1. This quote is from *Infinite Potential: The Life and Times of David Bohm*, by F. David Peat, his friend, colleague and co-author of *Science, Order, and Creativity: A Dramatic New Look at the Creative Roots of Science and Life*.

Chapter 1

2. Bohm, David. *Wholeness and the Implicate Order*. London and New York: Routledge, 2002. https://www.scienceandnonduality.com/article/david-bohm-implicate-order-and-holomovement.

3. *Infinite Potential: The Life & Ideas of David Bohm*, 2020. https://www.infinitepotential.com/.https://www.youtube.com/watch?v=06QlY9XehZo.

Chapter 3

4. Rodgers, Judy and Naraine, Gayatri. *Something Beyond Greatness: Conversations with a Man of Science & a Woman of God*. Deerfield Beach: Health Communications, Inc., 2009.

5. Freke, Tom. *Soul Story: Evolution and the Purpose of Life*. London: Watkins, 2017.

6. See the contribution by Frédérique Pichard to the bouquet of spontaneous experiences in Part III

Chapter 5

7. http://www.kosmosjournal.org/article/ecosophy-natures-guide-to-a-better-world/.

8. https://www.ethicalmarkets.com/a-tale-of-cities-and-cells-by-elisabet-sahtouris/.

Chapter 6

9. Carley, Joni. "The Case for a Systems based Values driven United Nations," 2016. https://www.academia.edu/6284502/The_Case_for_a_Systems_based_Values_driven_United_Nations.

10. Waller, Niels G., Kojetin, Brian A., Bouchard, Jr., Thomas J., et al., "Genetic and Environmental Influences on Religious Interests, Attitudes, and Values: A Study of Twins Reared Apart and Together." *Psychological Science*, Vol. 1, Issue 2, March 1, 1990. https://doi.org/10.1111/j.1467-9280.1990.tb00083.x

11. Carley. Ibid.

Chapter 8

12. See: www.centerforpartnership.org.

13. See: *The Chalice and the Blade: Our History, Our Future,* now in its 56th US printing, and *Nurturing Our Humanity: How Domination and Partnership Shape Our Brains, Lives, and Future,* Oxford University Press, 2019.

Chapter 9

14. https://humanenergy.io/projects/science-of-the-noosphere/.

15. Wrangham, R. *The Goodness Paradox: The Strange Relationship Between Virtue and Violence in Human Evolution*. Pantheon, 2019.

16. For more, see: Wilson, D. S. *This View of Life: Completing the Darwinian Revolution*. New York: Pantheon / Random House, 2019.

17. For more, see: Hoyer, D., and Reddish, J. (Eds.). *Seshat History of the Axial Age*. Chaplin, CT: Beresta, 2019.

18. www.Prosocial.world. For a book-length account, see Atkins, P. W. D., Wilson, D. S., and Hayes, S. C. *Prosocial: Using evolutionary science to build productive, equitable, and collaborative groups*. Oakland, CA: New Harbinger, 2019.

19. For more on the Latin America project, see: https://www.google.com/search?q=tvol+conscious+cultural+evolution+takes+root+in+latin+america&oq=tvol+conscious+cultural+evolution+takes+-root+in+latin+america&aqs=chrome..69i57.12537j0j7&sourceid=-chrome&ie=UTF-8

20. For more, see the episode of the "Science of the Noosphere" series titled "Cancer, Cheating, and Cell Communication." https://humanenergy.io/athena-aktipis-and-michael-levin/

21. https://en.wikipedia.org/wiki/The_Social_Dilemma.

Chapter 10

22. Konai Thaman is renowned as a national poet of Tonga and a now-retired longtime Professor of Education at The University of the South Pacific. It was during my time there as a professor that I was introduced to the

cultural concept of cyclical time. The poem at the start of this chapter is from Thaman's volume of poetry listed below in References.

Chapter 11

23. Neyfakh, L. "Where does good come from?" Boston Globe, 2011.

24. Hardin, G. "The Tragedy of the Commons." *Science*, Vol. 162, Issue 3859, pp. 1243-1248, 1968.

25. https://aboutmanchester.co.uk/75-of-us-put-compassionate-values-over-selfish-ones-shows-greater-manchester-research/

26. Holt-Lunstad, J., Smith, T.B., and Layton, J.B. "Social Relationships and Mortality Risk: A Meta-analytic Review." PLoS Med 7(7): e1000316. doi:10.1371/journal.pmed.1000316, 2010.

27. https://www.cmu.edu/news/stories/archives/2013/june/june13_volunteeringhypertension.html.

28. Gruber, H. "Creative altruism, cooperation, and world peace." In M. Runco & R. Richards (Eds.). *Eminent Creativity, Everyday Creativity, and Health.* pp. 463-79. Greenwich, CT: Ablex Publishing Corporation, 1997.

29. Dana Klisanin, PhD., Media Psychology Review. Originally published in 1987 by IONS. Howard Gruber was the grandfather, and a major influence to chapter co-author Rhiannon Catalyst.

30. Simon, E.B., Vallat, R., Barnes, C.M., Walker, M.P. "Sleep Loss and the Socio-Emotional Brain." *Trends Cogn Sci.* 2020 Jun;24(6):435-450. doi: 10.1016/j.tics.2020.02.003. Epub 2020 Apr 14. PMID: 32299657.

Chapter 12

31. Bahá'í movement for spiritual and social transformation, see Mustakova, E. *Global Unitive Healing: Integral Skills for Personal and Social*

Transformation, Fort Lauderdale, FL: Light on Light Press / Sacred Stories Publishing, 2021.

32. http://BeBeyonceshowmeartsacademy.com.

33. Gaston, E., "Dare to be Dauntless," TEDx, 2014. https://www.youtube.com/watch?v=Nw09D3GJrAE.

Chapter 12 / Spotlight Feature

34. See https://www.evolutionaryleaders.net/unitivenarrative.

35. See https://pwccc.wordpress.com/programa/.

Chapter 14 / Spotlight Feature

36. See https://greattransitionstories.org/

Chapter 15

37. https://www.codes.earth.

Chapter 16

38. www.masterclass.com/articles/a-guide-to-the-5-levels-of-maslows-hierarchy-of-needs.

39. Hubbard, Barbara Marx. *The Revelation: Our Crisis is a Birth*. Foundation for Conscious Evolution, 1993.

40. www.sourceofsynergyfoundation.org.

41. www.evolutionaryleaders.net.

Epilogue

42. See https://www.poetryfoundation.org/poems/43650/auguries-of-innocence.

APPENDIX: COMMUNITIES OF ACTION

The Holomovement is a movement based on Synergy, where the whole is greater than the sum of its parts. It offers humanity hope that we can and will return to the essence of Wholeness. Our future depends on mutually beneficial cooperation at a planetary scale. Luckily, countless Communities of Action within this movement of movements are igniting hope, healing and unity across the globe in common purpose, goals and actions. These communities are sharing expertise, resources and collective strengths and, as a result, optimizing the whole so that a truly synergistic society can unfold.

One group, the Evolutionary Partners Network, is made up of 45 organizations and conscious businesses. Led by members of the Evolutionary Leaders Circle of the Source of Synergy Foundation, they are committed to co-creating and synergizing a global network of organizations and individuals dedicated to accelerating the evolution of consciousness for the benefit of all life. This Network is being stewarded by an amazing team headed by Rev. Deborah Moldow, Director of the Evolutionary Leaders Circle, with the assistance of Dr. Kurt Johnson, Coordinator of the Evolutionary Leaders' Synergy Circles.

Please find a list of the current participating organizations below. This is just one example of wholeness-in-motion expressed as a fractal of the Holomovement. We stand as a unified field of consciousness with millions of other Communities of Action that are coming together and igniting this movement through collaborations in action.

Diane Williams

Founder, The Source of Synergy Foundation

Evolutionary Partners Network

Academy for Future Science
The Academy for Future Science is a non-profit corporation that examines new scientific ideas for the future. The principal goal of the Academy is to provide all people with educational and scientific tools that will help them meet the resulting challenges.

AgeNation, LLC
AgeNation is a global organization committed to providing the very best in information, inspiration and engagement to a rapidly growing audience of older GenXers, Boomers and elders who are committed to living vital, successful and conscious lives.

All Things Connected, LLC
Dr. Julie Krull serves as a midwife for the evolution of consciousness, whole systems health and a whole worldview. She works with evolutionary change-agents—co-creating greater connection and wholeness—as a best-selling, Nautilus Award-winning author, speaker, consciousness coach, mentor, host of "The Dr. Julie Show: All Things Connected" and founder of Good of the Whole.

Bridges In Organizations. Inc.

Bridges in Organizations brings diverse work combined with anthropology expertise to organizations: addressing everything from culturally-sensitive customer service to navigating messy conversations—conflict that can arise when operating from inaccurate assumptions or unconscious bias.

Children of the Earth

Children of the Earth inspires and unites young people, through personal and social transformation, to create a peaceful and sustainable world. One Earth…with all her Children smiling!

Choosing Earth

Choosing Earth offers many resources to help you learn more about the challenges and opportunities of our time of great transition. The Choosing Earth Project recognizes the world confronts much more than a climate crisis; we face a whole systems crisis that includes the mass extinction of species, growing shortages of fresh water, extreme inequities of wealth and well-being, and much more.

Community of the Mystic Heart

We seek to help each other grow and deepen in spiritual life and to be a prophetic voice for the emergence of a more just, sustainable and peaceful world. We nurture the continuing refinement and advancement of the Interspiritual message brought forth by Brother Wayne Teasdale and his teachers and we encourage each other in living out our vows to actualize the Mystic Heart, in service to the One, in which is included all of creation.

Contemplative Life

Contemplative Life is a central hub that brings many different practices under one umbrella, to easily find what's right for you and connect with others of like mind.

Create Global Healing

Founder Lori Leyden, Ph.D., MBA is an internationally known trauma healing expert and spiritual guide. Dr. Leyden works with successful leaders and influencers committed to becoming heart-centered leaders in service to global healing. She also works in traumatized communities that have experienced genocide, war and school shootings.

EARTHwise Centre

EARTHwise Centre serves to steward and actualize the possibilities for thriving worlds and futures, as an educational, training, coaching, research, publication and leadership centre for developing the necessary capacities, systems, governance, tools and pathways for a planetary civilization.

Everyday Knowings LLC

Founder Rev. Dr. Heather Shea is a Spiritual Leadership Coach for women executives, entrepreneurs and evolutionary leaders. She connects people to their inner wisdom and uncovers blocks that prevent them from stepping into their highest, authentic self for greater impact in their lives and the world.

Garden of Light

Garden of Light is a global community deeply rooted in a shared spirituality that transcends differences of circumstance, nationality, tradition, culture and even religion. The Garden of Light offers a virtual home for this community so that it can become visible for the powerful force that it truly is in uplifting the human spirit and approaching the global challenges we face as one global family.

Global Coherence Pulse

Global Coherence Pulse is a science-backed, social collaboration to Pulse the Planet with the frequencies of love and compassion, joy and appreciation, being monitored by global instrumentation networks to help science tell the story of our interconnectedness and of the power of our Collective Heart.

Good of the Whole

Good of the Whole is a growing community with a global mission and shared purpose. Good of the Whole creates whole-systems alternatives for the world's biggest problems, so that every person has an opportunity to evolve to their highest potential.

Great Transition Stories

Great Transition Stories is a virtual hub for illuminating the larger, often invisible, archetypal stories of our world, which can help us make sense of these times. By bringing to light the deeper patterns we're in and where they lead, we begin to have more choice in how we can consciously evolve our collective story towards wholeness, well-being, justice, beauty and regenerative culture.

Hygeia Foundation (For Health, Science and the Environment)

Hygeia Foundation supports holistic health education and research; fosters a common respect for all life on earth and promotes awareness of the interconnectedness of all creation. The Hygeia Foundation supports and sponsors a variety of projects that are aligned with this mission, particularly those that promote the principles and practice of sustainability.

Integral City Meshworks

Integral City Meshworks is a global constellation of communities of practice that nurtures cities as human hives. Through placecaring and placemaking, Integral City Meshworks inspires a Planet of Integral Cities as living, integral, evolutionary human systems, to become Gaia's Reflective Organs. An Integral City paradigm views the city as a whole living system. It is the Human Hive.

Like the beehive is for the species of the honey bee, the Integral City is the collective habitat for the human species.

Interstellar Community Foundation
The Interstellar Community Foundation is an organization made up of a worldwide network of conscious individuals working together to manifest the Vision of the Interstellar Universities and Universe Cities, co-creating the communities of the future whose purpose is to provide humanity with the necessary tools, skills and consciousness to grow into our cosmic nature, preparing humanity to interact with civilizations beyond our planet. The Vision has a three-fold purpose: Liberating our full Human Potential, Achieving Planetary Consciousness and Taking our Place in the Cosmic Community.

Islands of Coherence Community Network
Islands of Coherence Community Network is a heart-centered membership network, made up of communities of practice sharing evolutionary tools for embodied coherence, social synergy and planetary regeneration. Islands of Coherence Community Network aims to be an ecosystem of epic individuals, projects and solutions for the great shift of our species.

Karmic Warrior
The mission of Karmic Warrior is to teach time-proven principles and practices of Yoga wisdom that free us from continual cycles of ups and downs in life (karma) and give us direct access to lasting inner peace, clarity and connection so that we can awaken to our true nature and contribute to the flourishing of humanity.

Light on Light Publications and Media
Light on Light, a non-profit from the Interspiritual Dialogue Network, publishes books and e-magazines and hosts VoiceAmerica ("The

Convergence") broadcast media. Its books are an imprint of Sacred Stories; its free e-magazines from ISSUU are Light on Light, Convergence and Conscious Business.

Living Cities Earth

Living Cities Earth is an interdisciplinary action research network, connecting 10,000 cities and a web of integral experts serving Gaia's well-being.

NewStories

The purpose of NewStories is to help people, organizations, communities and systems navigate the tides of change towards well-being, compassion and deep collaboration. We do this through looking at the current stories in place and gently guiding shifts towards a new way of being.

One Humanity Institute

One Humanity Institute—a City of Hope, from I to We to ONE, from Hate to Hope. The overarching goal for this vision is to lay the groundwork for global solidarity that gives rise to what it means to be One Humanity. The Institute offers structured learning opportunities in a variety of forms for all ages, and will focus on the UN 17 Sustainable Development Goals, inter-and intra-faith studies, inter-cultural understanding and cooperation, conflict resolution, trans-rational problem solving, reconciliation, entrepreneurial social impact projects and leadership skills for the rising potential of the empowered individual.

One Planet Peace Forum

One Planet Peace Forum is a universal platform offering an annual interdisciplinary, Interspiritual gathering for living into a culture of peace. Approaching peace holistically, as an inner and outer evolutionary process, its mission is to inspire cooperative action toward building the future envisioned by the world's spiritual and wisdom traditions.

Peace Pentagon

The Peace Pentagon is a retreat and training center located in the Blue Ridge Mountains of Virginia along the ancient New River. We are committed to pluralistic and progressive values and host educational programs that provide hope for humanity. The Peace Pentagon also serves as a hub for planning and organizing regional, national and global peace-building and social justice campaigns. Our mission is to help YOU gain the information and tools to be a better advocate for the issues that matter to YOU!

Prosocial World

While Prosocial World is based on science, it is not just for scientists. It is also for activists, idealists, pragmatists, visionaries and contemplative change agents; in short, anyone who has a prosocial worldview. As such, it uniquely places the vision of spiritual seekers, who embark on different paths to self-discovery to consciously evolve a more harmonious and regenerative world, on a foundation of the most recent developments in evolutionary science.

Purpose Earth

Purpose Earth's mission is to fund and mentor purpose-driven people and projects with creative solutions to our global challenges.

Rainbow Circle

Rainbow Circle is a community supporting a system that contextualizes and synergizes knowledge, people, organizations and missions within a 12 domain multi-colored circle. Each archetypal domain contains keywords in a digital space, so anything can be mapped into a domain depending on its corresponding keyword. Through this design, Rainbow Circle illustrates how many visions can coherently align as one to regenerate the Earth and evolve humanity.

Self Care to Earth Care

The purpose of Self Care to Earth Care, representing the Ecospirituality Synergy Circle of the Evolutionary Leaders, is to provide space for the leading voices and activists across the interspiritual, ecospiritual, sustainability and other transformative landscapes; to vision and effectuate future programs, events and initiatives across these areas of passion; and to provide space for various constituencies and sectors to gather together that are committed to self-care and Earth care and are shaping a new, ecological society and culture.

Spiritual Life TV Channel

The Spiritual Life TV Channel features wisdom teachings from many spiritual traditions and gives a practical focus that shows how a person can use these teachings to live a more spiritual life.

The Center for Partnership Systems

The Center for Partnership Systems was co-founded in 1986 by Riane Eisler with the goal of shifting cultures worldwide from domination to partnership. It provides tools to this end such as the Partnership Technology toolkit and workbook, online courses, the Caring and Connected Parenting Guide and other resources that focus on the four cornerstones of childhood, gender, economics and story/language so we have foundations for a more equitable, sustainable and caring world.

The Great Turning at Findhorn

The Great Turning Initiative at Findhorn is an online spiritual education and resource center to support individuals and organizations to navigate and actualize The Great Turning—humanity's epochal transition from a life-destroying society to a life-affirming global family.

The Hague Center for Global Governance, Innovation and Emergence

The Hague Center for Global Governance, Innovation and Emergence is an organization and co-creative collective, serving the emergence of a conscious, harmonic, humanity. We innovate heart-centered, planetary governance with all domains of life.

The Heart of the Healer Shamanic Mystery School

The Heart of the Healer Shamanic Mystery School is committed to the co-creation of a heartfelt sacred community informed by the shamanic star-seeded wisdom of our cosmic origins. We support the eco-spiritual evolution of humankind through soul-honoring initiatory apprenticeships in the Pachakuti Mesa Tradition, Goddess Consciousness and Ancestral Star Knowledge.

The Interspiritual Dialogue Network

ISD is the original interspiritual organization of Brother Wayne Teasdale, the renowned interspiritual pioneer. It continues events and initiatives for interfaith and interspirituality, its well known newsletter, and is the parent of Light on Light Publications and Media. Its website centers on the message of The Coming Interspiritual Age.

The Interspiritual Multiplex

The Interspiritual Multiplex is a far-flung and dynamic network formed as of 2005 from the various constituencies and groups inspired by the work and writing of Brother Wayne Teasdale. It aims at carrying forward to a wider audience worldwide his vision of interspiritual dialogue and interspirituality as outlined in The Mystic Heart: Discovering a Universal Spirituality in the World's Religions.

The Interspiritual Network

The Interspiritual Network formed from combined constituencies of interfaith and interspiritual pioneers like Thomas Merton, Thomas Keating, Wayne Teasdale and many others. It includes resources from, and about, nearly one hundred spiritual leaders, teachers, authors and activists. It has been home for the "Dawn of Interspirituality," "Interspiritual Mandala" and other initiatives.

The Oracle Institute

The Oracle Institute is an educational charity dedicated to building a new world based on Social Justice, Interfaith Unity and a Culture of Peace. Our mission is to advance this global transformation by hosting pluralistic programs and anchoring progressive values.

The RIM Institute

RIM® (Regenerating Images in Memory) is a body-centered, transformational technique that frees you of negative thoughts, feelings and memories, so you are empowered to live your best life. Deborah Sandella PhD, RN is the originator of the groundbreaking Regenerating Images in Memory (RIM®) Method, which is a heavily-backed neuroscience tool proven to reduce stress and improve quality of life.

Sacred Stories

Sacred Stories is an award-winning conscious book publisher and multimedia company that believes wisdom coupled with the power of story—written, spoken, and lived—allows us to deepen into the Mystery of our souls. Their visionary publishing imprints include Light on Light Press, Haniel Press, and flagship Sacred Stories Publishing.

The Source of Synergy Foundation

The Source of Synergy Foundation is a not-for-profit educational organization whose purpose is to synergize individuals, organizations and efforts by tapping into the infinite source of collective consciousness, creativity and potential for the common good. The Source of Synergy Foundation recognizes that our essence is Source: a single, universal field out of which everything emerges, where we are united as one.

Touching the Stillness Ministries

Touching the Stillness Ministries is a global spiritual organization, synonymous with mindfulness and meditation practices designed to create exhilarating and meaningful connections, with that which we call God, as well as deepen our awareness in ways that will transform our lives.

Ubiquity University

Ubiquity's mission is grounded in the reality that history has reached a critical moment and people everywhere need to be nurtured with new mindsets, skillsets and tool sets to work together to solve global challenges. Ubiquity has an innovative combination of intellectual and artistic learning in which all students are required to engage in equal measure to balance the left and right hemispheres of the brain and thereby engage in integrated learning.

UNITY EARTH

UNITY EARTH is a growing network of groups and organizations coming together to empower solutions for unity, purpose and peace worldwide. Our calling is to weave threads of unity within the colorful diversity of the human family and the ecosystems that sustain us.

WholeWorld-View

WholeWorld-View is an emergent 'organism' that aims to serve and empower our conscious evolution through the understanding, experiencing and embodying of unitive awareness. We offer an underpinning framework and evidence-base that integrates the latest scientific breakthroughs and traditional spiritual and Indigenous wisdom teachings into a unified understanding of the nature of reality. We work co-creatively with a global network of collaborators to serve, explore and nurture a unitive and regenerative perspective for transformational change.

Wise Planet Media

Wise Planet Media helps to create a wiser and more just world through award-winning media storytelling.

ACKNOWLEDGEMENTS

This anthology is shaped by the passion and vision of extraordinary thought leaders and teachers. We are deeply grateful to all the authors who volunteered their time and generously shared their wisdom in a true expression of the Holomovement. Continuing with the spirit of the whole, proceeds from this book will support Purpose Earth's grant and mentorship program, launching purpose-driven projects into motion.

What an honor to have so many voices within these pages, gifting us with diverse language and insights all united in vision. A heartfelt thank you to all our contributors: William Keepin, Ben Bowler, Patricia Anne Davis, John Cobb, Ramesh Bijlani, Jude Currivan, Ervin Laszlo, Brian Russo, Sheri Herndon, Eli Kline, Tamsin Woolley-Barker, Harry Uvegi, Kurt Krueger, J.J. and Desiree Hurtak, Elisabet Sahtouris, Joni Carley, Phil Clothier, Scott Alan Carlin, Richard Clugston, Gordon Dveirin, Heidi Sparkes Guber, Daniel J. Stone, Lynne Twist, Mary Earle Chase, David Korten, Riane Eisler, Thomas Legrand, Doug King, Nomi Naeem, Ken Wilber, David Sloan Wilson, Jeff Genung, Peter Blaze Corcoran, Wendy Ellyatt, Nina Meyerhof, Rhiannon Catalyst, Elena Mustakova, Marty K. Casey, Amikaeyla Gaston, Audrey Kitagawa, David Lorimer, Chief Phil Lane Jr., Earl Possardt, Masen Ewald,

Duane Elgin, Lynnaea Lumbard, Julie Krull, Shamini Jain, Teresa Collins, Deborah Moldow, Justin Faerman, Jean Houston, Constance Buffalo, Jonathan Granoff, Olivia Hansen and David Gershon.

We are also eternally grateful for the meaningful conversations held with our dear friend, Terry Patten. His heartfelt energy and passion for this undertaking was truly inspiring and instrumental in the vision of this book.

Finally, we want to extend our deepest gratitude to our editor, Sandra Simon, and to Light on Light Press managing editors Kurt Johnson and Robert Atkinson and Ariel Patricia of Sacred Stories Publishing and Media. Their unwavering support and wise counseling on the editing and guidance of this project exceeded our highest expectations in countless ways. Their spiritual insight and practical knowledge combined to help us through every obstacle on the path of creating this book. They represent the kind of leadership that makes the Holomovement a living reality.

ABOUT THE CONTRIBUTORS

I t's an honor to have so many diverse voices within these pages, all sharing their wisdom and experiences to support our understanding of the wholeness in motion that is all around us. This inspiring team effort included a humbling number of contributors, making it a challenge to list everyone's biography as we would have hoped. To learn more about the Evolutionary Leaders Synergy Circle members who collaborated on this book's featured spotlight pieces, we encourage you to visit the Evolutionary Leaders website and its "Evolutionary Leaders" and "Synergy Circles" pages.

In Alphabetical Order:

Robert Atkinson, PhD, developmental psychologist, author of *A New Story of Wholeness* and *The Story of Our Time*, and founder of One Planet Peace Forum. www.robertatkinson.net

Ramesh Bijlani, MD, Indian writer, inspirational speaker, medical scientist and retired Professor of Physiology who has specialized in physiology, nutrition, and yoga.

Ben Bowler, executive director of Unity Earth, a global network for unity and peace. www.unity.earth

Constance Buffalo, tribal member of the Red Cliff Band of Chippewa, former corporate president and director of promotion with CBS TV.

Joni Carley, DMin, author of *The Alchemy of Power*, expert in values-driven leadership, and consultant with the private sector and at the United Nations. www.jonicarley.com

Dr. Marty K. Casey, motivational speaker, entrepreneur, activist, entertainer, and founder of UnGUN Institute. www.unguninstitute.com

Rhiannon Catalyst, multidisciplinary artist, vocalist, producer, manager, and community builder in the intersection of global cultures, art, and science. www.rhiannoncatalyst.com

Mary Earle Chase, author, educator, researcher, psychotherapist, activist, and documentary film producer. www.pachamama.org

Phil Clothier, senior cultural transformation advisor at the Barrett Values Centre supporting leaders to bring about ethical, sustainable, values-driven transformation.

John B. Cobb, PhD, theologian, philosopher, and environmentalist and preeminent scholar in the field of process philosophy and process theology.

Teresa Collins, cofounder of Global Coherence Pulse, educator, learning community developer, and whole-system strategic designer. www.globalcoherencepulse.org

Peter Blaze Corcoran, PhD, professor emeritus of environmental education at Florida Gulf Coast University and senior fellow at Forum 21 Institute.

Jude Currivan, PhD, cosmologist, futurist, author of *The Story of Gaia* and *The Cosmic Hologram*, and co-founder of WholeWorld-View. www.judecurrivan.com

Patricia Anne Davis, Indigenous elder of Choctaw and Dine' Navajo lineage and a Whole Systems Designer, specializing in peace-making leadership.

Riane Eisler, JD, PhD, social systems scientist, cultural historian, futurist, attorney, and author of *The Chalice and the Blade* and *Nurturing Our Humanity*. www.rianeeisler.com

Duane Elgin, speaker, visionary, educator, consultant, activist, and author of *The Living Universe*, *Voluntary Simplicity*, and *Choosing Earth*. www.duaneelgin.com

Evolutionary Leaders SDG Thought Leaders Circle Members
    https://sdgthoughtleaderscircle.org

Evolutionary Leaders Education Synergy Circle Members
    https://www.evolutionaryleaders.net/synergycircles

Evolutionary Leaders Unitive Justice and Global Security Synergy Circle Members
    https://www.evolutionaryleaders.net/synergycircles

Masen Ewald, executive director of A New Republic of the Heart. www.newrepublicoftheheart.org

Justin Faerman, visionary change agent, speaker, entrepreneur, and consciousness researcher. www.justinfaerman.com

Amikaeyla Gaston, Executive Director of International Cultural Arts & Healing Sciences Institute. www.icahsi.org

Jeff Genung, managing director of Prosocial World, and co-founder of Contemplative Life. www.prosocial.world

David Gershon, co-founder and CEO of Empowerment Institute. Designs second order change solutions for cities, countries and the planet. www.empowermentinstitute.net

Jonathan Granoff, JD, attorney, author, international advocate, and president of Global Security Institute. www.gsinstitute.org

Olivia Hansen, founder and president of the Synthesis Foundation and the Spiritual Life TV Channel. www.spirituallifetvchannel.com

Sheri Herndon, evolutionary social architect at the nexus of social networks, conscious evolution and co-creation.

Jean Houston, PhD, scholar, philosopher, and researcher in human capacities, and author of 26 books. www.jeanhouston.com

Desiree Hurtak, PhD, author, social scientist, futurist, and co-founder of the Academy for Future Science. www.futurescience.org

J.J. Hurtak, PhD, PhD, author, social scientist, futurist, environmentalist, and co-founder of the Academy for Future Science. www.futurescience.org

Shamini Jain, PhD, author, psychologist, scientist, social entrepreneur, and founder of the Consciousness and Healing Institute. www.shaminijain.com

Kurt Johnson, PhD, evolutionary biologist, eco-minister, author of *The Coming Interspiritual Age*, and founder of Light on Light Press. www.lightonlight.us

William Keepin, PhD, physicist, environmental scientist, gender equality activist, author, and co-founder of the Gender Equity & Reconciliation International project. www.GRworld.org

Doug King, integral theologist, and president of Presence. www.presence.tv

Eli Kline, founder of the Universal Foundation for Holistic Design to restructure societal systems to work within natural law for the benefit of all life.

David Korten, PhD, speaker, president of the Living Economies Forum, co-founder of YES! Magazine, and author of *The Great Turning*. www.davidkorten.org

Kurt Krueger, educator, speaker, trainer, and author of *Winning Ways for Living*. www.successsystemsinternational.net

Julie Krull, PhD, psychotherapist, co-founder of Good of the Whole, host of the Dr. Julie Show All Things Connected, and author of *Fractured Grace*. www.juliekrull.com

Ervin Laszlo, PhD, founder of systems philosophy, author or editor of more than 70 books, and director of the Laszlo Institute of New Paradigm Research. www.laszloinstitute.com

Thomas Legrand, PhD, social scientist, sustainability practitioner, and author of *Politics of Being*. www.politicsofbeing.com

Lynnaea Lumbard, PhD, transformational psychologist, interfaith minister, sacred activist, and president of New Stories. www.newstories.org

Rev. Deborah Moldow, interfaith minister, founder of the Garden of Light, and director of the Evolutionary Leaders circle of the Source of Synergy Foundation. www.revdeborah.com

Elena Mustakova, EdD, psychologist, counselor, educator, and author of *Global Unitive Healing and Critical Consciousness*. www.elenamustakova.net

Nomi Naeem, MA, integral studies scholar, and senior librarian Brooklyn Public Library.

Brian Russo, wholistic designer committed to crafting a regenerative earth.

Elisabet Sahtouris, PhD, evolution biologist, futurist, and author of *A Walk Through Time* and *Biology Revisioned*. www.sahtouris.com

Lynne Twist, global activist, fundraiser, speaker, consultant, author of *The Soul of Money*, and co-founder of The Pachamama Alliance. www.pachamama.org

Harry Uvegi, founding member of BiomimicryNYC, and founder of Brand Earth.

Ken Wilber, philosopher, visionary thinker, founder of the Integral Institute, author of *A Theory of Everything*, and over 20 other books. www.integrallife.com

David Sloan Wilson, PhD, evolutionary biologist, author of *Darwin's Cathedral*, *Does Altruism Exist?* and *This View of Life*, and founder of Prosocial World. www.prosocial.world

Tamsin Woolley-Barker, PhD, evolutionary biologist, bioanthropologist, biomimicry pioneer, speaker, and author of *Teeming*. www.teemlab.com

ABOUT THE EDITORS

Emanuel Kuntzelman is an entrepreneur, writer, philosopher, philanthropist and activist for social transformation. He began his adult life by traveling the world on a decade-long quest for his spiritual purpose before beginning his professional career as an editor/writer for *Readers' Digest,* where he authored dozens of articles for international editions. Upon discovering his right livelihood in the realm of cultural exchange, he founded and managed numerous exchange organizations in Spain, the U.S. and the U.K. Having created Greenheart International in 1985, he still serves as Chief Advisor to the organization. He is also the co-founder of *Fundación por el Futuro* in Madrid, Spain, and has been its President since 1995. His work in spiritual movements includes being a founding co-creator of the Global Purpose Movement and Purpose Earth, as well as his collaboration as a member of the Evolutionary Leaders Circle. Emanuel is a board member and/or advisor to: Greenheart, Humanity's Team, Unity Earth, Integral Transformative Practice International, and the Laszlo Institute for New Paradigm Research. He is co-editor of the anthology *Purpose Rising* (2017) and has contributed articles to a wide variety of publications. His vision of the Holomovement is a project he has been working on for over fifty years.

Jill Robinson is a writer and content creator supporting the important work of mission-driven leaders and businesses through purposeful storytelling. Jill has had the opportunity to collaborate with organizations such as Integral Transformative Practice International, Global Purpose Movement, the Mindful Agency, Sobremesa, Greenheart Transforms and Purpose Earth. She has also had the privilege to work closely with social entrepreneur and writer, Emanuel Kuntzelman, and the Holomovement project. Prior to pursuing her writing career, Jill served as the marketing director for Greenheart Travel—a branch of Greenheart International, based in Chicago, Illinois.

MESSAGE FROM THE PUBLISHER

L ight on Light Press produces enhanced content books spotlighting the sacred ground upon which all religious and wisdom traditions intersect; it aims to stimulate and perpetuate engaged interspiritual and perennial wisdom dialogue for the purpose of assisting the dawning of a unitive consciousness that will inspire compassionate action toward a just and peaceful world.

We are delighted to publish *The Holomovement* because of its fresh approach to understanding the totality of the cosmos, all dimensions of reality, and how all things interact and relate in this vast wholeness-in-motion. It does so first by exploring, from a range of perspectives, the nature of this wholeness and then by providing a similar range of experiential, practice and action-oriented ways in which we can apply this consciousness of wholeness to our lives in the world. In a time that calls so clearly for a light in the darkness, a compass to guide us in returning to the realization of who we really are, this book sets a rare standard in combining evidence-based visions of wholeness with inspirational accounts of how and where we can find avenues for engagement in living into this wholeness.

We consider this ground-breaking book, providing a broad and deep view of the cosmos and our role in it, to be both a cutting-edge vision and application of the many ways in which we can be an integral part of a movement toward holism, in which everything flows in orderly patterns of action. The scope of this anthology distinguished by a diversity of perspectives illustrates so well how there is harmony in the whole. The interplay and balance between these essential ways of knowing represented here helps us discover the greatest potential of wholeness and unity that human beings can know. This book offers a view of the living cosmos and our integral place in it in a way that unites science and spirituality as partners in revealing a wondrous creation that will inspire us to take an even more active role in supporting the wholeness-in-motion all around us.

If indeed a Holomovement toward "the world that works for all" is emerging globally, we are confident this book is part of that imperative visioning.

Managing Editors—

Kurt Johnson, PhD
Robert Atkinson, PhD
Nomi Naeem, MA
Chamatkara (Sandra Simon)